The Diary
Of the
Soul Crew 2

Annis Abraham Jnr

www.annisabraham.co.uk

First published in January 2009 by Annis Abraham Jnr.

Copyright © 2009 Annis Abraham Jnr.

ISBN 978-0-9561339-0-8

Printed in Great Britain by
Millcastle Printers Limited

Contents

Acknowledgements

Once again a big thank you and love to my wife Joanne for typing it all up and being patient with me (I did manage to learn to type a few lines he! he!) and special love to my children Annaise and Alexandra who are both True Bluebirds.

A big thank you to all the lads who helped put the book together with all their stories Pat Dolan (Chelsea), Jonathan Evans (Cardiff), Mike Dye (Ely Trendy Cardiff), Simon Neads (Neath punk), Dave Sugarman (Cardiff), John Simmonds (Simmo Cardiff), Mallo (Cardiff) , Kadjet (Cardiff), Simon Williams (Cardiff), Big Sam (Valleys Cardiff), Gwyn Davies (Valleys Cardiff), Mac (Cardiff), Pete Lintern (Little Pete Cardiff), Joe (Cardiff) Taffy Anton (Cardiff),Tony Ridgeway(Guff PVM Port Talbot), Tony Rees (News Reporter), Alan Swain (Bristol City), Danny (Plymouth), Nicky Muff (Leeds Utd), Ginger Bob (Millwall), Sooty Jason & J (ZULUS Birmingham City), Neil (Bristol City), John Newey (WBA), Barnsley (Five -0), Mick (Man Utd).

Thanks to my Godsons Connor Sullivan and Daniel Evans for being Bluebirds.

Thanks to Mike and staff at Millcastle Printers, Ely Cardiff, for all their hard work in helping me put the book together and of course printing it.

A special thanks to Jeff Marsh (Author of The Trouble with Taffies and Soul Crew Seasider's), Mike Morris Cardiff City unofficial website, www.Cardiffcitymad.co.uk, The Valley Rams Web Site and Andrew Turton (The Thin Blue Line Fanzine).

Thank you to all the following who gave me photos and newspaper cuttings Alun Griffiths (Jaffa Bridgend), Steve Wilson (Llanrumney), Darren Williams (Bridgend), Paul Williams (Canton), Paul (Clemos Love child & Pap Ratzi MB), Tim (Lawnmower MB), Richard Sandham (Skewen), Jerry (Gazza Llantrisant), Steve Williams(Suggs). Kev Ederle (Holyhead), Gareth Rogers, Wayne & Morgan Anderson, Pam, Lee, & Jermaine Simmonds, Sean Canton (For promoting my books), Steve Evans(Wolf MB), Martin (Cardiff 74 MB), Glenn Villis, Damian (Feedback MB), Nick Fish (MB), Chunky (Pontypridd), Callum (MB) and Peter Thomas (front cover photo & Jacks photos). Express Imaging City Rd, Cardiff (Dave, Rob & Angie). Mike Williams Press to print City rd Cardiff.

Thank you to Martin King for his Foreword and helping me with my previous books.

Simon Insole, Wayne and Mario for letting me take some lovely shots (From Ninian Park to Portugal & Germany).

The following Persons and Shops who have helped me and are also selling my books Ray, Lee , Ricky, Sam   A2 Clothing (Victoria Street, Merthyr), Paul   Mojo King   (Wellfield Rd, Cardiff), Nick   Original footwear Barnsley (Barnsley), Mark   Dudden News agents   (80

Albany Rd Cardiff), Sean (Cardiff Market), Billy (The Badge Man), "Here's News"(News agents 32 Albany Rd Cardiff), Phil Southall (Referee) Forget Me Not Card Shop, 26 Caroline Street, BRIDGEND, and Forget Me Not Card Shop, 87 Station Road, PORT TALBOT, Dave Roberts ICON Computer Shop, 26 Malpas Road, NEWPORT, NP20 5PA, Cheggers The Brunswick Pub, 5 Church Street, Merthyr Town Centre, MERTHYR and www.Casualsclobber.co.uk (WBA)

Thanks to Jamie Sullivan, Frankie Dimodica, Viking (Nils), Dave Bennett, Lyndon Cushing, Bradley Ashford, Conrad, Paul Corky (Valley Rams), Big Sams Wife Debbie and Daughter Kate Murphy, Jamie Francis, Dai Thomas, Lee Davies (Tonto), Ginger Jones, The Clemo brothers (Bridgend), A Rawlings, Darryl, Julian Jenks, Richard E, Paul Williams (Willie), Ian Thomas ,Alex Mannings, Kersy, Shep ,Terry, Staples, Wally, Jeff, Joff, James, Neil MacInnes, Andrew Jones , P Gregson, C Beer, Wayne Critchon, Jeff Lloyd, Rod, David Stanley, Granville, Caerwyn, Rob Hutchingson, Rotter, Winky, Taddy (RIP) Cwm Boys, Chris (Jelly Head), Paul Santos, Richard Cordle, Weller, Big Foot, Maxwell, Ivor, Oggy, Gary S, Ginger Nick, Jason (TGI), Neil Davey Ritchie (The Mod), Gabbsnewt (MB), Wilts Blue (MB), Steven (Brummy), Keith (The Kings Castle pub) Webber, Gonk, Simon, Julian Kelly, Toddy, Tongy, Kenny (Aberdare), Alistar, G Price, Mojo, Dayo, Wilts, Fisher, Marksy, Stud, Jaffa (Valleys), Ketty, Peter Morgan (Moggs) ,Mr Willimas, Sticky, Chris Smith (Snibs). Peter Morgan .Gareth Davies, Paul Morgan (Sect A and all the other lads who sit in there) , Big Tec, Little Tec, Chris Price, Craig McGowan, Vince & Matthew Alm, Leighton, Thomas, Christian, Dean,Wilbur, Lug, Chongo, Dobbo ,Wilo, Gabby, Jacko.

The following Ely Trendies Little Collin, Peter Mannings, R Moorie, Smiler, Nick, Penny, Baggers, Pip, Dean, Young Ant, Morgan, Justin, Glen J, Andrew , Ben, Jayo S, Jammo, Zub, Earnie Gee, Harry , Pie Face, Cissy, Mexi, Dulla , Derym and the main lad again Dio.

Dean (Roath), M Lyons, Chuggy , Big and Little Bubble, Mark (Penarth), Harvey, Nathan , Rob (Merthyr), Mcgrath (Australia) Nick and Dave (Bluebirds Fly), Marco, Jock, Nigel Lancastle, Dixie & Willie (Penarth), The Brownhills Dirty 30. Dave Allan (Topman), Jason, Catherine D, Helen Thomas, Nadia, Joseph & Sarah, Tony Dai H, Jona (Brighton), Pocock, Spud, Richie (Blackwood), Johnny Bywater, Ben & Chris Griffiths, Karl and Ashly from Hereford, Stan from Pontypool, Deacon, Glenn Waife, Ian Charles, Anthoney Rivers (Lakey), Dave Jones, Foster, Keith, Mark, Granville, Ginger John, Paul & Rob, Stanley, Sully, The Valley Commandos, The Rhondda Lads, Woody, Nigel, Quinny , Rotters, Kenny H , Wilbur (Canton)'s, Jerky, H (Thailand), Dibble, Wally, Matty (USA), , Scouse, Nigel, Gary J, AP, Phyllis (Port Talbot) , Tony Jeffries ,Allun Williams, Mike Flyn, Lee Beames, Chris Price, Newt, Beefy, Bevan, Blond Simmo, Chris (Caerphilly) , Wilbur's(Roath),Carlton, Dafyd ,Worzel (Gloucester), Ian (Older Blue), Jesse, Hue Boy, Rhys (Magor), Paul (Fairwater), Robert Maggs, Emlyn and Patrick (Bridgwater). Brian Edge, Pidgeon, Ching, Frankie Humphries, Ray Pill Blue, Leon & Harley Phipps, John a True Blue in Jackland, Gazza & Peter Bridgend, Joe Mullins, Beachy, Ducky, PVM (Port Talbot), Neath Blues, All The Bridgend Lads (especially those on Dib's Tours), 1927 lads, Ant Hill Mob, Milford Haven Blues, The Donut Crew, North Wales Blues, All the lads from The Neville Pub, Gethin and Chris (Original Soul Crew). Baker brothers, Steven Beards, Pricey, Lez , Jammo, Dowie, Shoulders,(and all the rest of the older lads from Llanrumney).The older Barry lads from The Zoo Pub, All the Merthyr, Pontypool and

Risca lads for their support.

To all the lads from Sunderland Brookie, Daz, Jason, Locky (The Twins) Joe, The Twins and the many more Sunderland that I have met who have always made me welcome and whoever has been with me you have always gone out to show great hospitality.

Dave Chappell (Crystal Palace), Rowland Pompey, George Calder Kilmarnock FC, Mark Forester (Villa), Fowler and all the lads from Villa and I know the following are your arch rivals but Big Al, Bones and Cuddles from Birmingham City, whenever I have bumped into them from Dublin to Glasgow, they've always bought me a drink and made me feel welcome.

David Williams (Author of Dessert England).

Mike for all his help (Plymouth), Diddy and Dave (Boro), Mark Gregory (QPR), Stefan (Hoffenbach FC), Steve Hickmont (Hicky) Terry Last (Chelsea), Prickett, Ian Woodruff, Adams and Dave Roberts of Newport County, Gilly Shaw (Wolves), Neil,Scoots, & Ponch of Wrexham. Marc Parcell & Angus, (Bristol C), Para Paul (Millwall). Paul (Reading FC). Mike (Wigan), Murco (Stoke City), Tony Reardon (Bolton W), Simon & Ian (AFC Wimbledon), Craig (Rangers Scotch Bar, Palmanova, Majorca), Bobby and Billy (Rangers Scottish Corner Pub, Santa Ponsa, Majorca), David McVey (Celtic).

RIP Derek Ford, Mike Rayer, Budgie and Ginger Jason (Cardiff C), Manny (Bradford C), Lemmy (Newport County).

My own Website is www.annisabraham.co.uk which you can purchase any of my books from.

FOREWARD

By MARTIN KING

I looked at the clock on my office wall and it said 11.55am, he'd said when I'd spoken to him on the phone that he was never ever late, then the phone rang the voice on the other end, said I'm 5 minutes away. I told him where to park when he eventually got here and I went outside to meet him. A couple of minutes later a four- wheel drive car pulled up and out stepped Annis bang on time. He shook me warmly by the hand opened the back door of his car and told me that before we could sit down and chat he first had to let his dog out and give her some water and stretch her legs. He lifted her out and she had a wander round. Annis explained that, Cleo his German Shepherd dog was getting on a bit and was nearly 13 years old and went everywhere with him. He'd had her from a few weeks of age and had been to most football grounds in the country and she had even worked with him behind the entrance to some of his father's nightclubs. Like me, it was obvious he was an animal lover. I'd spoken to Annis over the phone, over an idea he'd had about a book; our mutual friend Fat Pat Dolan had put us in touch.

Today he was here to discuss the book. What struck me on first meeting Annis was how tall he was. I'd heard his name crop up on loads of occasions, from football lads from all over the country. I'd heard that as a youngster he'd been with our lot at Chelsea and was well known at Cardiff matches. In the office he took his coat off and we chatted over a coffee and got on well, it turned out that we had many mutual friends and acquaintances. Anyway to cut along story short I published his first book "Shattered Dreams." We had the book launch at Ninian Park which was well attended with even the chairman Mr Ridsdale coming along and chatting to people and staying for a few hours and what a nice man he was. I took my 18-year-old daughter Kortney down there with me, and afterwards went out with Annis and his wife Jo and her brother Jamie for a meal. We had a lovely night and later I met up with Mac who for years has been one of the Soul Crews main faces. His hospitality was unbelievable and second to none, as he and his mate Tommy took us from bar to bar showing us the sights of Cardiff City centre. The three of us ended up carrying Kortney home at about 4am in the morning. She had a hang over for nearly a week after that. I did tell her to slow down and too not to drink so much. But she wouldn't listen and was sick in a Pole dancing club we were in.

It wasn't long before I was working with Annis on his second book, which was entitled " The Dairy of the Real Soul Crew" This was more of an hooligan book and recalled some of the battles had by the infamous Cardiff City Soul Crew. Annis, for the book launch had coincided it with a Cardiff home game with Bristol City. He booked a bar in the City centre from midday to about 2pm. I travelled down with the books with my son Rory and his mate Max who came along to help. We picked up Annis on the way through and headed to the venue about an hour before the launch, already the Old Bill were floating about and having a look at what we were up too? It wasn't long before people started to arrive and the books were flying out. People came from everywhere to snap up a book and in the end there must have been near on a thousand people there. The boys filled up four nearby pubs and because it was a warm sunny day the lads were standing out on the pavement having a drink and a chat and flicking through the book.

Fat Pat and Gilly from Wolves turned up and a few Forest lads made an appearance. More Old Bill turned up and stood across the road watching the lads have a beer or two? A few of the Cardiff lads had a chat with Simon their football intelligence officer who I've met before when I've been in Cardiff watching Chelsea at the Millennium Stadium, they all affectionately know him as Potato Head. Half an hour before the game Annis and me headed over towards the ground. It seemed strange walking the same streets after over thirty years.

I'd first come here with Chelsea in the Seventies. We were languishing in the old second division then, skint and fielding, mostly youngsters that had come through the ranks. A far cry from where we are now. I remembered I'd travelled to Wales on a packed football special train from Paddington with about 20 of the boys from Mitcham in South London. We took a few beers on board; you could in them days, and chatted about what we expected to face on our arrival in Cardiff. This was the first of four specials being run and all our top boys were on board. As the train pulled in at Ninian Park Halt station, we could see the floodlights. The doors were open and hundreds of the boys were off and running along the platform even before the train had come to a complete stop, that's another sport been done away with since the introduction of sliding train doors came in. A dozen or so local Old Bill were there to greet us and welcome us to Wales. We burst straight through them and out on to the street. Now where did we go? No one had a clue, which way the ground was? One of the boys asked an old couple out shopping which way the stadium was, and after a bit of pointing we were off. There must have been 500 of us marching through the streets holding the traffic up as we walked purposefully down the middle of the road, as we came to a railway bridge we saw the first mob of Cardiff fans waiting for us. The battle commenced and it went toe to toe before the police came in and broke it up. Every one on our side was now buzzing, we pushed our way out onto the main road in front of us and stood in the middle of the road. Cardiff were all around us, and by the looks of it they had some big lumps in amongst them.

There was a park off to our right and hundreds of them were streaming across it towards us, more Old Bill arrived and kept the two firms apart. We were herded towards the ground and as we were queuing to get in the Welsh boys came at us again. We paid to get in and found ourselves standing along side the halfway line opposite to where the masses of home fans were standing. After about ten minutes a fight broke out behind the goal to our right as someone unfurled a Union Jack flag who ever it was, they were soon coming under a furious attack as wave after wave of Cardiff fans tore into them. It turns out that it was Hickeys coach that had gone into the home section, and had come unstuck. One Chelsea fan found himself on the edge of the pitch and was being lead towards us with his shirt hanging out all tattered and torn, then when he reached the ranks of the Cardiff fans along the side, who were baying for his blood. He suddenly done no more and slipped the clutches of his police escort and leapt in amongst them and began trading punches. He lasted all of 10 seconds before he found himself back on the pitch. But he did get arousing reception from us lot. Before the end of the game a few of their lot appeared in our end at the exit which lead out onto the street, they began mouthing off on what was going to happen to us once we were outside. A few of the lads flew into them and they took a couple of whacks before they scattered. At the final whistle we stormed out into the street and in the park opposite us were hundreds of Cardiff waiting but between us and them, were some iron railing we were over them in a flash and walked towards the waiting Welshmen. A roar went up and we ran towards them, they stood as kicks and punches came in from both sides. A few of the Cardiff front line went down, and that was the signal for them to retreat. We gave chase for a couple of hundred yards then stopped and regrouped, we then turned to face another mob which had come up behind us, but before it could go off the Old Bill appeared and lead us back onto the street and towards the station.

As we got to the Railway Bridge, Cardiff came from everywhere and they were well up for it, bricks and bottles rained down on us and for a minute or so our mob lost its shape. The two mobs mingled with one another and one on one battles were breaking out. I was on the first special to leave Cardiff and the boys knew we'd been in a fight. As we pulled out we could still see fighting going on in the streets below us. We only got as far as Newport when the train stopped and the police boarded the train, apparently a couple of Cardiff fans had been stabbed in the fracas on the park and the old Bill were looking for the culprit. We were held for about an hour and then let on our way. As far as I know I don't think anyone was arrested?

Walking through the streets of Cardiff with Annis it bought back a lot of memories; it still looked the same. One thing I did notice was that the fence around the park looked new. But the Cardiff fans still have that same passion for their club, as they've always had. One thing for sure they will never ever lose it. Annis pointed out to me across the road the new stadium, the club was in the process of building and it looked impressive. I do hope like all new stadiums it doesn't swallow up the atmosphere and feel of the old ground. But some how with Cardiff City and its fans I don't think that will be allowed to happen.

Martin King - Base Camp Mount Everest 2009.

Introduction

After the success of "From Shattered Dreams To Wembley Way" and "The Diary of The Real Soul Crew"(1) and with a turn out of over 700 lads for the launch of the last book, I was inundated with people asking when's the next book out and lads asking if they can tell their stories.

Well I'm still in the middle of writing my own personal book of my accounts from the 70s to the year 2000, but I've put my own book on hold for the time being (end of 2009) and I've gone about meeting numerous lads, who have had some really interesting stories to tell, some of which were totally knew to me. Some were funny ones and others were more serious, also I was able to get an experienced reporters view from Tony Rees (ex News of The world) and the President and founder of The Valley Rams Gwyn Davies. Gwyn has seen everything from first hand experience and for 5 years was able to try stand up for the fans and tried to work with the authorities. I believe by putting the Cardiff's lads, other firms lads, Gwyns and a reporters view stories together, I was able to put a different type of book together and hopefully a good one at that.

There has been an increase in trouble at football in the last year, I'm not sure how that has come about, maybe because a lot of bans are now up, more younger lads coming through or maybe it never really went away and had gone underground and the media are just picking up on any incident, from a coin being thrown, to being drunk or to a fan swearing. The fact remains that any type of trouble nowadays is not on the scale of 5% of the type of trouble in the 70s & 80s.

The following lads have all given me their stories to tell and are as true as they can be, it is the way they saw it and everyone has their own version, some of these stories, many of you reading them will relate too, others you might relate to but have a slight difference off opinion, but that's life, we all have our opinions. This book has been able to give a cross section of lads from all over the country a chance to give their opinions on Cardiff and tell their tales regarding Cardiff.

Pat Dolan (Chelsea) now a legend in my eyes and still has got some interesting and intriguing stories to tell. A very good friend of mine for over 27 years and a well liked lad by all, even though in the 80s was probably most lads nightmare.

Jonathan Evans (Cardiff City), Wont ever bullshit and has no fear, but a good friend to have and a down to earth person. His son Daniel is my Godson, which I'm very proud off. Jonathan is the type of mate you can always depend on, no matter what. Jonathan cant stand all the nonsense that some lads talk about, he prefers straight talking, just like he did when he was on the frontline, He's currently on a 6 year ban.

Mikey Dye (Cardiff City Ely Trendy), we go way back to the mid 80s and have been good friends through all these years. Dio to which many know him as, still likes to go to away games in his own small group(be it 5 to 15), cant stand the days out with 300 lads, then being told go here, do that etc, he will never change and for that I respect him.

Simon Neads (Cardiff City Neath Lad). The famous Neath Punk who appears in many a book. Can be the funniest person around, but don't be on the wrong side of Simon as he will always have the last laugh, he's a lad who will always be on the frontline. Simon has been a great lad to know and a good friend too, right back to the early 80s.

Dave Sugarman (Cardiff City), got involved in the 80s like most lads did, you couldn't help It, if you followed Cardiff back then. Admits he was never an out and out lad, but saw the funny side of it. Got to know Dave well these last a couple of years and has become a friend.

John Simmonds (Cardiff City). Simmo famous for the battle bus(as everyone would call it in the 90s) and another Cardiff lad who everyone has heard off, another great character and a real character of a wife to go with it, never mind having Simmo by your side in the 80s , but Pam would off been just as good. Both good friends of mine and always there if I need them for anything.

Mallo (Cardiff City), Mallo was a bit of a tearaway in the 80s, probably because he was the youngest lad at that time down the football and was always trying to prove himself. Well you did Mallo and to this day a lot of lads have plenty of respect for you. We've remained friends for all these years, despite the odd disagreement.

Kadjet (Cardiff City), The best memory around that's Kadjet, you can ask him anything about the 80s and he remembers from the date to the time of the incident. He was one of the lads in the 80s, but has since totally come away from it, like a lot of the lads from the 80s he's settled down. We were good friends during those years and are still to this day.

Simon Williams (Cardiff City), my mate from the same village that I live in. When I first started getting involved in the Casual scene in the early 80s it was Simons group that I looked up to, as they were the main dressers at the time and always there, even though Simon was one of them, he will quite happily admit he was never on the frontline even though many a lad he was with in the 80s were, and probably most of them were the original Soul Crew.

Big Sam (Cardiff City Valleys) He's seen it all, been there when it matters and is known from one end of Wales to the other. He's also one of the most loyalist fans there is, we've become good friends through these years and have both been there when City have had less than 30 away. He looks the part and has done it when it mattered, but like most has moved on and just supporting his club is all that matters to him nowadays.

Gwyn Davies (Cardiff City Valleys), The type of lad who is friends with everyone, but will also stand up to anyone if they are out of order. He has worked tirelessly for the fans and has in a lot of ways got the authorities to work more with the fans,. I get on really well with Gwyn and it's a pleasure to know him.

Mac (Cardiff City) Probably the most well known lad Cardiff has and has earned that reputation without a doubt. Well liked and respected by every firm in the country. We've known each other for well over 25 years and have stayed friends through out. You will see

Mac at every game home and away, as also he is one of the most loyalist fans we have.

Little Pete (Cardiff City Valleys), Pete's obsessed with the hooligan world and is currently banned, I've known him for years and have always got on well with him, he's a game lad and for a small lad has no fear. Pete probably wishes he was around in the early 80s.

Joe (Cardiff City), I knew Joe in the 80s and he went on many a trip with us, a good friend during those years and now. He has done well for himself and has totally settled down, good on him.

Taffy Anton (Cardiff City Port Talbot PVM). A lad respected even in Jackland. Anton was a lad to always be found at the front, I've known Anton for many a year and we have total mutual respect for each other going back to the 80s. Anton is currently serving a 6 year ban.

Guff (Cardiff City Port Talbot PVM), Guff is a gentleman and a good person with it, way back in the 80s, he was as game as they come, as you will read, his story changed his life. He has also moved on and puts his family first and career first, fair play to him.

I've spoken to all the following lads and met quite a few, who even though they follow other teams, I have got on with everyone of them and there is total respect for each other and it shows that football lads are not all like animals as the media makes out. We can sit down and have a drink together and talk about the past, maybe this is what the media can't understand or maybe doesn't want to really happen, as it doesn't make a good story for them.

Alan Swain and Neil from Bristol City (City Service Firm), Danny from Plymouth (Central Element), Nicky Muff from Leeds Utd (Service Crew), Ginger Bob from Millwall (F Troop), Sooty Jason and J from Birmingham City (The Zulus), John Newey from WBA, Barnsley (Five-0) and Mick from Man Utd (Red Army).

I hope you enjoy the book as much as I have enjoyed meeting up with everyone and listening to their stories and then putting them together for them, its taken 5 months, with a lot of hours of hand writing behind me.

FOR THE RECORD THIS BOOK IS NOT ORGANISING OR TRYING TO ORGANISE FOOTBALL VIOLENCE IT IS JUST TELLING IT HOW IT WAS IN YEARS GONE BY.

January 2009 Annis Abraham Jnr.

www.annisabraham.co.uk

The following are Quotes from Lads who I have met over the years and many who have fought against The Soul Crew.

Steve Hickmott (Hicky The General CHELSEA)

We were smashed to fucking pieces and were now backing off or in some cases running for our lives on The Bob Bank.
We took the fences out of the ground in the park and we charged towards their mob using it as a huge battering ram, Cardiff were now in full flight across the grass park in all directions (Oct 1979).

Ginger Howard (6.57 Crew POMPEY)

A full scale riot, we got in Cardiff's Grange end, we ran them, they ran us, it was back and forth. The old bill tried to get in between us and break it up, but in the end the coppers disappeared under the sheer numbers fighting (approx 1973). I rate Cardiff in my top 5 firms.

Pat Dolan (Fat Pat CHELSEA)

CCFC a top Firm, with top people, I've fought against The Soul Crew and The Bob Bank Boys, we have been run by Cardiff and have also chased after Cardiff.

Coaville Daz (Baby Squad LEICESTER CITY)

Cardiff whether you love them or loathe them, you've got to say Cardiff are one of the top 5 firms, because they've got such a massive firm, they really have got a massive firm and you've got to put them up there, you've got to be honest about things.

Dave Chappell (CRYSTAL PALACE)

I've been with Cardiff with a thousand lads and I've been with them with twenty, no matter what odds, they have always obliged and in my opinion have never been bullies. I've seen them give quite a few lads walkovers, they are hard but fair, look for it at Ninian Park and your fucked.

Lee Spence (OLDHAM)

Cardiff are in my top 5 firms of today, because they travel to places.

Mike (PLYMOUTH)

Cardiff have always got a good mob and they always come to us.

Neil Clampit (Frontline WREXHAM)

Cardiff have a firm known as the Docks boys, there some of Cardiff's finest, who know how to have a row. In reality we have never taken what we should have done to Cardiff. We got battered on one trip, a Welsh Cup final in the Arms Park on a Sunday, 40 of us turned up and afterwards hundreds of Cardiff attacked us, as they do at Cardiff.

Teddy Bunter (ICF WESTHAM)

Cardiff like to put themselves about and I would put them in my top 5 firms of today.

Mark Jasper (Naughty 40 STOKE CITY)

Cardiff have come to Stoke and brought it right up to us

Daz (Seaburn Casuals SUNDERLAND)

Our supporters are like the Valley Commandoes mad and well game for it. I rate Cardiff, lets be honest everybody rates Cardiff, you know if you go to Cardiff your going to get it.

Gilly Shaw (Subway Army WOLVES)

The Soul Crew are a top firm, you know they are guaranteed to turn up, they'd never let you down. In the last 5 years they've been to our place with over 500 lads, where as there arch rivals Swansea in Oct 08 brought 40 lads max.

Stefan aka Hofmeister (Offenback FC GERMANY)

Cardiff on a good day is the biggest firm I have ever seen, but their firm is not organised, but this is pretty hard to do due to its size. They have so many separate groups.

Barry (NORTHAMPTON FC)

We had a home game against Cardiff, 40 Cardiff left the match early and bumped into a much larger Northampton firm. Cardiff initially stood their ground, but the greater numbers had them on the run. It was a good ten minutes toe to toe, but still hats off to them, as both sides were getting put down, but then getting stuck straight back in.

Dirk (Fortuna Dusseldorf FC GERMANY)

Met the Cardiff lads in Germany, top lads and I have a lot of respect for them.

Carl (PETERBOROUGH UTD FC)

We never go to Cardiff as we never have enough numbers, but there is always a welcome here for them and they always come.

Mark Gregor (Gregors Q.P.R)

I have a lot of respect for Cardiff as a mob, Cardiff have always had good reputation for coming to QPR and causing murder.

Diddy (The Frontline BORO)

All in all it was a day which I will remember, not only did we have a good off with one of the main firms in the country and come out on top, but also for the proper friends, I've made because of it (FA CUP 1994). To all the Cardiff lads respect.

Rob Silvester (6.57 Crew POMPEY)

Cardiff you've got to respect Cardiff, we've always had it at Cardiff and they've always turned out for Pompey. The old Cardiff firm or The Soul Crew Cardiff of today, we've got a lot of respect for them. The Soul Crew have a fierce reputation as any thug will tell you, in their huge catchment area it follows why they have so many. Even in the nineties they have been impressive, they have maintained this standard right into the present day and are considered over the years to be just about any ones equal on their day. Pompey rate them highly.

QUOTES FROM OUR FIERCEST RIVALS (as you can see there's no love lost)

Martin King has got the following quotes as I haven't got the time of day for them.

Have a laugh at this

Toozey (Jack SWANSEA)

In Milan every where you went Cardiff lads were on the look out for us. Cardiff had a huge 400 strong mob, our numbers were now down to 8, Come on you Jack Bastards shouted the Cardiff boys as they came straight into us, we stood our ground and had a set to with them.

If I had gone down I would have been dead, I looked around and 4 of our boys had disappeared, we still never moved in, at one stage we backed them off.

Stacko (Jack SWANSEA)

Still in Milan, 4 of them against 400 Cardiff, I Knocked one of them clean out and they were going down like flies.

The Scum have never had it toe to toe with the biggest mobs in England like we have.
They have never smashed our ground to pieces we have done to theirs.

In the media Chief Supt Graham Jones told reporters that there was a Cardiff mob who were "particularly" unruly while they were on the West Bank (away end in the old Vetch ground). They broke up part of the terrace and hurled pieces of concrete at policemen. Cardiff were an absolute vile crowd on the terraces he stated.

In the 1979/80 season there were 37 arrests mostly Cardiff fans. Police stated we had to send in squads of officers in the home end (North Bank) Swansea to remove Cardiff fans.

Another local paper stated Cardiff have stolen the head lines in recent years, no wonder Swansea hooligans like to wear England football shirts.

The mid eighties also saw a continuation of the trouble against Cardiff as at one home game Cardiff attempted to invade the Swansea home end but it was repelled in a violent way.

Another paper stated that Cardiff fans are annoyed that their rivals display English flags and sing English songs during Swansea games.

Aggis (Jack SWANSEA)

In the 80s and even now, Cardiff go looking for us to see if were about at a Wales game.

"WELL AT LEAST THE TRUTH IS OUT"

Chapter 1
Man United
The Red Army by Mick (Salford)

From this day, Manchester United's Red Army had total respect for Cardiff and they knew that if they ever came back to the Capital of Wales, they wouldn't be able to terrorise it, like they had done to virtually every major City in Britain and Europe. I have met a lot of Utd's lads over the years including Mick and they have always been honest about this day. Annis

It was the year that my club was relegated and in my time of watching them one of my only few bad memories, but as to the hooligan side of it, it was a great season and going to Cardiff was one I will never forget.

August 1974 Division 2 at Ninian Park
Cardiff City v Man Utd

I was just a schoolboy and although I'd been to plenty of games at Old Trafford with my mates, I had only been to a few away games where there had been much trouble at that time.

The Cardiff game was unlike anything I think I have ever seen before or since. We expected an 'interesting' day to say the least but nothing prepared 4 kids for an afternoon of absolute mayhem, the likes of which, (I'm sure anyone who was there will heartily agree) has never been seen since, with perhaps the exception of Man Utd/Man City , Millwall/West Ham or Leeds/Man Utd.

United fans were largely untouchable in those days, sheer weight of numbers plus a ferocious bravado that wouldn't allow them to back down from any resistance, even the southern counterparts - Chelsea, West Ham and to some extent Millwall were still lagging behind in both exploits and organisation.

So it was with that air of self confidence when we arrived at Cardiff train station "Manchester la la la" Manchester la la la" rang out all around as we walked and swaggered our way towards Ninian Park, We were with the big boys now the Red Army, the exhilaration of being surrounded by 200 or so ' grown men' of 20 plus.

There we saw a group of about 200 lads. A cheer went up, these were more of our own we assumed. To this day I'll never forget the scene. A handful of our lads from across the road ambled over, a reuniting embrace was no doubt to follow as these old friends joined the throng. Suddenly I noticed the crazed grin on the face of the approaching stranger and even with my limited knowledge of Football away trips, I had a feeling. All was not well.

Our mate with which we thought simply smashed his fist into the face of one of our lads. "Bloody hell, they're Taffy twats" came the cry. This one lad began wading in to at least ten of the United group, bodies were going down all around. His 199 or so mates did very little to assist this one maniac - either they were terrified of the situation or maybe knew his capabilities. Maybe this was Frankie Humphries the Legend from the newspaper stories.

At last the two mobs woke up from just standing there watching and charged into each other. Now when people say 400 fans were fighting 'toe-to-toe' they usually mean half a dozen at most, with the rest milling about looking stupid, but this was as it sounded, and I mean I've never seen anything like it since it was a full scale riot.

My mates and I stood there dumbstruck. It was over well over 20 years ago and I would love to have been able to recall how I joined in the scene of carnage, downing all-comers, but as a young boy I was horror-stricken and frozen with terror. I remember one Policeman ambling by and peering round the corner to see what all the noise was. He took one look at the scene and carried on walking ha ha. Classic!

By this time most of our group had been split into small groups and the walk to the ground was quite simply a journey you only have night mares about.

On every street corner the sight was the same, people scurrying around in all directions, I saw one outlandish figure - a United fan in a white boiler-suit and black bowler hat giving out instructions. All around were cries of "here they are" "don't run" "I've got one" over here. It was total confusion, a tidal wave of thundering red Doctor Marten boots and tartan scarves this was fucking mayhem.

We arrived outside the ground and met up again with some faces from the train. Some looked dazed and confused; others bloodied but still were up for it. "See this", said one half-caste Londoner with a bloody nose. "The next Taff I see, I'm going to give him three of these." We all laughed loudly at the ridiculous statement, though from some of the characters I had seen at the Station with scars down their faces and smashed noses I believe really did want more.

We started queuing at the rather oddly named 'Bob-Bank' whatever that was. Suddenly a group of Reds walked past us, full of contempt that we were planning to go into our own end. "Not in here you idiots, it's all down by the so called Grangend". We followed our these lads and paid in at the "Grange".

As we prepared to pay our money I noticed some of the lads around us were tying their scarves around their waists out of sight. I now realised that occupying the home end was more of a military operation than a consumer choice.

We gathered "inconspicuously" at a point close to the fence which had a huge no-man's land separating the rival fans. Insults were traded for half an hour, a few blood curdling screams of bravado followed by a couple of half-hearted charges by either side at the fence. A fat Cardiff fan with a scarf round his wrist, and tomato sauce stains around his chin, shouted something indistinguishable and launched a wooden stake, like a mini telegraph pole into the baying United mob.

A few cheers rang out as it hit an unseen target. Instantly a piece of concrete was hurled into the Cardiff boys to my right and I could see a small group of people huddled round a fallen comrade. The reality that someone really could die here today (possibly even me) hit home.

As if it wasn't bad enough, things were about to take a turn for the worse. A small group of Taffies began to take an unhealthy interest in the dozen or so lads to their left (us). One lunatic with a severely scarred face wandered over. "Not singing boys? We all sing in here, you're all a bit quiet today. You are all 'Care-diff ' I hope". I froze virtually shitting myself, and we knew they weren't going to go away now their suspicions were aroused.

The scout ambled back to the main group to report his findings. After a brief chin-wag amongst themselves, three or four more came over to ask more questions. Guess what it was those lunatic Taffies who attacked us earlier by the train station.

Then some of the top lads from the Red Army came flying over and said we'll give you a song UTD UTD

That was the signal for all out attack from both sides. The dozen or so UTD lads charged upwards at the massed ranks of blue-scarved Taffies in a suicidal attack. Fists flew and a massive gap developed between the fans as the visitors gained some amazing ground. I hid behind one of Utd's lads,

Suddenly the 'Red Sea' in front of me became just a pond, as the Cardiff boys realised the small numbers involved in the Suicidal mission. It finally stopped as Utd's lads ran straight out the entrance they had come in.

The 4 of us were now totally left on our own, we should have followed, it was now clear that we were in serious trouble and we seized the chance to make for a gap in the faltering fencing, weakened by numerous charges. We raced towards the safety of our fellow fans, who, to our horror, on seeing the onrushing mob charged into us, and a number of fists flew before our identity was established.

We were suddenly being applauded like heroes as though we ourselves had done the suicide mission, which I guess it had been. I don't really know what I was thinking I was still in a daze, one minute I thought we were dead the next we were heroes, as huge lumps of brick, concrete and wood were flying over from both sides, the Police were desperately trying to contain the two Lunatic mobs who charged continually at the terrified looking thin blue line and at several points it looked as though the fence would give way.

As a veteran of away trips at home and abroad throughout the 70's, 80's and 90s, I can honestly say I couldn't imagine the carnage that would have taken place had that terrified police line given way on that day.

Thankfully it held, and despite sickening chants of "Munich" and occasionally even "Aberfan" the severe injuries were low and sometimes I think about that day and I'm shocked nobody died. People were being carried out from both side on stretchers, many with horrifying head wounds, struggling yobs were being plucked from both ranks by those Policemen plucky enough to try. Others were met with a volley of missiles and feet.

Every so often a small group of United fans would emerge in the home section and the same scenario would be played out - a suicidal charge followed by submersion beneath a frenzy of kicks, stamps and punches.

We decided it was time we got away from this area and got as far away as possible and just stood there and watch the war continue.

The match continued but I don't know how as today it would have been called off with in seconds of what I saw that day, and on the final whistle, both sides burst from the terraces into the street.

Just as before, during the game, it had seemed that I had an awful knack of arriving just as major disorder was breaking out, so it was to be the pattern on the journey back to the station.

Sporadic bottles and missiles flew but no major incidents occurred until the station was in sight. Suddenly this was to be the major convergence of both main mobs, and hundreds of Cardiff and Manchester boys tore into each other. There was none of this bouncing about of the modern 'offs' as they became known. No pushing the bloke in front of you into action in order to hide behind him. Just straight in no mouthing, fight till you dropped.

I will tell you this not only was I relieved to be on that train home but so were many of Utd top lads.

Utd's Red Army that season went to all the other Towns and Cities and pulverized them and in years on we've had many a battle on foreign grounds but nothing will compare to the hatred and violence I saw that day from The Taffies.

Cardiff fans continue to wreak havoc around the country and some how have got bigger in numbers while other firms have either dwindled or even vanished. Believe it or not that day got me hooked on being a hooligan and years on I was part of The Red Army.

Chapter 2

"NEVER TAKE CARDIFF LIGHTLY"
By Ginger Bob Millwall (Rob Payne)

Ginger Bob, he's old school and has been there right through the 70s and is still going just like they do at Millwall, I don't think they ever give it up. Bobs one the main faces at Millwall and is well respected by all who know him. I've had the pleasure to meet him on a number of occasions and he's just like Chelsea Pat, got plenty of stories to tell of the old days, so when he agreed to give me some stories for the book I knew I was getting them from the horses mouth and not any second hand tales. Annis

I first met Annis at the Millwall Chelsea game in the early 90's and later on we were to meet up on many occasions when he was with Pat from Chelsea and when he was in London for a Cardiff game. Annis was also invited to drink with us the night before the Millwall v Man Utd FA Cup final at Cardiff, The lads who have got to know Annis up here through the years have got a lot of time for him, as one thing he doesn't do is bull shit, and he's Cardiff through and through. He asked me if I would give some stories of the old days at Cardiff and I said yes, but it will be the way I and Millwall saw it at the time.

Older Millwall over the years have come to respect Cardiff's firm as they have always come to Millwall be it the 70's, 80's or 90's, they have always turned up, no matter even if their team was bottom of the league.

28th March 1976

One of the games that I will always remember was Cardiff v Millwall 28th March 1976 at Ninian Park, I remember it was a top of the table Div 3 clash and at the end of the season Cardiff went up and we went up instead of Palace. We had all got the early morning special about 500 Millwall were on the train with about 300 boys all together and all of the 300 were quality top Millwall.

If I remember correctly we got to Cardiff about 12 o'clock and the place was swarming with old bill, all waiting for us. We were put straight into an escort and marched to Ninian Park and other than the odd Welsh nut case sticking his head out of some pub window, it seemed pretty quite. Along the way a few Millwall had given the old bill the slip, as the streets had been quieter than the old bill had even expected, so they weren't on top of us any more and eventually about 40 Millwall had got away. We were feeling pretty confident, as the year before about 60 Millwall had run Cardiff out of a section of the Grandstand at Ninian Park, which was the away end at the time. Fair play to Cardiff for trying, not many teams outside London have tried to infiltrate the Millwall section before. I know it was at Ninian Park and it was their manor but at first they gave us a bit of a shock, but we soon sent a 100 Taffies packing. So it seems we were lulled into a false sense of security because at what had happened that season.

So the same as the year before, they put us in the left hand side of the ground next to the Grange end. This time it was really weird as we couldn't believe how quite it was, we were expecting to get attacked at any time, but as time went on we all started to relax.

My best mate Dave Rand, who was like a brother to me and at the time was Millwalls main lad (from the mid 60s to the mid 70s) .He was also known by Millwall as the Captain, because of his black beard, he looked the spitting image of black beard the pirate. He and another guy called Winkle(cos he had a massive cock) had also given the escort the slip and had decided to go into the Bluebirds Supporters club bar for a drink, they had managed to sneak in as I think you had to be a member in those days, by what they later told me.

After ordering one drink, they were immediately sussed, but their luck was in as at the same time about 40 of the rest of the Millwall who had also slipped the escort came steaming straight through the doors, game on. Then fucking hell over 200 Cardiff attacked them, led by at the time a bloke I later found to be called Frankie Humphries, Millwall were smashed and run right out leaving Dave Rand and Twinkle behind, Dave was hit over the head with a wooden chair, but managed to stay on his feet, and even though he was staggering around and the blood was pouring out, he new no matter what he had to stay on his feet, as if he went down it was curtains for him. By now they were both at the front door and fighting for their lives. Finally some luck really did come their way as two of the doorman stepped in and stood between them and the mob of Cardiff. One shouted "this is enough" and shielded them till the police came, who then took them to hospital for stitches and a lot of bandaging up.

Dave got back to the ground just before half-time, looking like the red Indian Geronimo, with a whole bandage covered in blood, wrapped around his head. I've since met one of the doorman from that day when I was down for the Millwall and Man Utd FA Cup Final, I listened to his side of the story word for word and it was the same, apparently the guy who hit Dave over the head is dead now.

Anyway back to the match, which as far as I remember ended up 2-2, with the usual abuse and banter branded about between the two mobs, " You're going to get your fucking heads kicked in" and "we'll see you all outside" came from the Taffies. At the end of the game, when we came outside, fuck me there must have been over 2,000 Taffies waiting for us and on this occasion the old bill seemed to be very thin on the ground. The Taffies had filled the main road and were refusing to move, the thin blue line of old bill tried to escort us, a mere 300 lads. As we walked along at a slow pace, the Taffies attacked both sides of the escort, our ranks stayed together and with the old bill having a right baton charge at them, between the two of us, it meant the Taffies weren't having much success, so we were able to hold them off.

However on the way back to the train station, maybe another 200 yards or so , further down the road, myself and about 20 Top Millwall who were all at the back of the escort, where there was a lot less old bill, Cardiff were able to do their best attacks and I mean vicious attacks. We decided to make a sort of stand and went for it, a proper toe to toe, fuck me it was tiring, as when we threw a punch they must have thrown a dozen. In the mean time, un-noticed one of our guys , had drifted back into the middle of the Cardiff hordes and who upon sussing him, battered him to the floor and were mersivilly kicking him. I recognised him as my pal Winkle who had previously been fighting in the Bluebirds club with Dave Rand (it just wasn't his day).

I thought I should stop you there and tell just you something before I go any further. My good mate Chelsea Pat, who I first met working the doors in London (before all that licensing shit), his lovely placid manor as you all think. Well when it comes down to it , he is one of the nastiest cunts around in a row and that makes him one of the best people to have on your side when it comes on top with another firm or working the doors. We could write our own book about just working the doors together, ha ha that would open some eyes Millwall and Chelsea together!!! . Pat didn't know me in my prime as when I was young and fit as a fiddle, I was a boxing, Judo, and wrestling champion in London. I was ruthless and fearless in them days and for a big man lightening fast.

As to clothes I was never lucky, as that day in Cardiff I had a brand new cashmere jumper on , nice strides to my eternal regret and a pair of hush puppies on, instead of my usual steel capped boots like the rest of Millwall. When I had seen Winkle being attacked by Cardiff, I took it upon myself and without any communication to the others, to do a charge into the mob of Cardiff . The adrenaline was pissing out of my ears, and at first I stunned the Taffies who were kicking Winkle, I was able to drag him back into the escort, he was semi conscious by now. I then had a bit of a battle with two Taffies, I hit one with my right had flush, (they had attacked me from the side) he was out cold. I then managed to hit the other one with an upper cut and had him on his arse. Winkle was still lying on the floor, the escort all over the place, I was then clocked by another 2 Taffies, this time I kicked them in the bollocks, it was a pain full lesson for me as well, as I was wearing hush puppies, and I never wore them again.

I managed to drag Winkle once again back into the escort and at the same time I was punched, nutted, even bitten, everything you can imagine from all sides. It must have been the adrenaline that kept me going and upright, if I had gone down it would have been RIP Bob and Winkle. As I reached the escort Millwall at the back saw my predicament and finally came to my aid and between the lot of us managed to shore up the escort and some vicious toe to toes took place. Police reinforcements eventually came to the back of the escort, while at the same time taking Winkle to hospital. Now with protection at the back of the escort, we were now moving forward, instead of continually walking backwards or running back to help others. The Taffies were still coming at the escort and the old bill were fighting them back from all angles of the escort.

As we looked to our left and to our amazement and shock, we saw the police fighting with 4 girls, 2 black and 2 mixed race (obviously Tiger Bay), they were about 17 or 18 years old wearing multi coloured tops. The old bill had decided to turn these girls virtually up side down only to reveal they were carrying blades for their Welsh counter parts. We had never seen anything like this before and people think Millwall are "crackers". Anyway murder continued right the way to the station, but some how no one dying (fuck knows how).

In them days Cardiff station had a big wooden gate outside it and once they had pushed all our lot inside they locked it with huge padlocks. A train was now waiting for us and the police were now concentrating once again on the Taffies outside the station. They temporary forgot about us, bad move as only 50 Millwall got on the Penny lane train, leaving 250 of us on the platform. The police had gone thinking we had gone too, as the train had left we had gone through on to another platform and waited there for 10 mins quietly.

The police were still battling with the Taffies, but had managed to clear them from outside the station .Myself and a few other Millwall rallied the troops and said we had been humiliated by the Taffies and what they had managed to do. We said we are Millwall the best fucking firm in the country and we are not leaving it at that. "Come on lets fucking do them" the cry went up. It was dead outside the station as the old bill and Cardiff were well away from the front. Another big roar went up and we smashed the gate down and steamed forward like Vikings." WAR WAR WAR WAR" we shouted as we went looking for the Taffies, we then smashed anything in our way, pubs, cars, and any one who looked like they could fight. ""Come on were Millwall we shouted as we headed straight into the old bill. They charged us with horses, dogs and batons , eventually getting us on the next train home, weather we liked it or not.

That was a typical away day in the 70s, if you had the arse to go to a naughty gaff.
At Cardiff you always had to graft BIG TIME.

Chapter 3

THE EARLY 80s. THE 3rd DIVISION WAS TOUGHER THAN WE THOUGHT
By Simon Williams (50yrs old Ex Director) CARDIFF CITY

A mate of mine Simon who I have known down the football since I was 12yrs old, has written about the next 3 teams, I was there and Pompey,Wigan and Lincoln all made a day of it with Cardiff and tested Cardiff to the full. I've let Simon tell you what he witnessed. Annis

I remember Annis when he was a kid as he was about 7 years younger than me and by the time he was 15, he was hanging around with all the older lads and eventually going to all the away games with some of the top lads at the time.

I have never ever pretended to be one of the top lads, but just one of the lads who enjoyed the scene and all who know me will agree with this. I have supported Cardiff City football club for 42 years now and all the boys I used to go to games with were a great laugh and top boys. Many of whom used to travel with me week in and week out to every game for more years than I care to remember, they were Paul (the Rumney baboon) Tony (Nanna) Little Colin, Dave (the postie) Dai (Hooligan) Mark (from Portmanmore Rd, Splott) Carlton, Dav, Jonna and probably some great lads that I have missed out ...sorry.

I have seen both sides of this great and famous football club, from the terrace all the way to the boardroom where I was a director for 3 years under the Rick Wright regime in the early 90s, and then back to my season ticket in Sect A of the grandstand. The club is in my blood it a massive part of my life and now my son, who I take to most home games is also addicted to this great tradition, this is Cardiff, we are Cardiff " Blue Army ".

I've seen it all with the City from small scuffles to near riots, I've been there when the crowds have been as low as 1,500 and I've been there when Ninian Park has been packed to the rafters. I've got to know the lads on the terraces who eventually became the original Soul Crew in the early 80's.

1982/83 Season.

It was the 1982/83 season which stands out in my mind as that was the year that you could say was the year that Cardiff terrorised the third division and it was the year that the Soul Crew was formed.

LINCOLN CITY..... everybody was looking forward to Lincoln City away as most of us had never been to Sinsil Bank and also Lincoln were one of our main rivals for promotion from the old division three back to the second division.

We all met up early at Cardiff Central station and travelled by intercity train via Birmingham new street to arrive in Lincoln at about 12.30pm on the Saturday.

We made camp in a local pub near the ground and up to this point there had not been any major disturbances that I can recall, just the odd scuffle and mini battle around the streets of the town centre.

I had travelled with the same mates that I went with for most games, Paul (the Rumney baboon) little Colin, Dave (the postie) and Tony (Nanna) all great guys and very very game lads. Their was also a lad called Parsons from Cardiff, who at the time lived in London and to many including myself felt Parsons was the one who started the Soul Crew and also came up with the name, a leader and a game lad but at the same time he upset many a Cardiff fan with his obnoxious attitude.

We stayed in the pub for a while until everyone who was suppose to becoming had arrived. After leaving the pub Parsons wanted us to all go in the seats in the main grandstand, which was something that most firms had now started to do around the country. There had been a lot of rumours coming back to us, that a few skirmishes had already taken place between some of the Valley lads and Lincoln. So off we went about 40 of our lot to their home section seats in the ground.

The game passed by pretty uneventfully, as at half time we were all allowed to wander around from the stand and near to the pitch side unchallenged. This gave Parsons an idea that he wanted everybody onto the pitch at the final whistle. The main bulk of approx 1,500 Cardiff fans were fenced off to our left on an open terrace. At the final whistle, a game which I think we lost 2-1, we rushed onto the pitch and basically just meandered around the penalty spot, some of the lads were urging Lincoln who were not fenced in to join Cardiff on the pitch, this they did in there hundreds and hundreds, there must have been about 40 Cardiff on the pitch and 300 Lincoln, I remember thinking this is not too clever, it was well on top, with no chance of the main Cardiff firm helping as they were battling with the Old Bill themselves trying to join us, Cardiff stood their ground in the centre circle before eventually being legged out of the ground by biting snapping Alsatians and the Old Bill whacking their batons into us, along with hundreds of Lincoln fans baying for blood.

As soon as Cardiff got outside the ground it went mental, Lincoln were well up for it and very game and at one point it looked like we were going to get over run again, however as soon as the massed ranks of the main throng of Cardiff lads arrived from the opposite side of the ground it was pretty much all over with Lincoln, having to retreat fast as they had attacked us, as waive after waive of Cardiff's firm attacked them.

There was then out breaks of trouble all the way back to the station, this was mainly damage caused by marauding Cardiff supporters attacking or damaging pretty much what ever got in their way. I was later told that Lincoln then had battles with the Valley lads who had come by vans and busses and that Lincoln were well up for it.

On the trip home some one had a radio and we all listened on radio sports report at 5,ish about the trouble that had just unfolded as this had reached the national radio station.
When the train pulled into Birmingham new street, Cardiff all disembarked, there was probably 50 or 60 lads on this train, the next one due in had the bulk of Cardiff on.
People were milling about the concourse waiting for the connecting train to Cardiff, when somebody shouted that WEST HAM'S ICF had just arrived on one of the platforms, Cardiff went steaming down the escalators and straight into what must have been only about 20 to 30 ICF, Cardiff through sheer numbers were having the better of this until another train pulled into the station within minutes of the first packed with West Ham, they poured off and went straight into Cardiff who had to make a quick retreat up the stair's as overwhelming numbers were piling into the Soul Crew.

Up on the main concourse after being backed right off, the Old Bill and dogs restored order and normality. We all kept thinking, if only the next train of Cardiff would arrive but that was half our behind us so West Ham won the day.

This was one of the best away trips in this promotion season and all credit has to go to Lincoln City's lads, this is what I can remember all be it many years ago now.

PORTSMOUTH…. I think we've both got a lot of respect for each other. The amount of trouble with the 6.57 lads was always big as you have to rate Pompey as one of the top UK firms, especially after Pompey got into our seats in Block A of our main grandstand at Ninian Park and tried holding out for as long as they could.

Cardiff had massed under the stand and then poured into the seats, all hell broke loose and as well as thick wooded seats being hurled at each other, Pompey were getting thrown over the adjoining wall into the enclosure below, this went on for no more than three or four minutes but it was a nasty situation for the Pompey lads to be in and fair play they took it to us.

One of my best mates Dai (hooligan) was due over the wall the next day and was using his final day of freedom to rid our seats of Pompey, as was another good mate of mine called Willie who was banging Pompey over the wall into the enclosure below.

PORTSMOUTH AWAY

Probably the biggest firm of Cardiff to travel to the South coast was the season both clubs gained promotion from the old division three to the second division.
The main mob of Cardiff gathered at Cardiff central station to travel the three hours by train, and Parsons was there as if to marshal the troops and make sure every one was present correct and up for it, even down to the fact he seemed to be inspecting what some people were wearing to make sure he was happy.

When we pulled into Portsmouth Harbour everybody imagined there would be hundreds of

Pompey waiting, but there weren't, as 400 to 500 Cardiff piled off the train they were looking for confrontation and started marching all over the City, some then started blaming Parsons for messing up what they believed was going to be a meeting with Portsmouth infamous 6.57 firm, and believed he had got the station wrong, whether this was true or not I am not too sure.

Eventually after a pretty uneventful day so far Cardiff's Soul Crew had reached Fratton Park, Cardiff must have had upwards of four to five thousand out that day, and in those days it seemed as though 85% to 90% of Cardiff's away support were mad lads always looking for a battle at every away ground in the country.

During the game there was a lot of scuffling with the local police, and major damage was caused to Pompeys famous "pompey chimes clock " when a well know chap named "Freddie the gargoyle" climbed up the main stanchions and grabbed the hands of the clock and hung there till the hands of the famous old clock snapped, Pompey as you can imagine went mental, as well as both sets of fans trying their hardest to get at each other inside the ground and were pelting each other with anything they could throw at one another, they couldn't wait for the final whistle to blow, as it did the police tried holding Cardiff back in the ground, but they heaved and pushed their way out and the Police lines broke and hundreds of Cardiff met hundreds of Portsmouth outside, all hell broke loose it was chaos both firms going for each other neither giving way and it took a massive effort from the police to keep both battling firms apart, all the way back to the station, mass disorder was taking place as well as mass destruction as I witnessed more than one vehicle lying on its roof, that's how bad things were becoming, as well as that everything was raining through the air from both sides and many people were taking some right nasty cuts to their heads and bodies. Both firms really wanted it and no matter how many police tried to keep us apart, battles between us and them went on for a good half hour.

Eventually we got back to the station and if truth were told, the running battles all the way back were pretty even affairs, some of the events that day were pretty unbelievable to witness especially the damage inside the old stadium. Back on the train Cardiff were another point closer to their main aim promotion back to the second division and hopefully more meetings and days out which they had just experienced.

WIGAN ATHLETIC…. The old Springfield Park ground was the scene of probably the longest battle I have ever witnessed on another teams end in all my life. I had travelled up by car with my usual mates and after parking up a few streets away from the ground, we saw a few well-known faces outside a pub near to the ground, so we headed for a drink there. We had a few drinks and then waited to see what the order of the day was going to be.

After a few outbreaks of trouble before the game between small mobs of Wigan and Cardiff, Parsons who founded the Soul Crew had the idea that every one was going to get organized and get on Wigan's end. And so all the lads who had been drinking together at the same pub close to the ground all left on masse about ten minutes or so before the kick off, unbelievably unimpeded

by the police and left to their own devises, but making no noise and trying to look very inconspicuous.

After queuing up and getting into the ground, about thirty or so Soul Crew made their way over to the fence on Wigan's end closest to the main bulk of the Cardiff support.
I think the local constabulary had forgotten about this fixture, as they just did not turn up for a very very long time. As soon as the game started so did the trouble. The two sets of fans on Wigan's end just went at each other toe to toe for what must have been the best part of 5 to 10 minutes uninterrupted by the police. Eventually the Police arrived to try to restore order, which eventually after several arrests they did. Cardiff were all led out of the end and allowed entry into the away terracing (how things have changed).

During the game albeit there was a lot of chanting from both sides, you could sense that as soon as these two sets of fans could get at each other then they would, and they did. Outside both sets of supporters charged into each other and were both as up for it as the other. Friends later told me, as we had to get back to our car, that this went on throughout the whole walk back to the railway station as both mobs fought running battles with each other and on many occasions the old bill lost control of the situation. Wigan wanted it as much as Cardiff that day and took the fight to the Soul Crew who were happy to oblige, honours even. That day was talked about for the rest of the season by the Lads.
This was a top away game between these two clubs, which has never really been rivalled in all the fixtures between the two since.

Pompey we expected it but Wigan and Lincoln had showed the Soul Crew that they weren't going to take the mick in their manors.

Chapter 4

Dont Ever Underestimate The Taffy's By Pat Dolan Chelsea

Im sure I dont need to introduce my old mate Pat from Chelsea as he's probably one of the most well known lads in the Country and a True Legend with it. In the "Diary of the Real Soul crew 1", Pat told some really great stories of how we met and many more stories on Cardiff, I had to ask him back as a book with out Pat wouldn't be complete without him. Annis

Chelsea V Cardiff 1983

Much has been made of the famous 3-3 draw, Cardiff V Chelsea match in 1984 but although not on the scale of this match the game at Stamford Bridge earlier in the season had it's moments as well.

I remember the talk during the week, there was to be a meet at Paddington station in the morning, at the bar in the station, so bright and early, I was at the pub by about 11.30am.

By 12.30 we had about 25 boys. It turns out there was a documentary about football violence the same day and they were filming in the Swan at Fulham Broadway, which was one of our main pubs. Apparently most of our lot wanted to get their boat races on T.V. It wouldn't happen nowadays and that's why it was such a shit turnout.

About 1 o'clock we noticed 10 dressers had come off the Cardiff train and were stood on the concourse staring at us lot. Three of us walked over and before we reached them (these Cardiff who were younger than us, about 16 years of age), they nervously edged over towards a group of transport old bill who were at the end of the platform. "No trouble boys", one of our lot said, "We just want to know how many you are bringing today?" The Cardiff boys in a Patrick (light blue, dark blue) waterproof jacket said "We've got 300 lads, but they all got off in Slough and went on the piss, so we're not going to get to your place until late". "Fair enough mate" we said. To be honest I wouldn't have fancied our chances with our 25 against 300 of Cardiff's finest. We all then went back to the bar, had one more and then headed up the taxi rank onto Prags Street to get the underground.

As we got to the top of the ramp, we noticed about 40 lads drinking outside the Dickens Tavern. "How the fuck did they get past us?", I said, "never mind", said one of ours , "it's, game on, come on you taffy bastards". We charged towards the Cardiff, who had just woken up to the fact that they were being attacked. As one they turned and ran back into the pub closing the door behind them, We were all stood in the street feeling pleased with ourselves, when the door went flying open and glasses, ashtrays, barstools and even a plate of spaghetti came flying towards us. I picked up the board outside the pub and launched it into the mob of Taffy's who were now slowly edging out of the pub. This backed them off at first, but more and more glasses came at us and we were now backed off into the street.

Cardiff then poured into the street with at least 100 boys. There must have been about 60 in the pub when we ran the first lot in. After standing for a while under a constant bombardment of glasses the old cry of "fucking stand Chelsea" went up. A sure sign that we were about to get put on our toes. Anyway we got chased round the corner back into the station, but Cardiff stopped at the entrance luckily for us. I think they thought we were leading them into an ambush, so they didn't follow us.

Back at the ground, apparently the Cardiff who had come on coaches had got run by Chelsea down at the Princess Royal, all the way up to the North Stand entrance. It was later shown on the documentary they were filming that day. It shows about 150 chelsea chanting "Ooo, Ooo, Ooo" as they chased Cardiff up the street, and then the old bill nick a wedge headed Taffy in a ski jumper and tight Lois jeans, Nike Wimbledon trainers for trying to do a suicide stand, when all his mates have fucked off.

After the game, (the other Cardiff boys did turn up, late by the way and got drenched on the North Stand), there was talk of revenge for our little reversal before the game, so it was all set for round 2 at Paddington.

We had about 200 waiting at Paddington, when all of a sudden the shout goes up, "here they are!", up came the Cardiff boys in an escort and they were pushed through the middle of the station by the old bill, with us lot trying to get at them from both sides. As they got to the platform entrance, me and Brains fronted a few of them and they backed off. This old bill saw what was happening and jumped between us drawing his truncheon and shouting to me get back. I'll never forget what happened next. A Cardiff lad lent across the copper and spat a big greeny which hit me full in the face. I was fucking speechless, as Brains was crying with laughter next to me. I swear to god, I was incandescent with rage. If I had caught that cunt, I would have beaten that prick to death, given him the kiss of life, then beaten him again. To coin a phrase, I would have done 28 days later on his fucking head! Anyway I could keep my rage in check until the return a few months later.

Chapter 5

THE MATCH WASN'T FINISHED By PAT DOLAN CHELSEA

Cardiff v Chelsea 1984

Ah, the famous 3-3 draw, which I would put in my top ten in matches for trouble before, during and after the game.

Dave Jones did a very good summary of what happened from a Cardiff point in the Soul Crew book and Annis has asked me to write it from the Chelsea side. Luckily would you believe there is actually a tape knocking about of the actual match. A ninety minute ******* tape with no commentary. Fuck me, I was laughing my head off, it is non stop action in the Grandstand and Canton stand with fans being led around the pitch and coppers dragging lads out, etc... I'm glad I watched the tape as the memories of back then are not the sharpest, so it was a good help.

The morning of the game, we arrived about 1.30pm. The first train had already dropped a big firm off and they had already clashed with Cardiff, as mentioned by Dave Jones (Soul Crew). The old bill tried to hold us at the station entrance, but if I remember correctly there was a John Menzies shop in the station and we all cut through it and escaped into the city. Soon the old bill saw that everyone was now out of the station and jogging down the road towards the ground. The old bill just said "fuck it" and just let everyone go, so we were about 600 handed walking towards Ninian Park with the old bill behind us. It was god's grace that we didn't bump onto Cardiff, because there would have been murder. In fact we didn't see one boy all the way to the stadium.

In the early 80's all of our firm used to go into the seats, because at the end of the match you never got held back and you could leave 5 minutes before the end and walk outside or attempt to invade the home section as the home fans were leaving. Anyway as usual we all piled into the seats in the Grandstand and the Canton stand (we had a fucking massive firm that day).

We were surprised to see a small firm of Cardiff in the seats next to us in the Grandstand. There were only about 70 of them and they were soon getting terrorised, so the old bill and stewards took them down into the enclosure and round the pitch to put them back in the Bob Bank, Not to miss a chance of mischief, a load of our lot jumped on the back of the Cardiff escort going back to the Bob Bank. As they passed the Canton Stand the Chelsea mob in there steamed down and a few punches were exchanged through the fence.

The old bill then opened a gate on the Bob Bank to let the Cardiff lot back in, when it all kicked off the 20 or so Chelsea invaders got sussed as they entered the gate. Apparently this is where some Cardiff got squirted with Ammonia as the Chelsea boys were being driven back out.

Throughout the game the there were so many incidents I couldn't possibly remember them all. But with 10 minutes to go we were 3-0 down, we were now sat in the Canton Stand and could go wherever we wanted as the old bill didn't have a Danny La Rue. The shout went up "Come on, we're leaving". With that about 250 of us walked round behind the Canton Stand with the intention of getting on the Bob Bank.

I can remember us walking through all the early leavers and looking up and seeing two lads at the top of the stairs starring down at us. They both sussed us and ran back into the Bob Bank, within seconds hundreds of Cardiff came flying down the stairs towards us, Game on. It went toe to toe for about 20 seconds until we started to get the upper hand and chased Cardiff back up the stairs into the home end. Apparently the Chelsea in the Grandstand saw all the Cardiff run back onto the Bob Bank and then they all tried to leave and join in the fun. For whatever reason, I forget now but we all stalled at the bottom of the stairs enabling one fucking copperand a dog to pull the gate shut on us. Cardiff then came back down the stairs and we all started to trade punches through the gate until the old bill forced us back onto the road.

There were now 1000's of Chelsea boys outside while the old bill locked Cardiff in the Bob Bank, it's the first time I've ever seen the home fans kept in while the away fans were let out. Anyway about 500 of us walked up to the Ninian pub and plotted up, there were no old bill with us. About 5 minutes later some Chelsea came under the railway bridge and were calling us up the road. Obviously it was going off outside the ground, here we go again as everyone charged down the street. I don't know what exactly happened as the old bill now chased everyone back to the Ninian. It apparently went mental outside the stadium with Chelsea getting the better of it but Cardiff giving a good account of themselves.

Back at the Ninian we started to walk back towards Canton and we noticed off the road we were on, there was a load of Coronation type streets leading back to the road towards the train station. As we reached one side street, we couldn't believe our luck, as at the top of the road was a huge mob of Cardiff 500-600 handed about the same as us. The old bill were behind both mobs so this was it! "Fucking walk at em, Don't run at em" , went the shout. However being youngsters and keen and dafter, some people walk quicker than others. At the other end of the road Cardiff came charging down the road towards us, launching everything at us. We noticed that as Cardiff were getting closer but at the same time slowing down. The charge had now gone to a jog, then to a walk, then at about 100 meters to a stop. Then we could here the stand "Cardiff stand", as they started to back peddle up the road. On the junction of the main road they managed to regain some composure and had made a stand right across the road.

Us lot (the younger ones) reached the junction first and bounced up and down in front of the Welsh hoards, "we're fucking Chelsea, come on you mugs," just then the biggest skin head I've ever seen came out of the Cardiff crowd and fronted the lot of us. I nudged my mate C, who by the way is one of the gamest most fearless football lads I've ever met. "go on then C", I shouted as the skinhead called us on. "you fucking go on then", said C as we were debating which one of us was going to be killed first. It was then I noticed a "draught" behind me, as in our haste to get to the fight, the rest of our mob were still casually strolling down the road about 100 meters behind us.Luckily for us it was as Cardiff started to sense the chance of a turning point in the row, a police van pulled up in front of them, while another one drove straight at us sending our whole mob scampering back down the road. Further on we cut down another side street and were now behind the Cardiff mob with a few token old bill in the middle. It went mental all the way back to the bus station, with Cardiff going toe to toe with us, then back pedalling, then standing again, all the way back to the train station. I couldn't believe how many Chelsea had been busted up with bricks and bottles etc..

When we got to the train station, it was only then that we realised how many lads had been hurt. There were load of cut heads, busted hands etc.. If looks could tell the truth it looked like we had been in the wars, literally. All the talk on the train was what would have happened if we'd got on the Bob Bank. In my opinion, I think we would have got killed. From my experience of going on the other teams end, you need three things, the element of surprise, to get behind the home mob and to hold the high ground. We didn't have any of this with Cardiff. Also when you go on a home end you can end up fighting everyone from hooligans to fans, even women and children want to kill you.

As we got off in London a ticket inspector said, "fucking hell boys, who have you been fighting with, the Welsh rugby teams?", "near enough mate, near enough", said one of our lads, sporting a nice black eye and chipped front tooth ensemble, the inspector then said, "good result on the pitch", "are you taking the fucking hit and miss?", I said angrily, "you drew 3-3 mate, you scored 3 in the last 5 minutes", we just stood there opened mouthed. There had been so much trouble, we didn't even think of the score. What a fucking day!

P.S. To the fucking huge Cardiff skinhead, I still see you in my nightmares!

MARCH 31, 1984

Cardiff   3 Chelsea   3

Ninian arrests

AT least a dozen arrests were made before half time at this afternoon's Cardiff v Chelsea match as violence flared on the terraces and outside Ninian Park.

A major police operation had been mounted in a bid to prevent problems.

Many Chelsea fans climbed from the enclosure into the grandstand, preventing ticket holders from taking their seats. Others climbed over a wall into areas containing City fans, and began chanting their team's name.

City followers retaliated, and police moved in to separate them.

Chapter 6

What A fucking Let Down
By Nicky Muff (MUFFY)
Service Crew Leeds Utd

I first met Muffy when I lived in Bradford in the early 80's, unusual circumstances to say the least which you will later see that Muffy has touched on and I have written about in my own life story book due out later this year.

He knows my thoughts on Leeds, so we've always agreed not to discuss them and that way, we stayed good friends, he was a good mate during the 80's and still is today even if he does support Leeds. Fair play to him he's Leeds through and through and Muffy is a lad who will stand by your side no matter what. He's probably one of their gamest lads. Leeds don't rate many other firms in fact ,I don't know any one they do rate from Millwall to Man Utd, they haven't got an ounce of respect for, so to even get a mention means something, perhaps this was one of the main reasons I disliked them so much when I lived up that way for over a year. Well here are Muffy's stories on Cardiff. Annis

I've been a Leeds fan since I was knee high, my dad though was Bradford and the rest of the family were too, but Leeds was the team for me and will be till I die.

If ever there was an appropriate way to meet a football hooligan then it was going to be a kick off, not anything major but a bit of a set too, I was 15 years old at the time and was on my way to see Leeds v Chelsea, It was the 1982/83 season and you cant get any better than that fixture in those days. I was at Bradford train station at 9am with a couple of my mates Woody being one of them. We were school kids at the time but were already into the casual scene and had been watching the Leeds Service crew rise to the top, so playing Chelsea was far better than going on a geography field trip to Hebden Bridge.

Ten minutes to go for the train, 20 minutes to Leeds Central, then we would be in up and coming hooligan heaven. We didn't have to wait to long, as whack straight to the side of the head, I stumbled back and as I did I looked up to see a glimpse of a fleeing sheepskin, faded jeans and a pair of adidas trainers, we were at it already. Not sure what had really just happened and by who, but we decided to get the next train to Leeds and we would then be amongst our own.

Twenty four years later, I with my family would be sat at a table along side Sam Hammam and his wife and many Cardiff lads celebrating the wedding of the very person who had given me that first taste of the enemies' fist. Annis.

Over the years I have witnessed and been involved in many incidents with Annis, but for now it's the ones involving his beloved Cardiff City and the Soul Crew which I now tell. It took a couple of years to come across a Leeds/Cardiff game and after many stories from Annis and members of the Bradford City Ointment, so it was with great anticipation I found myself again in Leeds at 10 in the morning.

Having been to many a game up to then it was well known that many firms didn't come to Leeds, whether through fear or lack of organisation I do not know. So Cardiff's arrival was a great shock to Leeds, The Black Lion pub was just about to open for the days gathering of Leeds, around 50 Leeds were already waiting for the doors to open, not even thinking of Cardiff.

From the entrance of The Black Lion you can see the arrival of anyone coming into Leeds City Centre via the train station. You could wait all day long in the hope of some firm being daring enough to have ago which we longed for. Ten minutes is all we had to wait that day, they were here in mass around 250 of them had made the trip from South Wales to have a go at Leeds. We 50 to 60 thought yes here we go this is it. Remember organisation they had that, remember fear they may have had that as they were now in Leeds, because up to then it seemed they would be coming straight at us and with no escort what's so ever and they got one. What a fucking let down, I had waited 2 years of tales of this and tales of that and what Leeds got was a hard looking Welsh male choir. They started singing behind the barriers, Ca'rdiff Ca'rdiff and with that the old bill came from every where and that's where it ended.

I did here from other Leeds lads that a rogue coach of Cardiff attacked the Peacock pub at 3pm and chased a few Leeds, a pity they didn't get there earlier.

We would meet some months later down in Cardiff, in those days Leeds took various divisions of firms to matches, one being the lads from Bradford, on a good day we could number over 100 easy and I mean some good lads came from Bradford who followed Leeds, we had many a Saturday night battle with Bradford's Ointment in Bradford town Centre. So the trip to Cardiff, we had a very good coach full.

We made our way to Cardiff via some country villages and soon found our way into Cardiff. Our coach driver being originally from South Wales he took us to a road called Penarth road and dropped us off and the 50 of us made our way for a mile at least to Ninian Park, We never saw a lad, another let down. It was now approaching kick off so we went in. Nothing happened during the game but after, the 50 of us came steaming out straight for the Soul Crew, we were met by hundreds of lads and yes we were backed off but for Cardiff to claim that as a result with their numbers well that's up to them. I will admit when I was on the floor, lads who I've got to know from Cardiff over the years and who came to visit Annis when he lived up this way, Mannings and Little Collin, Moorie etc when they saw me, saved me from a hiding and I owe you one.

Annis later laughed at me and said you idiots you walked down a road no one ever uses, once again we decided not to talk about Cardiff/Leeds as we would both not agree on anything.

I never came to the FA CUP match in Cardiff in 2002 as I was abroad, I had enough texts of Annis though after the game, laughing at us. I know for a fact over 200 of Leed's top lads went to Hereford before the game and tried their best to get into Cardiff and near the end of the game they also fought like mad to get out on the streets and knowing Cardiff were massive that day.

Also when Cardiff played their first league game up here for years when we were first relegated we had thousands of lads out for Cardiff and many went to prison for it, fighting the old bill outside the ground for over 2 hours.

Annis still says Cardiff are way ahead of Mighty Leeds in lads well we beg to differ once again.

Chapter 7

Seventeen
By Dave Sugarman CARDIFF CITY

Dave Sugarman, as you will see is not a hooligan, but if you supported Cardiff through the years, whether you liked it or not you would probably of got caught up in it. I wanted Dave's story in this book as I thought it would be different and it sure is as Dave is probably one of the best writers down the City and remembers everything, he's known as TLG on the City Message Boards. Annis

Seventeen. That's how old I was when it became painfully obvious that I wasn't cut out to be a football hooligan. My experiences during a six month period from March to September 1984 left me in no doubt that I was never going to make the grade as a member of the Soul Crew. If you're hoping this will be another collection of anecdotes from somebody who was one of Cardiff's top boys in the Eighties, you'll be disappointed. On the contrary, mine is a cautionary tale about a young lad who was drawn to football violence like a moth to a flame, but who soon learned that getting involved was more hassle than it was worth.

My father took me to my first Cardiff City game in March 1975 on the day before my eighth birthday. A trip to Ninian Park was his idea of a special treat. Sheffield Wednesday were Cardiff's opponents on that glorious occasion. The Owls were rock bottom of the Second Division table, while the Bluebirds were just one place above them. Predictably, the match ended in a goalless draw. The crowd jeered, slow hand clapped and chanted 'what a load of rubbish' at regular intervals throughout the ninety minutes. Midfielder George Smith ripped off his shirt and threw it at manager Jimmy Andrews after being substituted. His replacement, Johnny Vincent, missed a late penalty, and City were booed off the field following the final whistle. Both teams were relegated to the Third Division a month later. Happy days.

Although I'd been given a grim introduction to life as a Cardiff supporter, I was nevertheless bitten by the Bluebirds bug and became a City fanatic from that day forward. After my father had taken me to the remaining four home games of the 74/75 campaign, I pleaded with him to buy me a season ticket for 75/76, which he duly did. Our seats were situated in the back row of Block C of the Grandstand, directly in front of the old press box, and the view from up there was superb. I have lots of terrific memories from my first full season as a City fan, which was a very successful one for the club. The likes of Willie Anderson, Adrian Alston and Tony Evans played some brilliant football as they fired the Bluebirds to promotion to the Second Division, but it wasn't just the action on the pitch that kept me entertained. Back then, visiting supporters were usually housed in the enclosure, which was an area of terracing to the left of the Grange End. It was directly below our section of the Grandstand, so those of us in Block C had a clear view of what went on down there. In the mid-Seventies, the sight of rival fans smashing lumps out of each other in the enclosure was as common as the sound of fireworks on the Bob Bank during winter and the smell of cigars in the Grandstand at Christmas. Teams such as Crystal Palace,

Brighton and Millwall brought decent numbers to Ninian during 75/76, so there were plenty of scraps to be seen on the terraces.

As a young child I was fascinated by hooliganism, but that's hardly surprising as I began attending matches at a time when violence seemed to go hand in hand with Cardiff City. In those days, crowd trouble was such a regular occurrence in and around Ninian Park that I never considered it to be anything other than normal. As far as I was aware, fighting was simply something that young men were supposed to do at the football. There was nothing unusual about it at all.

Sometimes, after matches had finished, the clashes on Sloper Road would get so bad that the stewards in Block C of the Grandstand would advise anyone with women and children to wait in the Players' Bar for twenty minutes or so. Our exit onto the streets was the same one used by the away fans in the enclosure, so we were told to stay in the ground until things had calmed down outside. I can remember several occasions during the mid-Seventies when I was sat in bar watching through the upstairs window as scores of lads fought pitched battles on the streets below.

Naturally enough, the majority of the football songs I was hearing and learning as I was growing up were about violence, or Cardiff aggro as the boys preferred to label it. City's lads proudly proclaimed they came from the valleys where the grass was green and were the hardest fans you'd ever seen. Visiting supporters were warned they'd have to keep off the Grange End if they wanted to stay alive. They were also told they were going to get their fucking heads kicked in, they'd never make the station and they were either going in the Taff or going home in an ambulance. Ninian Park was such a warm, welcoming place for visitors back in the Seventies.

While I'd seen numerous minor skirmishes on the streets and terraces during my debut season as a City supporter, the first major outbreak of trouble I witnessed came at the end of the 75/76 campaign. The occasion was a European Championships quarter final second leg between Wales and Yugoslavia at Ninian, and the crowd disturbances on that sunny May afternoon were so serious they ended up making headline news all over Europe.

The Yugoslavs had beaten Wales 2-0 in Zagreb a month earlier, so Mike Smith's team had a mountain to climb in order to reach the semi-finals. Nevertheless, the demand for tickets was high and Grandstand seats were very hard to come by. My father managed to get us tickets, although he couldn't get two together. His seat was halfway up Block E, while mine was a couple of rows from the front of Block F. Not too far apart in reality, but it was a little daunting for a nine year-old to be separated from his dad in a crowd of over 30,000, especially given the volatile atmosphere.

The man who took centre stage on an afternoon those present will never forget was an East German referee by the name of Rudi Glockner. He was considered to be one of the best officials in the world at the time, having previously refereed the 1970 World Cup final between Brazil in Italy in Mexico, but for whatever reason he didn't seem to like the Welsh. Within twenty minutes of the kick-off he'd upset the crowd when he awarded the visitors a penalty despite a blatant dive by striker Dan Popivoda. Defender Josif Katalinski tucked away the spot-kick to leave Wales 3-0 down on aggregate and in need of a miracle, although Crystal Palace centre-half Ian Evans equalised seven minutes before half-time to give the home fans a bit of hope.

An unlikely comeback looked possible shortly after the break when John Toshack scored from close range. A bicycle kick from John Mahoney had set Toshack up, but Glockner ruled that Mahoney had been guilty of dangerous play and disallowed the goal. Despite the fact that Toshack's effort would have been deemed legal by any British referee, the East German was having none of it, so Ninian Park went mental. Beer cans rained down on the playing surface from all angles, several lads scaled the fences and invaded the pitch in an effort to attack the ref and the rest of the crowd aimed Nazi salutes in the direction of the officials. Play was halted for five minutes and Glockner threatened to abandon the match, which was something he did twice more before the afternoon was over.

A second Toshack goal was disallowed for offside ten minutes after the first, which prompted another volley of beer cans from the terraces along with more pitch invasions, more Nazi salutes and another lengthy stoppage in play. The crowd's misery was complete when Terry Yorath missed a penalty twelve minutes from time, so the fans contented themselves by abusing the East German officials for the remainder of the game. Play had to be stopped again after linesman Siegfried Kirschen was hit in the neck by a stone thrown from the Bob Bank. When Glockner eventually decided to blow the final whistle, hundreds invaded the pitch from all four sides of the ground. Between twenty and thirty policemen sprinted onto the Ninian turf and surrounded the referee in an attempt to escort him to safety and they just about managed to do so, but not without a serious casualty. One of the pitch invaders grabbed the flag from the corner where I was sitting and threw it like a javelin in Glockner's direction. It landed in the shoulder of one of the coppers who was trying to shepherd him off the field. Images of the stricken officer were used by many of the national and international papers in the days that followed as Welsh fans were roundly condemned by the world's press. 'Ninian Park's Day of Shame!' screamed the headline on the front page of the Western Mail, while talk of possible European bans for both Cardiff City and Wales filled the back pages.

That day was a hell of an experience for a nine year-old kid and it made a huge impression on me. The atmosphere inside Ninian Park was so hostile it was frightening, but it was also strangely exhilarating. I can clearly remember my bewilderment as the entire crowd were standing and chanting 'Sieg Heil' at Glockner during the second half. I didn't have a clue what that was all about, but everyone else was doing it so I joined in regardless. I can also remember my mother giving the old man an almighty bollocking when we arrived back home. We'd returned well over an hour later than scheduled due to a combination of the large crowd, the various delays during the game and the fighting on the streets after it had finished. Mum had heard about the trouble on the news and she'd been convinced that something terrible had happened to us. She was right too. We'd been knocked out of the European Championships.

Three more major outbreaks of violence I witnessed in my first few years as a City fan occurred during games against Wrexham and Everton in 1977, and Chelsea in 1979. The Wrexham match was a dramatic fourth round FA Cup tie that the Bluebirds won 3-2 courtesy of a last-gasp strike by Scottish midfielder John Buchanan. The attendance at Ninian Park on that occasion was almost 30,000 and the fighting in the enclosure was incredible. It was almost non-stop during the first half. So many lads were involved that the police seemed powerless to do anything about it.

Cardiff played Everton in the fifth round in front of a bumper 35,000 crowd. Some bright spark came up with the idea of putting four thousand visiting supporters on the Canton side of the Bob Bank with only a temporary plastic fence separating them from about eight thousand City fans on the other side. The segregation measures lasted all of two minutes. Everton won the tie 2-1 but the Scousers who came down to South Wales won't have happy memories of their trip. Many of them got battered.

The Chelsea match in 1979 is one that has gone down in hooligan folklore. A group of around fifty Londoners invaded the Bob Bank shortly before the game started and they were given an almighty hammering for their troubles. There were bodies flying all over the place while it was kicking off. A couple of Chelsea lads got thrown over the wall at the back of the terrace and about a dozen had to be carried away on stretchers once things had eventually calmed down. There was also chaos outside the ground after the game had finished. Jubilee Park was like a mini war zone. The press later reported that two pubs in the city centre had been badly damaged, twenty four fans had needed hospital treatment and the police had made almost a hundred arrests.

My father usually took me to three or four away matches each season during my first five years as a City supporter. The games he picked were generally local derbies in places like Bristol, Hereford and Swansea. Unsurprisingly, there was always trouble of one sort or another at such matches. He also took me to games against several of the London clubs including Charlton, Crystal Palace and Fulham, along with a couple of England v Wales home internationals at the old Wembley Stadium. They were lively affairs to say the very least. If memory serves, more Welshmen were using the rotten wooden seats as weapons than were sitting on them during a 0-0 draw there in May 1979. Wembley was a dump when we arrived but it looked considerably worse after we'd left.

The first time I ever travelled to an away match without the supervision of my father was in April 1981. I'd just turned fourteen at the time. Cardiff were playing Swansea in a Second Division game at the Vetch Field, but the old man refused to take me because of the violence during the previous season's fixtures between the two clubs. It was a vitally important match as the Bluebirds were battling against relegation and the Swans were going for promotion. I was determined not to miss it, so my mate Dan Beynon and I cobbled together as much money as we could in the week leading up to the game. After telling our parents on the Saturday morning that we were spending the day at our local youth club, we caught a bus into town, then jumped on a National Express coach and headed for Jackland. Having left Cardiff at around 9-30am, we were able to walk from the bus station to the Vetch without any problems, but we'd arrived so early that the ground hadn't even opened by the time we got there. We were both as green as grass and didn't have a clue what we were doing. We ended up sitting outside the away end for at least an hour before the turnstiles eventually opened.

The terraces began filling up pretty quickly once the ground did open and it wasn't long before missiles of various descriptions were flying back and forth between the West Stand and the North Bank. I can remember an enormous skinhead dislodging a large piece of one of the terrace steps shortly after his arrival in the away end. Once he'd smashed it into hundreds of pieces, the air was thick with lumps of concrete for a while. About half an hour before kick-off, the word went around that a gang of Cardiff lads were going to attack the North Bank at ten to three. Sure enough, when the time arrived a group of thirty or forty City fans made themselves known in the top left-hand corner of the terrace and it was bedlam over there for a few minutes until the Old Bill managed to drag them out.

The game itself proved to be a decent contest. The Jacks were well on top during the first half and Leighton James put them ahead just before the break, but he wasted a chance to increase their lead when he had a second half penalty brilliantly saved by Ron Healey. Striker Peter Kitchen nodded in an equaliser from a John Lewis cross with ten minutes remaining and Tarki Micallef almost won it for the Bluebirds in injury time with a header that went inches wide. Following the final whistle, Dan and I somehow managed to get back to the bus station unharmed, which was quite a feat considering there were running battles taking place all over the town centre and we didn't know where we were going. I'm certain we found our way to the station more by luck than judgement. After we'd been sitting there for a while waiting for our coach, we were surrounded by a gang of local kids who pushed us around a bit and nicked my beloved City scarf. I can remember being seriously pissed off at the time, but looking back now I reckon we got off pretty lightly considering we'd been wandering around enemy territory like a pair of lost sheep for much of the day.

About twelve months after that Swansea game I began drinking in my local pubs in the Rhiwbina area of North Cardiff. The regulars in the Deri back then included a group of City fans who were a few years older than me and who were more than familiar with hooliganism. They included the likes of Carlton Jones, Spragg, Dafydd May, Foxy, Simon Williams and the infamous Dai H. The casual culture had begun to kick in by that stage and the Deri crew were already wearing all the right labels. As a young punk rocker, I was none too impressed by their clothes, but I looked up to those lads all the same. Listening to them tell stories of their numerous escapades on their travels encouraged me to go to more away matches.

The 82/83 campaign proved to be an excellent one for the club and it was also a big learning curve for me personally as it was the season in which I began to travel away regularly. My usual mode of transport was a coach run by the Barry branch of the Supporters' Club, but occasionally I'd travel on the train with a couple of my mates from school and a few of the older lads from the pub. I took in a total of fourteen away games during an incident-packed year and there are several that stand out in my memory. One was an early-season match at Oxford that ended in an exciting 2-2 draw. City fans celebrated a late Jimmy Mullen equaliser by running riot in the streets around the Manor Ground. A couple of cars got overturned if I remember correctly. Another memorable encounter was a fiery affair up at Lincoln, where Dave Bennett was sent off, City were beaten 2-1 and I got sparked out in some dingy side street after being caught in the wrong place at the wrong time as I headed back to the bus. I've still got a small scar on my chin from that incident. Then there was a first round FA Cup tie at Wokingham, where a wall collapsed during the second half, badly injuring a policewoman. A load of us spilled onto the pitch when that happened and I ended up being spotted on the evening news by my old man. He went berserk when I eventually got back home, which was much later than planned. A couple of our coach windows were put through by a gang of Chelsea fans while we were making our way out of Wokingham, so we had to hang around at a bus depot in Reading for a few hours while we waited for a replacement vehicle to arrive.

The biggest game of that season by far was a promotion battle with Portsmouth at Fratton Park in March 1983. Pompey were top of the Third Division table at the time and Cardiff were second. The match attracted a crowd of around 25,000, which included almost 4,000 travelling Bluebirds. The contest on the field wasn't the best and ended in a 0-0 draw, with the highlight being an incredible save made by City keeper Eric Steele from a Billy Rafferty header. I think it was later voted as Match of the Day's save of the season or something similar. However, the most exciting action that day took place on the terraces. Fighting broke out in the home end on several occasions during the first half, while the scenes in the away end were chaotic from start to finish. Numerous fixtures and fittings were destroyed, including a huge old clock which stood at the back of the terrace. At one stage during the second half, a mobile hot dog stand that had been parked in a gap between two large sections of the away terrace was smashed to pieces, resulting in burgers, sausages and bread rolls being used as missiles against the Old Bill. I've seen many bizarre sights during my thirty four years as a Cardiff fan but that one must be close to the top of the list.

Some of the clashes with the police after the game had finished were amongst the most violent I've ever witnessed. Everything went crazy when a load of Pompey fans started launching bricks and stones into our section from an alleyway behind us. We were locked inside Fratton Park for ages while a huge City mob vented their fury on the local constabulary and there were plenty of injuries on both sides, some of which looked serious. It was also pretty hairy when we got outside the ground. I remember feeling mightily relieved when I eventually made it back to the coach in one piece.

Cardiff went on to secure promotion in the second week of May with a 2-0 victory over Orient at Ninian Park. John Lewis and Dave Bennett scored the goals that lifted the Bluebirds back to the Second Division. Seven days later, thousands of us travelled to a meaningless end-of-season game at Bristol Rovers' Eastville ground, where City fans celebrated the team's promotion by going on the rampage. There was loads of trouble before, during and after a match that is best remembered for an unfortunate incident involving striker Jeff Hemmerman. He'd been brilliant all season and had netted twenty six goals in fifty two league and cup appearances but, sadly, he damaged his knee ligaments in a second half collision with Rovers keeper Phil Kite and had to be stretchered off. The injury proved so severe that it effectively ended Hemmerman's career. He did attempt a comeback towards the end of the following campaign but he was never the same player again and was forced to retire from the game in 1984.

I left school in the summer of 1983 with few qualifications and even fewer ambitions to get a full-time job. Football, music, drinking and chasing young women were the only things that interested me at the time. I did a few fiddles for a local landscape gardener called Keith Oliver, who had previously been City's groundsman for many years, and I also did a bit of labouring work for my mate Tommy, who was a roofer, but apart from that I was perfectly content with life on the dole. Provided I had enough money for football, weekend drinking and the occasional gig, I was happy. Working was for mugs as far as I was concerned.

It was during that summer that I began frequenting a place called the Lexington, which was on

Queen Street in Cardiff city centre. It was situated where the Capitol shopping complex now stands. The ground floor of the Lex was supposed to be an American-style restaurant, but in reality it was little more than a glorified burger joint, while the basement was a small bar where all the punks and goths used to hang out. It had a fantastic jukebox which featured loads of great singles by punk bands such as the Sex Pistols, the Clash, the Buzzcocks and the Stranglers, as well as lots of stuff from early-Eighties alternative acts like Bauhaus, the Cure, Killing Joke and the Psychedelic Furs. I used to love it down there, particularly on Friday and Saturday nights, when it was packed with punkettes and goth girls.

Among the many weird and wonderful characters I met in the Lex was a lad called Carlton Seymour. He was several years older than me but we got on like a house on fire, particularly as we were both keen City fans. I think I'm right in saying that Carlton was originally from Aberdare. He was around six feet two inches tall with a wiry frame and a distinctive tattoo of a sheep wearing Dr Marten's boots on his right arm. Hard as nails, nutty as a fruitcake and pretty much fearless, he'd spent a bit of time behind bars but was one of life's loveable rogues. Despite his obvious faults, he had a heart of gold and was always great fun to be around. We became firm friends very quickly and began going to matches together as soon as the 83/84 season started.

At that stage, our Saturday routine when the Bluebirds were playing at home would often begin with a mid-morning haircut at Harry's Salon in Mackintosh Place, where barbers Andy and Nicky were both staunch City supporters. They specialized in flat-top and mohican-style haircuts, so all the sharpest punks and psychobillies used to go there regularly. After Harry's, we'd head to the Lex for a few lunchtime pints, and then it was off to Ninian Park for the match. When the game had finished we'd return to the Lex for a few hours, and then stagger around the corner to Nero's nightclub on Greyfriars Road, where the upstairs bar was full of punks, goths and psychobillies on Saturday nights. How on earth we used to manage all this with so little money is a mystery, but we usually did.

Overall, the 83/84 season was a mediocre one for City. The team spent the majority of the campaign in mid-table and consequently never looked likely to go up or down. Nevertheless, we had some good trips to places like Charlton, Fulham, Brighton, Portsmouth and Cambridge, even, if the results were a little erratic. By then, the casual look was well and truly established on the terraces, so Carlton and I must have stood out like sore thumbs. He always had a bleached-blonde flat-top, while my hair colour and style used to change regularly. At various stages during that particular season it was jet black, orange, yellow, half black/half white and bright red. We both dressed similarly in denim jackets, checked shirts and drainpipe jeans, but while Carlton usually wore a pair of moccasins, I favoured either Dr Marten's boots or leopard skin effect brothel creepers. I think it's fair to say there weren't many other lads travelling around the country with Cardiff during the mid-Eighties who looked like us, which was probably just as well, as we weren't exactly inconspicuous.

As we approached Christmas 1983, Carlton decided that we should get ourselves Pringle jumpers specifically for the football because so many other City fans were wearing them. Consequently, he turned up in the Lex one Friday evening with a couple of brand new Pringles in a Tesco carrier bag. The one he chose for himself was a light blue effort, while the one he gave to me was bright yellow. God knows where he got them from, and I didn't like to ask. One thing's for sure though, he certainly hadn't paid for them as he never had a penny to scratch his arse with, never mind enough money to buy expensive golf jumpers. We wore them to numerous games before the season had finished and to be honest we must have looked a right pair of clowns. After all, punk rock haircuts and Pringle jumpers could hardly be described as a perfect match.

In late-March, a small group of us celebrated my seventeenth birthday by travelling up to Maine Road to watch Cardiff take on MANCHESTER CITY. The Mancs were on the fringes of the promotion race, while the Bluebirds were eleventh in the table. We went up there on one of the Supporters' Club buses, which in those days were far removed from being the pop and crisps affairs they are now. In fact, a couple of us were so pissed by the time we got to Manchester that we could barely stand up. We arrived pretty early and I can't remember any significant trouble before the game, but things became much livelier inside the ground. City took an early lead when Gordon Owen converted a Trevor Lee cross and they played well for most of match, but sadly they collapsed late on. David Johnson scored an eighty fifth minute equaliser for the home side and then Graham Baker bundled in an injury time winner from a Neil McNab corner. That was the signal for chaos on the away terrace as hundreds of City lads began fighting with the police and stewards. Apparently, there were a number of ferocious battles on the way back to the train station, but we didn't take part in any of those as our coach was parked near the ground and the Old Bill had cleared the area by the time they let us out. While we'd lost the game in unfortunate circumstances, the day hadn't been a total disaster as the Manchester fans to our right had been throwing coins at us all game long. Carlton and I picked up that many ten and fifty pence pieces during the course of the afternoon that we ended up returning home to South Wales with more money than we'd set out with, which was good news for a couple of dole bums like us. Oddly, the 20,140 crowd at Maine Road was the biggest in all four divisions that weekend, which goes to show how far attendances were dipping at the time.

A week later came a game we had been looking forward to for months – the visit of arch enemies CHELSEA to Ninian Park. The Londoners were joint-top of the table and their fans were the undisputed heavyweight champions of the hooligan world at that point in time, so the fixture promised to be a stern test of Cardiff's credentials both on and off the field. To say the afternoon proved to be an eventful one would be something of an understatement. By the time it was over, I was left with cuts, bruises, aching limbs and a nagging feeling that perhaps this hooliganism lark wasn't all it was cracked up to be.

During our pre-match drinking session in the Lex, Carlton demanded that we sit in the Grandstand as opposed to stand on the Bob Bank for this one. He'd heard on the grapevine that Chelsea were planning to take over the Grandstand, and he'd also heard that a lot of our top lads were going in there in an attempt to stop them. He told us he felt it was our duty to join up with them and do our bit, so that's what a small gang of four or five of us decided to do. Apart from Carlton, who was in his early-twenties, the rest of us were teenagers. The group included an old mate of mine named Vaughan Roberts, who I've been friends with ever since we were toddlers. I was skinny enough back in the Eighties, but by comparison to Vaughan I was like some kind of muscleman. He was so thin it was unbelievable. There was more meat on a whippet's lip. Nevertheless, I remember we were full of ourselves on the long walk to Sloper Road and we were proudly singing Cardiff songs all the way to the ground. Luckily, we didn't bump into any of the four thousand Chelsea fans who were making their way to Ninian Park, which is quite surprising in retrospect.

When we arrived at the turnstiles, we paid to get into Block A of the Grandstand and took our seats in the middle rows. There appeared to be plenty of City boys around us, including a couple of faces I recognized. One of them was Marksy, a lad from Aberdare who I didn't know well at the time but who I became friendly with a few years later. With his long hair and droopy moustache, Marksy was an unmistakable figure in those days. He looked like a cross between a Mexican bandit and Dylan, the hippy rabbit off the Magic Roundabout, although he definitely had more in common with the bandit than the rabbit. While he wasn't the biggest lad in the world, Marksy always seemed to be there or thereabouts whenever it was kicking off and he was never afraid to get stuck in.

We confidently began chanting Bluebirds songs shortly after the teams took to the field and I was immediately struck by the fact that so few people in Block A were joining in. Chelsea looked to have occupied every part of the ground other than the Bob Bank. There were visiting fans in the Grange End, the Canton Stand and both enclosures, and it was soon evident that there were also plenty of them in the Grandstand. City started the game brightly and were well on top for the first quarter of an hour. By that stage, a suspicious gap had begun to open up all around us and it was becoming apparent that there were no more than thirty or forty of us in total. To make matters worse, it was clear that most of us were kids. Then the visiting fans struck up a chorus of 'One Man Went to Mow,' which was Chelsea's anthem at the time. Cardiff supporters also often sang that song back then, so we decided to join in. The problem came when the London lads stopped at 'Three Men Went to Mow,' while we stood on our seats and carried on until we reached 'Ten Men Went to Mow,' which we followed with a chant of 'Keyaaardiff!' That was like a red rag to a bull as far as the visiting mob was concerned.

All of a sudden the Chelsea fans in Blocks A and B turned to face us and started punching the air while bellowing 'War, War, War!' They then began clambering over the seats towards us. There must have been a couple of hundred of them, and many were considerably bigger and older than our lot. The majority of us instinctively backed away into the top right-hand corner of the stand, as that was the only place we could go, but two or three lads decided to throw caution to the wind and steam into the visitors. Those brave souls included the indomitable Carlton, who was in his element. He managed to take several Chelsea boys out of the fray before they were able to drag him down.

I was on the outside of our group towards the left. The first Chelsea lad to reach me was an enormous acne-scarred monster with a face like a bucket of smashed crabs. He towered over me and shouted something along the lines of "come on Taffy, let's 'ave it!" in his broad Cockney accent. He effectively stuck his chin out and gave me a free shot. My legs had turned to jelly by this point, but I summoned up all the courage I had left and attempted to hit him as hard as I could. He barely flinched. If the truth be told, I'm not sure if I even connected properly. I thought my life was going to end there and then, so I just curled up into a ball, hedgehog-style. In fairness to him and the other Chelsea lads alongside him, they didn't go over the top. I was given a few cuffs around the head, a couple of blows to the back and a boot or two in the ribs, but I came out of the encounter unscathed apart from some minor cuts and bruises.

Meanwhile, Vaughan hadn't fared quite so well. He'd been at the front of the group when Chelsea attacked and was thrown around like a rag doll. He was also booted down the stairs just as the police began pouring into the stand. It obviously wasn't his lucky day, as he was grabbed by a copper and mistakenly thrown back into the Chelsea mob, where he was subjected to another kicking. While all this was going on, midfielder Roger Gibbins had apparently put City into the lead with a spectacular volley, but we hadn't seen it. At that point, Carlton was busy fighting, I was busy being hit and the only thing Vaughan was seeing were stars.

Once the Old Bill had managed to restore some sort of order, they quickly decided to get us out of the Grandstand and put us on the Bob Bank. As we began moving out of Block A, a very strange thing happened. The Chelsea fans in the stand began applauding us. To this day I'm not sure why they did that. With the exception of a couple of individuals, it wasn't as if we'd managed to offer much resistance, but it appeared we'd amused them all the same. Perhaps they were acknowledging that we were mainly a bunch of kids and that we'd at least attempted to take them on, even if it had proved to be a really bad idea from our perspective.

After getting us out of Block A, the police took us down the stairs and under the stand. While they were doing so, a roar went up outside, which turned out to be City fans celebrating a Gordon Owen penalty. Incredibly, our team was 2-0 up against the league leaders with a little over twenty minutes played, and yet we hadn't seen a goal. We were then led out into the players' tunnel and kept there for a minute or two while the Old Bill prepared to escort us around the pitch. As we were standing in the tunnel, Nigel Vaughan stroked home a Karl Elsey cross to give the Bluebirds a 3-0 lead. I didn't see that happen but several others did, so they started jumping up and down and the rest of us followed suit. Seconds later, a Chelsea fist came flying over the enclosure wall and caught Vaughan right on the side of the head. I think it's fair to say he wasn't having the best of afternoons, and neither was I. City had banged in three goals in a sizzling seven minute spell, but I hadn't had the pleasure of seeing any of them.

As the police started escorting us around the pitch, we were spat at from the enclosure and had coins thrown at us from the Canton Stand. There were Chelsea fans everywhere and they weren't happy, which was hardly surprising given the score. We got another round of applause from the City fans on the Bob Bank as we were being led onto the terrace, and they sang 'We're Proud of You.' While that was undoubtedly well-intentioned, it wasn't much of a consolation for the hammering we'd been given, especially in Vaughan's case. He'd taken such a pounding that his legs had gone, so he was effectively being held up by the copper who was escorting him. Carlton was a different matter altogether, though. As a natural-born hooligan, he'd been having a whale of a time and was as happy as a pig in shit.

Cardiff continued to play well for most of the game and looked destined to run out comfortable winners until Kerry Dixon pulled a goal back for Chelsea in the eighty fourth minute. The Bluebirds started to panic at that stage and conceded another goal a couple of minutes later when Colin Lee scrambled the ball home from close range. Nevertheless, a City victory still seemed certain, so hundreds of Chelsea lads began pouring out of the ground as the game went into injury time. A large mob of them made their way around to the back of the Canton Stand and for a brief moment it looked like there was going to be murder, as the Bob Bank gates had been left wide open by the stewards. Only a couple of coppers and a solitary police dog stood between the rival factions, but one of them quickly managed to swing the gates shut while the other sent his dog flying into the Londoners. They probably averted a mass brawl by doing so.

Within seconds, another loud roar went up inside the ground, so those of us who had congregated at the top of slope on the right-hand corner of the Bob Bank headed back towards the terrace, while most of the Chelsea mob ran back into the stands. It transpired that the visitors had been awarded a penalty after John Bumstead had blasted the ball at David Tong during a goalmouth scramble. The referee adjudged that Tong had handled the ball, although television footage later showed it had struck the midfielder on the right side of his chest. He even had a mark on his shirt to prove it, but the ref ignored City's protests and Nigel Spackman converted the spot-kick to rescue an unlikely draw for Chelsea.

After the final whistle, the supporters on the Bob Bank suffered the indignity of being kept inside the ground while the visiting fans were let out. When the Old Bill finally did open the gates for us, they formed a human barrier which they maintained right up until we got to the railway bridge next to the Ninian Park pub. From that point onwards it was mayhem. Loads of Chelsea boys were still rampaging through the area, so there were running battles all the way back to the city centre. The scenes on the streets leading to Central Station were unbelievable. There were hundreds of lads from both sides heading in the same direction and fights were breaking out all over the place, but nobody seemed sure of who was who. As we ran past one of the Chinese supermarkets on Ninian Park Road, I had a big Chelsea lad breathing down the back of my neck and screaming "Come on, you Taffy bastards!" I spotted a milk crate full of empty bottles on the pavement, so I swooped down, grabbed it, swung around and launched it at him all in one movement. He crumpled in a heap, although I didn't hang about to see if I'd done him any damage for fear of him getting back up and killing me. Instead, I ran all the way back to my bus stop on Kingsway.

Having had more than enough excitement for one day, I decided to go straight home once we eventually got into town, but Carlton and the revitalized Vaughan opted to stay and have a few pints in the Lex. Later that evening, they ended up drinking and swapping stories with a group of Chelsea lads who Carlton had become friendly with on the gig circuit. Something that surprised me when I read the local newspaper reports over the next couple of days was the fact that the police had made a total of just thirty eight arrests. That was amazing considering what had gone on in and around Ninian Park. My guess is they'd been so busy trying to keep the rival mobs apart that they didn't have the manpower to detain many people.

The South Wales Echo's report included a large photo of the fracas in Block A. In the accompanying text, journalist Joe Lovejoy wrote: "This is the picture that sums up one of the main reasons why attendances at Football League games have halved since the Second World War. As we watched the skirmishes between rival sets of so-called supporters on Saturday, one season ticket holder told me he no longer takes his son to watch Cardiff as he fears for his safety. It seems the Grandstand no longer guarantees immunity from these hooligans who travel to matches intent on causing trouble." I must admit I felt a bit guilty as I was reading that, especially as the photo featured a father and his young child who had got caught up in the middle of the disturbance.

Three weeks after the Chelsea game, City were scheduled to meet Swansea at the Vetch in an Easter Saturday fixture. I initially planned to travel on the football special, which was due to depart Cardiff at around the 1pm mark. However, Carlton insisted that we should leave on a much earlier train as we'd miss all the best action if we went on the special. I reluctantly agreed, so me, Carlton, Dan and another mate of ours from the Lex called Jim Frampton ended up setting off from Central Station at something silly like 9am. I don't remember Jim as being that much of a City fan and I can't recall him ever going on another away trip with us, but the way things turned out it was very fortunate for Carlton and I that he'd decided to join us on this particular occasion.

There were a couple of hundred loonies on the train as we left Cardiff, and plenty more got on at Bridgend and Port Talbot. When we arrived in Neath, everybody piled off and headed straight for an off licence, which was quickly ransacked. It was a boiling hot day, so we spent the next half hour or so drinking and sitting around in the sun before everyone made their way back onto the train. Upon our arrival in SWANSEA, we were greeted by a small handful of police outside High Street Station, although there was no sign of any Jacks in the vicinity. The Old Bill made a token effort to hold us there, but a shout went up from the front of the mob and within seconds we were all sprinting off in the direction of the town centre. When we got to the Quadrant shopping complex, most of us went inside and it wasn't long before Gilesports had their windows put through. We weren't in there more than a minute or two, but nevertheless numerous items were grabbed from shop displays and lots of damage was done.

After running amok in the Quadrant, everyone started heading towards Oystermouth Road, but the day's entertainment was about to come to an abrupt halt as far as Carlton and I were concerned. A couple of police riot vans suddenly appeared on the scene, so most of the lads began to scarper in the direction of the seafront, but our small group decided to play it cool and keep on walking. We'd been at the back of the mob ever since we'd left the train station, we hadn't done any damage or stolen anything in the Quadrant and none of us had committed any crimes as far as we were aware, so I was confident the Old Bill wouldn't give us any grief provided we stayed calm. However, that confidence was misplaced. As one of the wagons passed us, its back doors flew open and two burly coppers jumped out. They grabbed hold of Carlton, wrestled him to the floor, handcuffed him and dragged him into the van. I couldn't believe what was happening, so I ran towards the driver's door, banged on the window and demanded to know why my mate was being arrested. The driver's response was to tell me to fuck off or I'd be joining him. I protested that Carlton hadn't done anything wrong and was given the same reply, so I foolishly kicked the side of the van and shouted something ridiculous about the police being fascist bastards. Unsurprisingly, I was sat alongside Carlton in a pair of handcuffs very shortly afterwards.

While we were being driven to the police station, the officer who'd arrested me began making snide remarks about my hair, which I'd dyed bright red a few days earlier. He was sporting a thick, bushy moustache and looked like an extra from a Village People video, but nevertheless he decided that my appearance was worthy of his derision. "Why do wankers like you have such stupid haircuts?" he asked. "The same reason why tossers like you have stupid-looking furry things stuck in the middle of your faces," I replied. Apparently, that was the wrong answer, as he grabbed me by the throat and banged my head against the side of the van. Carlton went nuts and started screaming at the copper to leave me alone, so he was also given a couple of hefty whacks across the head. When things had settled down a little, he quietly told me to button it and said he'd deal with our moustachioed friend later.

When we arrived at the station, and once we'd gone through the formalities of being signed in by the desk sergeant, Carlton was asked if he'd calmed down yet. He confirmed that he had, so his handcuffs were removed by one of the officers who'd apprehended him. After gently rubbing his wrists for a few moments, he casually turned towards the copper who'd arrested me, grabbed him by the ears and butted him in the face. Naturally enough, all hell broke loose and Carlton received some severe punishment, but not before he'd managed to dish out a few decent punches of his own. While all this was going on, I was cowering in the corner. If I'd have had my wits about me, I suppose could've tried to make a break for it, as the station doors were wide open and the Old Bill were too busy trying to control Carlton to pay any attention to me. Still, on reflection, running away probably wouldn't have been the wisest of moves. After all, how long would it have taken the police to track down a drunken teenager with a bright red mohican?

Once Carlton had been subdued, we were put into separate cells which stood opposite each other. The match was due to kick off at three o'clock, and yet we'd managed to get ourselves locked up well before midday. It was almost an hour until anyone else joined us, but the cells started filling up steadily as the afternoon wore on and the lads who were arriving had plenty of tales to tell. Apparently, something in the region of four thousand City fans had descended on Swansea and there had been pitched battles with the police and the Jacks at the train station, in the town centre and at the Vetch Field. The first bit of information we were given about the game was that it had been held up for a few minutes shortly after kick-off when around a hundred Cardiff supporters invaded the pitch from the East Terrace and confronted the home fans on the North Bank. Then the coppers told us that the Bluebirds had taken a 2-0 lead. That news was greeted with prolonged cheering and a spontaneous burst of City songs from most of the cells. Next they informed us that the scores were level at 2-2. Finally, they took great delight in telling us that Swansea had come back to win 3-2. To begin with, nobody believed it and everyone thought they were winding us up, but then a few boys who'd been nicked after the final whistle arrived and they confirmed that the final score was indeed 3-2 to the Jacks. Dean Saunders had scored two of their goals, including the winner. I was gutted, especially as defeat for Swansea would have seen them relegated to the Third Division.

The eventual number of lads arrested on what had been a very busy day for the boys in blue was sixty eight, and more than two thirds of us were Cardiff supporters. Therefore, some of the cells at Swansea Central were packed to overflowing. At one stage, my cell contained no less than nine of us, including a well-known Bluebirds fan named Seddie. He told me he was going to give up football as he was getting himself into too much trouble. Three weeks later, I spotted him on the Ninian Park pitch battling with a group of Sheffield Wednesday fans after the last game of the season had finished, so that's one resolution that didn't last long. Carlton's cell contained four other Cardiff lads and an ugly Jack skinhead. Suffice to say he was given a hard time for much of the duration of his stay, but nevertheless the filthy bastard still managed to spit across the hallway at us on several occasions.

After our statements, fingerprints and mug shots had been taken, the lads slowly but surely started being released. As Carlton and I had been amongst the first to be arrested, I naturally assumed that we'd also be amongst the first to be let back out again, but that's not the way things panned out. In fact, we were the very last City fans to be released along with five other lads, most of whom were Cardiff-based. It was fast approaching midnight by the time we were finally let out of our cells. While we were being turned loose, the coppers informed us that the last train back to the capital had already gone and there were no more services that night as the following day was Easter Sunday, so we were well and truly knackered. No explanation was given as to why the seven of us had been detained for so long, but in our case I reckon it was a straightforward act of revenge for the incident in which Carlton had nutted the officer who arrested me.

While we were standing around in the foyer planning our next move, a couple of the lads poked their heads out the station door and spotted a group of Jacks across the other side of the road. They were obviously waiting for any stray City fans to emerge, but none of us were in the mood for any more hassle. We just wanted to know how we were going to get home, so initially we refused to budge. The desk sergeant told us he couldn't care less how we got back to Cardiff, but he wanted us out of his station. After a few minutes of angry bickering, he made arrangements for us to leave via the back door and get a lift in a riot van to the outskirts of the city. From there, he expected us to either hitch a ride or walk home.

The van dropped us off at a roundabout on the A483 just outside Swansea. After a brief discussion, we decided our best bet would be to walk the remaining six miles to Neath and see if we could arrange some sort of transport from there. As it had been such a hot day it was still pretty warm, so at least the temperature wasn't a problem. We christened ourselves the Magnificent Seven and set off on what proved to be an eventful late-night hike along the side of the dual carriageway.

We hadn't been walking for more than a quarter of an hour when one of the lads spotted a white transit van moving slowly past on the other side of the road. The driver wound his window down and shouted a tirade of anti-Cardiff abuse, so we returned his insults with interest and thought little more of it until a few minutes later, when the van reappeared on our side of carriageway. On that occasion it was travelling considerably faster. As it drew level with us, the passenger door opened and one of the occupants hurled a couple of bricks in our direction. I couldn't believe it. Thankfully, nobody was seriously hurt, although one of the boys did get hit on the leg if I remember correctly. The van went past once more a short while afterwards, but by that time we'd collected up a few bricks and stones of our own. Once we'd lobbed them at the vehicle, we decided to make ourselves scarce for a while in case the driver went back into the centre of Swansea and called up some reinforcements. After leaving the side of the dual carriageway, we walked through a series of fields for the next mile or so, and then returned to the road. There was no sign of the van for the remainder of our journey.

It was around 2am by the time we made it to Neath, and naturally enough everything was shut when we got there, so we decided to head for the station and keep our fingers crossed that some kind of train would eventually turn up. Happily, we didn't have to wait more than half an hour before one did. To be honest, I can't really remember what sort of service it was. It might have been a Royal Mail train or something similar. All I know is that we were very glad to see it, and although we ended up going back home in the middle of the night, we were all in remarkably high spirits by the time we pulled into Cardiff Central.

The Magnificent Seven returned to sunny Swansea a few days later for our initial court hearings. The majority of the forty six City fans who'd been arrested on the Saturday were on the same train as us and plenty had brought mates along with them, so it was like a mini football special. There were some chaotic scenes in and around the court buildings after we arrived. Fighting broke out on the steps outside on a couple of occasions and the proceedings inside had to be halted numerous times due to a variety of misdemeanours from those in the dock and the public galleries. They included the chanting of football songs, the screaming of insults at the magistrates and police, the smoking of cigarettes and the drinking of alcohol. After hearing the ludicrous charges that were being levelled against us, Carlton and I pleaded not guilty, so we were granted legal aid and our case was adjourned.

The police had concocted a ridiculous story that involved us being seen leading a large mob on a destructive rampage through the Quadrant and then being arrested after a violent confrontation with a group of Jacks near the seafront. They made out that we were the imaginary gang's ringleaders. It was a complete fabrication, but it was worrying nonetheless as the charges were serious and the alleged offences were at the top end of the public order scale, so the punishments were likely to be harsh. The Swansea-based solicitor we were appointed was very sympathetic to our plight and he seemed to genuinely believe the Old Bill's allegations against us were false, but he warned that there was every chance we'd be found guilty as it was our word against theirs. He predicted that Carlton would be looking at several months inside due to his previous convictions, while I would probably be liable for a heavy fine because it was my first offence. However, he added there was a possibility we could both get custodial sentences if the worst came to the worst, as the police were clearly trying to make examples of us.

It was around six weeks before our case was eventually heard. In the meantime, Carlton dreamed up a hare-brained scheme that involved our girlfriends, Judith and Carol, turning up at the courts with cushions stuffed up their dresses in a bid to convince the magistrates that they were pregnant. He told us he believed this would result in more lenient punishments if we were found guilty. Thankfully, he was outvoted three to one. When the day arrived, the girls opted to simply try and look sad instead. I can remember feeling extremely anxious as we re-entered the court building, and Carlton was as quiet as I'd ever known him to be. Jude and Carol were alongside us to offer their moral support, while Dan and Jim were present as our witnesses.

The two arresting officers were first to give their statements and fortunately they weren't particularly convincing. They offered up no evidence other than what they had allegedly written down in their notebooks on the day and they had no witnesses, so our solicitor got stuck into them and managed to pick several holes in their story during his cross-examination. Carlton was up next, and his testimony was a nervous one. He looked worried throughout and didn't speak very well at all. I followed him, and although I was shaking like a leaf as I made my way up to the stand, I grew in confidence when I got there and ended up putting in a fairly decent performance. During one heated exchange with the prosecution solicitor, I even managed to make the magistrates laugh with a sarcastic remark about the quality of his questioning technique. Dan was called up next and he did reasonably well for us, although he wasn't in front of the court for long before our solicitor played his trump card. That was Jim, who neither looked nor sounded like a potential football hooligan despite having a flat-top haircut. He proved to be a brilliant witness. Jim was a well-spoken lad and he delivered his testimony calmly and confidently. Having eloquently expressed his outrage at the inaccuracy of the police evidence, he then gave his own version of events and stuck to it rigidly under questioning by both solicitors. By the time he'd stepped down from the stand, the prosecution's case was in tatters. In the end, the magistrates retired for little more than a couple of minutes before returning to declare a verdict of not guilty on all charges. I don't think I've ever felt so relieved in my life. When we got back to Cardiff we celebrated our acquittal with a few beers in the Lex, but we didn't stay there long. To be honest, I think Carlton and I were too drained to genuinely enjoy ourselves.

While my arrest in Swansea and the subsequent court case had been an experience, it wasn't one that I was keen to repeat in any great hurry. Therefore, I promised myself that I'd be much more careful at future matches, but it wasn't long before I was in trouble again.

Three weeks into the 84/85 season, Cardiff played old enemies Leeds United in a midweek fixture at Ninian Park. Leeds were top of the Second Division table going into the game, having won all four of their previous matches, while the Bluebirds were rock bottom, having lost all three of theirs. City's attendances were getting so bad at the time that only 6,800 supporters turned up on the night and a large percentage of those were from Yorkshire. Despite the team's pathetic start to the campaign, they began this particular match brightly and took the lead in the twenty fifth minute when Paul Bodin struck from close range. Scott Sellars equalised for the visitors on the hour when he crashed in a thirty-yard thunderbolt, but Phil Dwyer secured a well-deserved victory for the Bluebirds ten minutes from time when he powered home a header from a David Tong free-kick.

The atmosphere on the Bob Bank had been superb all night despite the small crowd, although the Leeds fans in the Grange End didn't look very happy. As we exited the ground from the alleyway behind the Grange, loads of Yorkshire men were hanging over the back wall throwing coins and various other missiles down at us, and they were getting plenty back in return. The gates to the away end were locked as usual, so the bulk of the visiting supporters were contained, but Leeds also had around fifty lads in the Grandstand who were able to leave Ninian at the same time as the City fans. Fighting broke out from the moment they ventured out of the ground and the police were taking no prisoners, so things got ugly very quickly. Although I was supposed to be being careful and I should have been heading straight home, I just couldn't resist joining the mob on Sloper Road. The whole situation was much too exciting to ignore and my adrenalin was pumping, so I chose to stick around. A minute or two later, a line of angry coppers charged into the City boys with their truncheons flailing, so I jumped into one of the gardens opposite Jubilee Park and ducked down behind a hedge. I imagined that would be the best way to avoid a battering, but it didn't prove to be the wisest move I've ever made. Having waited for a few moments until I thought the coast was clear, I stuck my head up above the hedge to see what was going on. Out of the corner of my eye I spotted a copper lunging towards me, but I didn't see him until it was too late. Before I was able to take any evasive action, he'd swung his truncheon and smashed it into the side of my skull. I hit the deck like a nine-stone sack of shit, and for a while I didn't know who I was, where I was or what I was doing there. It felt like my head had caved in.

As I slowly clambered back to my feet, the officer who'd clobbered me grabbed me by the scruff of the neck and dragged me out of the garden. I'm absolutely certain he was going to arrest me, but then he was attacked by several other Cardiff lads, so he let go of me and turned his attention to them. I made my escape while I had the chance and staggered off in the direction of the city centre, where I caught the next bus to Rhiwbina. The pain inside my head was already severe, but it got a whole lot worse during the journey home, as I was treated to a loud and lengthy analysis of the match by legendary City fan Dai Hunt. Although he's as mad as a box of frogs, Dai is about as genuine a Bluebird as you could ever wish to meet. However, he is positively the last thing you need when you've got a screaming headache.

While I lay in bed that night, unable to get comfortable because of the pain I was in, I asked myself if getting involved in football hooliganism was worth the kind of hassle I'd endured during the Chelsea, Swansea and Leeds incidents. After a couple of sleepless hours, I decided it wasn't. Ever since that day, I have always endeavoured to stay out of trouble at the football, but as I'm a Cardiff City supporter and a regular away traveller, it hasn't always been easy. Although I've consciously avoided confrontations with rival fans and officers of the law, I've nevertheless ended up in a whole host of tricky situations over the years. For instance, I was arrested before a Friday night game against Chester in 1989, having allegedly been seen fighting with Bristol City fans a month earlier. Thankfully, my explanation for what had happened with the Wurzels was accepted and I was let off with a warning. Then I was subjected to a dawn raid following the infamous home match against Swansea in 1994. That was a straightforward case of mistaken identity. I was released without charge after a few hours of questioning once the Old Bill had established I wasn't the man they were looking for. There was even an occasion in 1987 when I got head-butted by a police horse during a disturbance outside a train station in Stoke, but the less said about that incident the better. Life as a Cardiff City fan often has its ups and downs but one thing's for sure, it's rarely dull!

Unfortunately, my story has a sad postscript. I lost touch with Carlton Seymour during the late-Eighties when Carlton moved to London. While he was living there, he apparently fell in with some heavy characters from the West End who were involved in all manner of dodgy activities. After marrying a Swedish stripper, he moved over to Holland for a brief period and then worked in Bath on his return to Britain. It was while he was living there that he disappeared one weekend in 1998, and he's never been seen since, His wereabouts are a complete mystery. Although the police are still in contact with his friends and relatives from time to time, they haven't got a clue what happened to him, as his possessions remain untouched and his passport has never been used. He is listed as missing presumed dead. If Carlton is still out there somewhere, I'd like to think he may get to read this and eventually he may even be tempted to get in touch. Like many, many others, I would dearly love to hear from him again. If he's no longer with us, then I'd simply like to say thanks for the memories mate, and rest in peace.

Carlton Seymour - CCFC - 1984

Dave Sugarman - CCFC - 1984

Chapter 8

NEWPORT COUNTY FULL ON

By S Kaged.

CCFC

Kaged, is a mate from the 80's and who has always kept in touch with me, we had a right old time in the 80's and Kag was on board for a lot of them. He was a game young lad, who took a couple of bad beatings for his bottle. He was a City fan through and through in the 80's and was one of them who would be on the long away trips on a Tuesday or Wednesday night to the Rochdale's of this world. One thing about Kag is that he has an unbelievable memory as you will read. Annis

'Willie, Willie Anderson, Willie Anderson on the wing' they all sung in their masculine voices when I first went to Ninian Park. 1974 was the year, Flares were the fashion, and bands like the Rubettes were in the charts. Bloody hell, we were a tasteless lot weren't we.

I had already fallen in love with football, watching Match of the Day and The Big Match every Saturday and Sunday religiously. I could name all the players of all the teams in the first division parrot fashion. But actually going to Ninian Park introduced me to a different world that day (28th April 1974). Hearing the real roar when Gil Reece equalised against Orient was deafening, aggressive and real. For a 6 year old this was edgy stuff and much more exciting than visits to the park or the zoo.

For the next few years I went to 3 or 4 games a season. I was aware that there were lads who went to the games only for the warfare. They were of course, all bigger than me and just as hard as Dennis Waterman in Minder. I had seen the occasional outbreak of fighting as well, matches such as Chelsea '79, Stoke '79 & Tottenham '77 spring to mind, but I don't recall much about the specific incidents, I was too interested in the football.

Inexplicably, I was to be just as gripped by matters off the field in 1981. I was now 14 and able to attend games on my own. I had a school friend called Vincent, his brother was a well known face at the football and I used to overhear the conversations his older brother had with his mates, and let's just say when they spoke about their plans to attend the games, they didn't dwell on the merits of playing the 4-4-2 system. No, they were pre-occupied with 'christening' their Doc. Marten boots.

Britain in the early eighties was a pretty depressing place to be, with the inner city riots & mass unemployment. There seemed to be a succession of personnel & social upheavals that for the average working man that took a long, long time to recover from. The song "Ghost Town" by The Specials was influenced by both the Toxteth and Brixton riots, with the lines "All the clubs are being closed down" and "Bands won't play no more" talking about bands, not willing to play during the riots due to fear of being attacked, it did sum up the nations feelings.

I had decided that the 1981/82, I was going to attend every home game and some away games too. The stories that I heard from my afore mentioned friends older brother had certainly got me interested in attending games on a regular basis. So, true to my word I attended all 3 home friendlies that year (Birmingham, Wolves & Coventry) and was excited with anticipation.

Oldham away kicked off the season, and my appetite for attending was further wetted by the stories of Vincent's brother on his coach trip that day. I was ready; this was too be my season of adventure. So next week we are home and who are we playing ??????????, CHELSEA. I remember informing all my friends at our local hang out (the bomb patch in the Roath area of Cardiff) that I was attending the Chelsea game and the comments that were made were on the lines of 'bloody hell, Chelsea are mad' and 'I'd watch yourself down there', to which I would defiantly reply about not being at all worried.

The game that day was played in beautiful sunshine, we stood in the family enclosure, and this was due to the fact that if you found an adult to escort you in your entrance fee was 30p. When I arrived in the ground I was amazed and impressed to see all the Chelsea fans with their yellow away tops on in the grange end singing way. Early on Peter Kitchen scored for Cardiff but Chelsea rallied and won 2-1.

Throughout the game there were outbreaks of ferocious fighting in the 2 x side enclosures, suddenly I wasn't safe and this scared me. Maybe I should have listened to my friends in Roath after all. When the game ended everyone left ground as normal, but the faces of the older lads were different to normal that day, they seemed to be pre-empting the ensuing mass skirmishing that by now seemed inevitable, they were tense, aggressive and antagonistic.

Vincent and I were outside very briefly and we were walking away from the ground when we bumped into Vincent's older brother, who told us in no uncertain terms that we would be best off out of it, as there was 'going to be murder' at any moment.

Roar !!!, Chelsea are out and there is mass panic amongst the group of early teens that I am with. Chelsea then seem to make what was 4 or 5 charges, the panic spreads and worsens and I was petrified. Chelsea are now in the side streets also and there seems to be no escape, I just want to vanish into thin air when we see Vincent's grandfather coming out of a betting shop, he lives a couple of doors away and takes us to the safety of his flat. This was a first floor flat and was on the main road where chaos was ensuing. For the next 5 minutes I watched from the safety of that flat, transfixed, the bedlam in the street outside. Vincent and I then made our way to Cardiff Central bus station. On arriving at the station, there are still pockets of trouble, while we wait for our bus.

That night, I made my way to the bomb patch and informed my mates, who earlier had the foresight to know that if you were too young to defend yourself, Ninian Park was not the place to be, I informed them all of the days happenings. Whilst telling them the events of the day, that's when it happened, I realized I was in a real life adventure that day and I wished we could play Chelsea every week, I felt like a rock star.

That season I began going away and the following season I didn't miss many. The first friendly of the 82/83 season was at home to .... wait for it, yes, Chelsea. I met the author of this book that day. I was to next meet him and soon get to know him more was before an away game, he was sat outside the cafe that used to exist under the bridge by Ninian Park. We were due to play Millwall away and he was as excited as me to be making the trip. Not long after that season started, Annis moved to Bradford, so for obvious reasons, his appearances at games became spasmodic. Don't misunderstand me, I still saw him at varying home games and away games such as Lincoln, Huddersfield, Sheffield United, Doncaster, Preston, Wigan, Portsmouth etc.

The next time I really came into contact with Annis was April 1984, by now he had moved back to South Wales and was living in Barry. In the early months of his return he ventured into NEWPORT for a shopping trip with a friend of his (little Coll) and was promptly threatened. What happened that day was to be the catalyst to one of the most eventful times ever, as wars waged between the 2 cities and for a group of 15-18 year olds things would never be the same again.

As in the early 80's, life and opportunity in Britain had certainly not progressed by 1984. This was the year of the Miners strike, Band aid, Frankie goes to Hollywood, Tommy Cooper died and I had a perm, wore pink and was 17.

Wearing pink and having a perm it then became inevitable that I would hang around outside Olympus sportswear on Queen Street in Cardiff and pose like a peacock, very majestic and with a touch of attitude. There was about 50 regulars from Canton, Ely, Splott and Grangetown mainly and varying other people would venture outside Olympus from an array of areas at a range of times.

Every mob has its own unique blend of personalities, this one was no exception. Within our crew ranged the full spectrum of types. From the flamboyant, to the demure. From the repellent, to the ideal. Somehow, we managed to fit together in a kind of fragile alliance. One for all, and all for one. With one exception: Patrick boys (those stupid awful cagoules) anyone wearing one was most defiantly not welcome.

Most days were the same, we used to mess around, try and pull any girl who would have us, talk about clothes, walk around St. David's shopping centre 10 times in a day, anything to pass the time and not spend money as most of us were on a maximum of £30 per week. There were the occasional 'dust ups' with the mod's and whomever else took the liberty of walking down Queen Street, in a group and that happened to be our age. This was our street, our manor, we were untouchable. Then Newport started paying their uninvited unwelcomed visits. Let's put it this way, they didn't used to come to Cardiff to discuss the price of eggs.

NEWPORT is a rough little ex trading port 15 miles east from Cardiff situated on the River Usk. The town itself is relatively small and therefore everyone seems to know everyone else's business. The suburbs of the city have grown outwards from the inner-city, mainly near the main roads, giving the suburban sprawl of the city an irregular, aggressive and somewhat ugly shape.

Newport, or as they call themselves in their own unique way KEWENTY (county), had a tight little firm of around 50-60 lads who were very loyal to each other. If Newport as a team never existed and these lads would have followed Cardiff and were around in 1945, we would have given Adolf Hitler and his troops a run for their money.

Before I relay these events to you, I'd like to make a couple of points. The series of events that took place in the spring of 1984 were extraordinary. Two sets of lad's who hung around in their relevant town centres fought a series of battles that caused chaos on a regular basis. None of these events happened at football games or grounds, as if this was the case it would have been a massacre to Cardiff. The advantage for Newport was there town was smaller, therefore there mob was tighter. On regular Saturday's as any stranger stood out like a beacon, it's like walking into a local pub, the connections are tighter and stronger. Whereas, Cardiff was bigger, therefore, it took longer to mob up and a mob coming of a train station could've meant Rugby, Stag nights, lads out for the day etc. Also, there were a lot of pubs in the vicinity of their Train station and therefore this attracted men of all ages who had no interest in football to become involved in what they saw as a free for all.

But the main point, as earlier mentioned, these events did not base themselves around football. Remember it's easier for a group of lads from say ...... Exeter to walk around Manchester rather than vice versa, as word would spread and every local would gang up ready for a pop. I just wish it had been at football as this would have been a miss match.

For me, my first encounter with our rivals from 15 miles east came on a Wednesday night in early April 1984. Cardiff had just had an amazing on and off the field encounter with Chelsea and we were smarting from our City being totally over run by our cockney invaders 4 days earlier. So we ventured to Newport, to sort what had happened in the afore mentioned incident with Annis and little Coll.

We took the number 30 bus to Newport town centre Annis, myself, Moorie, Dio, Eugene, Chris B and a handful of others. Apparently Newport knew we were coming, so we all agreed it was all hands on deck as soon we get there. When we got to Newport, nothing. after about 15 mins. of chasing any lad who was hanging about to suss what all the fuss was about, we were soon becoming bored and made our way to the bus station home. Unbeknown to us, whilst we had been there we had wiped up a storm and every local was up for a bit of Cardiff blood. From the local pubs and down the alleys of the side streets they came about 50 of them all lashed up and ready to rumble. We were in trouble and backed off fast, in Newport bus station that night a few us were given a bit of a slap, at first we were doing OK, but the sheer volume meant they overpowered us. We returned that night beaten but unbowed and hell bent on some sort of retribution.

That retribution came a fortnight later over the Easter period, when Annis, Little Coll, Bobby M, Myself and Tony G paid Newport a return visit. In 1 car we drove up, early evening and were ready for action. As we pulled into Newport and parked opposite the Train Station there was about 10 or so lads who were hanging around and did not take any notice of what was coming their way. As we got closer one of these lads nodded as if he recognised us, I think he thought we were Newport, his faced suddenly changed as we broke into a canter and he realised his little gang was in trouble.

Wallop! In went all of us, when something like this happens you just hope you haven't picked out a black belt in your own personnel duel. Fists flew and Newport were gone. One tall thin lad was trying to make a stand and was screaming at his mates to come back and fight. We all went at him and he turned and ran .... straight into a lamp post. We all fell about in hysterical, yes this was defiantly a "Wish I had a Camera" moment. We all returned home happy with our nights work.

The first Monday in May is known as May Day. It is the time of year when warmer weather begins and flowers and trees start to blossom. There is also another bank holiday at the end of May called the Whitsun bank holiday. It is said to be a time of love and romance. It is supposed to be a time when people celebrate the coming of summer with lots of different customs that are expressions of joy and hope after a long winter.

If that's true, I don't know what the hell happened in May 1984. In 34 years of going to football matches I have never been involved in so many incidents over such a short time. As well as trouble at the Brighton and Sheffield Weds home games there, we also invaded Blackburn's end at Ewood Park, the usual crew, Mikey Dye (Dio), Annis, Little Coll, Mannings , Mallo , myself etc. We actually scattered the whole end about 20 of us, 5 mins before kick off. Oh yes! There was also the littler matter of a further 4 x incidents with Newport.

I was present at most of these events and will detail this in chronological order with the facts as told or witnessed.

May 7th – Bank Holiday Monday 1984.

Meanwhile, at Cardiff central train station, a few Cardiff fans were coming back from Barry Island. They were met by a group of a dozen or so Newport who caught them by surprise and chased the small group of Cardiff. Newport did not stay around and were attacked by a reorganised Cardiff, on the train platform whilst waiting for their return journey.

On returning to Cardiff after the 1-1 draw with Blackburn this was the story that was reported to us. It was starting to become obvious that this was turning into more than just tit for tat one up manship.

May 15th – Tuesday

Whilst queuing to enter the under 18's Ritzy disco that night about a dozen or so lads including Tony G, Bear, Mallo, Eugene M, Moggy, Ivor and several others plus of course the author Annis and myself went on a completely unplanned journey to Newport. This existed of 1 x Car & 1 x small train mob. We arrived at Newport around 08.00 was stood in a car park just outside the station waiting to meet the car load of others. The first person we actually 'met' was an old Newport lad called Dino, who was in a donkey jacket on his way home from work and riding a bicycle. He proceeded to ride into us waving a metal chain. This unnerved everyone and we were waiting for what now seemed like an inevitable attack. We met the car full of Cardiff and soon enough Newport arrived. We were outnumbered that night and we were all kids, but everyone who was there did their bit, some Cardiff were as young as 13 but everyone stood up and were counted. We charged at Newport who ran, they came back and called us on, but we chased them again. This went on for about 5 minutes with Cardiff coming out on top. No punches were thrown as it was just a case of one group chasing another.

We made our way back to Cardiff and still made it to Ritzy that night and told all the other lads of the happenings 15 miles east. I felt like a giant.

May 19th – Saturday – F.A. Cup Final Day 1984.

Some Saturdays are just the same, nothing happens, just a repetition of previous Saturdays. But, there are certain days that right from the start look, sound and feel different.

That cup final day I had declined the invite to go to Wembley with the Author that day for a look around, so I made my way into town with my then girlfriend, Vicky. Vicky was a Scandinavian looking girl who looked older than her 16 years, she had a blond bob and curves and had a healthy and pretty smile. As soon as I saw her, I realized she was the kind of girl I'd wanted to meet ever since I was old enough to want to meet girls. This was my first taste of that terrible thing, love in your teens. I thought I was the perfect catch, with my wedge, pink and yellow attire, gel, hair spray and Blue Stratos deodorant and she was my prized possession. We ambled along at our usual leisurely pace into Cardiff town centre where she would met her friends and go for coffee and I would meet mine and we would act like something out of the film the Wanderers. We would then walk meet up about 5 O'Clock, catch the bus back to her house meet up later in a park or if we were feeling brave the pub and be 16 year olds for the night.

There were no two ways about it. When I was sixteen... I was a pretty cool (remember that word) kid, or so I thought,. Not in the ninety-ninth-percentile of coolness, maybe, but definitely top third of the Cardiff Trendies. I knew the walk. I knew the talk. I had my own kinda... style. Vicky was part of that style, the perfect fashion accessories, a pretty and popular girlfriend.

This day, when we arrived in town, a local rogue called Greeky ran past us chased by the police and hid by a fruit barrow. On seeing he was safe he asked if we wanted to buy the new Madness album called keep moving (he had about 7 x copies under his arm) of a box of chocolates (he had about 4 x boxes under his arm), we refused. The sight of Greeky panicking with his arms full of stolen goods amused us greatly. He followed us back to Olympus and proceeded to ask everyone who was between the ages of 6 – 93 if they wanted to buy his goods. On arriving at Olympus Vicky then left to meet her friends and do whatever girls do.

I had been outside Olympus about 5 minutes when a young kid called Dave from Grangetown plonked a complete case of Orange Fanta on the floor in front of us that he had stolen from some newsagent. Next, a few lads who were slightly older than me and were from my area were going to watch the Cup Final in a pub. Wow!, I thought, a pub, that'll be really grown up. So I went with the slightly older lads to watch the game.

On arriving at the pub it became immediately obvious that I hadn't a clue about drinking on regular basis as the pub was not serving alcohol due to the time restrictions and I tried to call the bluff of the barman & told him that the previous Saturday I was in the same pub at the same time and they had served me that day.

His reply of 'we close at 2 o'clock every Saturday and we are only open today for the cup final' exposed me for the charlatan that I was and I became completely embarrassed.

We were in the pub about half an hour when someone came running in 'Newport are here'. That was enough for me to leave the pub and make my way to the central station. On my way to the station I noted that there must have been 40-50 Cardiff hastily making their way to give these Newport lot a taste of real Cardiff. With a confident spring in my step I continued my way to the station, I was looking forward to this one.

On arriving at the station it was obvious that whoever had run into the pub that day was correct, Newport were here, about 100 of them. By the time I was at the station little one on one's had started, Newport were fast advancing. Moorie from Canton was first into them, he was holding his own too, next, in went Subb, he actually flew into them almost feet first. And at that moment I learned a little something about fear, and courage. If these 2 lads were brave enough to take life by the horns maybe I could too. Newport continued advancing. By now Moorie and Subb weren't faring so well and Newport had by now gained momentum, I noticed that these weren't just kids, a big fat dark haired lump of about 30 with a moustache was throwing his weight about, still Newport advanced. Suddenly I was right at the front with Tony G, a look of inevitability drew over our faces and we began to back off, but we were almost within touching distance.

I noticed 2 x tall half caste lads who had to be brothers calling us on, they had picked us out and sensed blood. One made a charge and into Tony on my left who fought back and gave as good as he got, me, I had my Light Blue Kappa polo shirt half over my head exposing my back and started to get a beating. The next few seconds are a blur, but Tony was by now on the other side (right) of me getting a bit of pasting form about 4 or 5 guys, he was trapped against the metal barrier outside Asteys Café & in trouble. I made probably the most pathetic attempt in the world to rescue him, I held my hand over my face and hunched my back ready for my anticipated further beating and looked like a girl protecting herself from a snowball and made a feeble grab for Tony, when Bang!, someone caught my clean on the nose and my nose spread all over my face.

To my horror, there was more bad news as the Police arrived and began to chase whatever Cardiff were left into the city centre. I ran along Westgate Street and into a department store called James Howells out of the way of the Police. So I'm now in James Howells covered in blood, I'm in the shop a matter of 30 seconds and I bump into Vicky. She gives me 'that' look and walks on, her friends are more sympathetic and I am taken upstairs where the blood is washed off me in the middle of Circles Café in James Howells.

After about half an hour I lefty the café and shop with Vicky and made my way to Olympus for the Autopsy of that day. I slated a lot of Cardiff that afternoon, saw Subb he was Ok apart from some scrapes, bought Automatic by the Pointer Sisters and then left for home. That day there was no Little Coll, Annis, Dexy or Richard E etc but fair play to Newport they came down to us bigger than usual. Result to Newport.

May 26th – The following Saturday

I was in town early that day, I was walking passed Boots in Queen Street, when Gary from Rumney came running past, 'Newport, Newport' he said in a high pitched excited and energized tone. This time they were on Queen St., Cardiff's main thoroughfare. One lad from Ely called Jamo had already given them his own welcome of a table or chair from a nearby café called, Lord Sandwich over some Newport lad's head.

By the time Newport arrived outside Olympus there was hardly opposition, this was early and they caught us by surprise. Once again, this was the same lot as the previous week, grown men, moustaches, etc. One of their lumps caught Cairnsy from Canton smack in the face, Cairnsy has a blond wedge and when he was punched his wedge haircut almost hit the floor. But Bang! Fair play to Cairnsy he hit him straight back, this stopped them in their tacks. Meanwhile little Coll was having a one to one with someone twice his size and age and was also giving as good as he got. I stood next to Little Coll and noticed that a stray Newport lad had tried to sneak behind him &and grab him, me and Subby pounced, Subby hit him with his brolley and he soon ran back into his mob.

The police then rounded their lot up and they were escorted back to Newport via Cardiff Central station. In the escort back, they were then attacked as Cardiff by now had mobbed up as people arrived into the town centre. Although that week they made it onto Cardiff's main centre, I felt that Cardiff had fared better than the previous as the small numbers stuck together and never took a step backwards, we gave them a better run for their money. Would a handful of Newport have done that to a fair sized mob fronted by men twice their age? I doubt it.

May 1984, what a month. In a matter of weeks I had turned from a novice of a lad into a battle scarred experienced combatant. We started to realise that not everyone who stood outside Olympus was ready and willing to throw their fists about, that not everyone had the courage of a lion and when it came to it there were not many raving banshees among us. What this did was make Cardiff as a mob tighter, we knew who we could trust and who was there to make up the numbers.

By the end of June 1984 we were drinking in pubs on Saturday afternoons and the summer had set in, Vicky and I were still an item I had an Ellesse polo shirt and Diadora Bjorn Borg trainers. Minor midweek incidents with little to nothing worth reporting happened but sure enough Newport made their way west.

As usual word spread of their presence; by the time I arrived at the bus station Cardiff with their en masse, Newport were hesitant of leaving the station and stayed in the foyer. Cardiff went at them, first about 6 of us and then as more came Newport fancied their chances less. Jamo and a few Ely went across to confront and beckoned them on and fists flew. Then the second charge, and they were ready to do the Canton mile, Newport were now getting picked off and were scattering. Then the police came in their dozens and we were all off. Off to Dumfries place which would be the route the bus took.

We were now well and truly up for carnage, as we got to Dumfries place the bus stopped and a few of us had a couple of Newport out the windows by the scruffs of their necks, me included. When I felt someone grab me in a forearm lock, I was arrested. Sixteen / Seventeen, true heroism has not less to do with actual logic and more to do with pure stupidity.

Earlier on that year I had been arrested at Portsmouth and fined £100 for running down the street and shouting, this time I was in real trouble. I thought I was going to be spending some time at Her Majesty's pleasure. To my amazement, as this was addressed not a football related incident I was only fined £25.

By the time the football season had arrived there was anticipation over another season of the unknown. It's always exciting looking at the new fixtures when they are realised and planning your trips, a real Pandora's Box. The first game I made an effort to go to that season was at Newport, they were playing a friendly against West Brom on a Friday night in early August 1984 and in torrential rain. About a dozen of us, including the usual lot Annis, Mannings, Joseph ,Moorie, etc with an average age of about 18 made our way to Newport. We arrived in Newport late and with the length of the walk from the station to the ground being lengthy we decided to catch a bus to the ground. On the bus were 3 very nervous Newport lads avoiding eye contact and looking sheepish. As they numbered only 3 nothing happened but a chat. This was a mistake. As when we alighted from the bus they led us to the back of the Newport end, and it emptied. We dozen were now stood at the top of some concrete steps and Newport were advancing up the stairs like a pack of swarming ants. We remained where we were until the advancing mob just overpowered us, Annis was demanding we stood but we were being backed off and whacked every where eventually we were run. That chase in the back streets of Newport was pretty scary to say the least. We were chased into a Chinese takeaway where we tried to hold the door shut. They tried, unsuccessfully for some time to get in that take away until the Police came and saved our bacon. A pretty scary night.

It was a risk going there that night, but if there's one thing every kid learns growing up, it's that life is a series of risks. It's a cause and effect relationship. Nothing ventured, nothing gained.

By the autumn of 1984, things quietened down on the Newport front, due to the continual 'ad hoc' midweek raids that Cardiff dished out. During that autumn the Author's nightclub was near its completion and one afternoon whilst I was actually working on Newport Train Station and had seen about 10 lads make a midweek afternoon venture into Cardiff, I knew a few of the faces, one of which John Charlton was distinctive by his mop of curly hair. As this was way before the time of mobile phones there was no way of informing anyone of our friends pending visit to Cardiff. I had planned to finish my shift (at 14.00) and head to Caesars where the decorating was in mid process and 'word' the lads up that the enemy were in town.

All my plans changed when I caught the train back to Cardiff and in the foyer of the station were the 10 Newport lads. I immediately spotted them and as I was in British Rail uniform was able to walk through them unnoticed around the corner to Caesars. Lying in wait in Caesars were a few lads working at the decorating as well as a few other faces (Annis, Tony G, C Beer, Harris), who on hearing the news made haste around to Cardiff Central station and we pounced. Newport did not know what hit them, they were immediately on their toes and hiding on the platform, where we all ended up picking them off. Priceless.

There are many, many, many, many, many, many, many more memories there of that golden period when everything happened so fast and so often and all for the first time. I guess magic doesn't last forever no matter how much you wish it would.

Over the next 24 years I have maintained my friendship levels with the Author. In fact at Cardiff home games we sit several seats away from each other in the same row and have done now for a number of seasons.

Whenever I think of those intervening years 1 memory always springs to mind, 26 April 1986. I was to be engaged and I asked to use the Author's nightclub called Caesars for the venue of the Party. That day, Cardiff were at Wolves and if they lost would've been relegated to the bottom tier of the league (the old Fourth Division). Wolves's fortunes were not much better and they were also struggling in a big way, so a lot hinged on the game, but I had not planned to go due to the fact of my pending engagement.

During the week leading to the game and my engagement I made a trip into Caesars where I was met by the Author and his parents who were charming to my Mum and Dad. We agreed to use the venue but as it was a Saturday night we had to share the establishment with regular Saturday night clubbers but could have an area closed off.

For the trip to WOLVES there was to be a mini bus of which the 'usual suspects' were to be present. I was invited, but due obvious matters declined.

On the morning of the game all plans were complete and there was nothing more to do. So, along with my parents (both of whom are avid Cardiff fans) we decided to make the trip. I miss the days when you could make last minute plans to go away without the coach booking, tickets etc. that has become so prevalent now. We arrived just before the kick off; the game was full of incident on and off the field. There were disallowed goals; skirmishes in the town centre, outside the ground and in the seated are on the right hand side of the way end. Cardiff lost 3-1 and were relegated, an old Cardiff player called Jimmy Mullen was on his knees at the end.

As we left the ground the inevitable happened underneath the subway just outside the ground and to the right of the away end. Our car was parked to the left & along with my parents I walked the opposite way of the shenanigans that were unfolding just yards away. Then, who do we see? The crew of about 12 from the minibus that I was invited on, they had been in the afore mentioned seated area, where there was trouble during the game. They were obviously making their way to the unfolding chaos under the subway.

As they run passed us the Author (unaware of the fact that we could see him) says words to the effect of 'under the subway lads, come on', obviously referring to the bedlam that had by now well and truly kicked off.

With that, my Mum turned to me and said 'doesn't that look just like your friend who owns that club'. I nearly roared laughing.

The author and I have both left those days behind us and are both family men. The author would rather be with his children nowadays and fair play to that, as he is now a true family man .Myself, I have an expanding waistline, a walking or in this case waddling cliché for a 40 something but still never a dull moment.

I like to think that during those days we built a foundation for the future. Because within 2 or 3 years, the firm that started following Cardiff became amongst the best in Britain.

It would be remiss for me to inform you that I was there through thick and thin because I wasn't. During the mid to late 90's I was only an occasional visitor to Ninian park (4 or 5 games a year). The same cannot be said for the Author who's fanatical support didn't dwindle one bit, for over 35 years he has stuck by supporting the City.

I returned on a regular basis during the 99/2000 season just before Sam Hammam years. When I preceded to form friendships with about 15 lads who had balls the size of SOMETHING BIG. These lads I would prefer to remain nameless but came from Roath, Splott, Ely, Fairwater & Tongwynlais. There were about 3 or 4 little mobs of that size from the Docks, Llanishen, Port Talbot and Neath and collectively, If there has been a better crew before that time in Cardiff I would be shocked.

Some of these guys were way out of my league and they used to unnerve me with their total lack of fear. **'YOU ALL KNOW WHO YOU ARE, SO GIVE YOURSELVES A PAT ON THE BACK AS THE BEST CREW THAT I'VE EVER SEEN.** I just wish that I could turn the clock back and this lot would have been there when Shakatak, Billy Ocean, Chaka Khan & Grandmaster Flash were in the charts when shaggy perms were fashionable and when Kelly LeBrock was gorgeous, because they all would've loved it, loved it, loved it.

Don't misunderstand my meaning, during the years 1982-84 a basic footprint was created. To me the Soul Crew as a firm had not yet fully formed. By 1987 the numbers had trebled and by the mid nineties it was out of control. It s like building a wall, first you lay the foundations and from good foundations comes something that is strong and unbreakable.

☐ It was the worst violence in 30 years'   ☐ Stones and bricks were flying through air'

SOCCER MOB ATTACK POLICE AT CITY GAME

Pc Ken Tilley recovering at his Cardiff home today with his police dog Kaied.

Echo men forced to flee

WEDNESDAY, AUGUST 26, 1987

FRIGHTENED FAMILIES told today how a vicious soccer mob showered police with a hail of stones, bricks and bottles after a South Wales cup tie last night.

More than 250 fans turned on officers after the Cardiff City and Newport County clash — with one constable taken to hospital with head injuries.

THREE Echo reporters were caught up in last night's violence — and had to flee in the running battle between police and thugs.

After leaving the match at Ninian Park, Echo men Jeremy Bacon, Jim Clarke and Paul Horton were trapped in the middle of the warring soccer fans.

Frightening

"Suddenly a roar went up of 'They're out' as Newport fans were allowed from the ground, and the City fans ran back up Sloper Road," said Mr Bacon.

"We saw the mob clash with the police and the air was full of bottles and bricks. It was horrific."

After a few minutes, the mob broke up and ran as police counter-attacked onto a garage forecourt.

The Press shows a crack in a window at the Ninian Self-Serve Garage and part of the pavestone thrown by fans during last night's violence.

Two police dog handlers had to ask residents to dialled 999 for reinforcements as the pack of teenagers began attacking them.

"It was the worst violence we've seen in more than 30 years living here. We were terrified and the police were really worried," said 63-year-old Mr Kenneth Dawkings.

Four fans were arrested during the five minute attack including one girl carrying a hockey ball in a sock as a weapon, said police today.

More than £2,000 damage was caused to windows at the Ninian Self-Serve Garage and crates of milk bottles were stolen and used as missiles against police.

'Gang were going wild'

Detectives were today studying a video of the violence taken from a security camera on the garage forecourt in a bid to identify more of the hooligans.

Garage owner Mrs Pamela Thomas said: "The gang were trying to break into the garage and were going wild. I've never seen anything like it."

Now people in the Sloper Road area are worried about matches with Swansea and Wolves over the next 10 days — and Mrs Thomas says she will shut up her garage.

Wounded policeman Ken Tilley, aged 35 was today recovering at home after being hit on the head by a brick.

"There were only two of us with dogs trying to get the fans towards Penarth

Road when they just turned on us," he said.

"We managed to push them back the first time but then they started throwing things.

'Fell over when hit'

"We called for help but the radios were not working, so we had to ask residents to phone for reinforcements," said Pc Tilley at his Cardiff home.

"I fell over when I was hit by the brick and the next thing I remember is trying to get up but I fell again."

Pc Tilley's head injury was X-rayed and he was today on sick leave.

Chief Superintendent Alan Chadwick blamed the trouble on a "hooligan element of City supporters" who were intent on attacking Newport fans.

He said the four people were arrested for carrying missiles, obstructing the police and disorderly conduct.

Buses carrying the Newport fans were later escorted away from the ground by more than 50 officers.

'We were all terrified'

There were more than 100 police on duty for last night's match — three times the number that usually work the football ground. People in the area say the major police presence was at the opposite end of the ground towards Ninian Park Road — the scene of violence last week on the first leg of the cup tie.

"We never have any trouble down this end — until last night. We were all terrified," said Mr Dawkins.

"The crowd shouted 'charge' and just turned on the police. There were broken milk bottles over the road," he said.

The mob rampaged through the gardens in Sloper Road and picked up missiles from the houses to hurl at the officers.

"I was shaking from head to toe. It was like something you see on the television," said 56 year-old neighbour Mrs Betty Ham.

"The police asked me to call for reinforcements. It was a terrible sight," she said.

Cardiff supporters saw their team to a 3-2 draw in the local derby — a result that knocked them out of the Littlewoods Cup as the County team went through on aggregate.

Mr Chadwick said it was unfortunate that the first two matches of the season were against Newport, because the fans were especially volatile.

'City fans very bitter'

"At matches of this nature we try to escort the fans away while we hold the Newport supporters in the ground. Officers were trying to clear the area so we could let the Newport people get to their trains, when they were pelted with bricks and bottles.

"The incident only lasted for a matter of minutes before the trouble makers ran off down Virgil Street.

"The city fans were very, very bitter last night. They always have this bad feeling when they are playing against Newport, but it was worse last night.

Soccer fans in mass train arrest

By MARK O'CALLAGHAN and GRAHAM EVANS

TERRIFIED policemen stood by helpless as soccer thugs gutted a packed rail coach in the latest episode of Welsh football madness at the weekend.

In an unprecedented move everyone travelling in the carriage was arrested on suspicion of causing criminal damage and public-order offences.

The fans smashed lights, windows and fittings in the coach after a local derby match.

Transport Police arrested 103 Cardiff City supporters after the train carrying around 600 people pulled into the city station, and transported them in groups of 10 to cells throughout Cardiff for questioning.

The explosive match against rivals Newport County trouble flared before, during and after the match

A Gwent Police spokesman

● **Traffic Superintendent Gwilym Thomas (left) and Chief Superintendent Fred Wyer examining the broken fence at Somerton Park.**

said 25 fans of both sides were charged with a variety of public-order offences. Fighting erupted and a banner bearing obscene slogans was set alight by Cardiff supporters.

Some City fans also took wire-cutters to the game to break through the new reinforced £60,000 segregation fence.

Secretary of the Welsh Football Association Mr Alun Evans, who was monitoring the match after the violence by Cardiff supporters at Peterborough on the previous Saturday, said last night he was "infinitely depressed" by this latest hooliganism.

He said he would be meeting his officers tomorrow to hammer out a report for a full council

meeting of the Welsh FA on Wednesday. Measures to be considered would include a ban on Cardiff City fans, except holders of season tickets and members of the supporters' club, travelling to away games.

The commander of British Transport Police South Wales sub-division, Chief Inspector Stephen Chapman, said it was the worst example of soccer violence he had known in 20 years in the force.

Of the 103 male supporters arrested from the one carriage, 67 were adults and 36 were under 17, their ages ranging from 12 to 27. No one was charged and they were all given police bail to appear again for questioning on December 14 and 15.

In the short journey from

Newport Station to Cardiff Central fans in the rear coach wrought a trail of destruction.

The catalogue of trouble started before the train even left the platform after the emergency cord was pulled three times.

Although British Transport Police officers Sgt Gil Tyler and Pc Derek Lawrence were in the rear carriage they were powerless to stop the unbridled mayhem as vandals ripped lights from fittings, smashed five large windows and some luggage racks on to the line.

Sgt Tyler said yesterday, "Some of the rats came out of the sewer. I have never seen anything like it before."

The police officers were surrounded by the hooligans who shouted verbal insults including a chant of "Kill, kill, kill."

As the train drew into Platform Three of Cardiff Central station they were met by British Transport Police officers after Sgt Tyler had radioed a message ahead.

A BTP spokesman confirmed that some of the vandals jumped off the train on to the line as the train grinded to a halt and escaped.

Those left in the rear carriage were told by loud-hailer that they were all being arrested and

were taken to Cardiff Central, where the holding cells at the city's crown court had to be used as an overspill, Rumney Police Station, and BTP's own offices at the station.

Chief Inspector Chapman said his own force, Gwent Police and South Wales had all taken precautions for the potentially explosive Newport County-Cardiff City match.

He said damage would run into thousands of pounds and BTP scenes-of-crime officers were examining the carriage yesterday while two teams of detectives followed up leads.

Chief Inspector Chapman promised that charges would follow as part of a new get-tough policy, and said that in the aftermath of the violence he would be making special recommendations to both British Rail and the Welsh FA today.

These include:

● Calling on British Rail to ban football supporters from travelling on regular service trains and confining them to policed soccer specials.

● Calling on the Welsh FA to

ensure all-Welsh derby matches are played in the morning to minimise the amount of alcohol available.

The train-wrecking fans were branded as outcasts by Cardiff City chairman Mr Tony Clemo.

He said, "I don't want these people travelling to away games or coming to our home games. They are not interested in football, only in causing as much trouble as possible.

"We have no trouble at all with the supporters who travel on the trips arranged by the supporters' club.

"These are the fans who we want supporting us. We don't need or want anyone else."

Mr Clemo said it was difficult to stop the hooligan element going to and from away matches but a method must be found.

Trouble also flared before, during and after the game in Newport.

A Gwent Police spokesman said that 25 fans including supporters from both clubs had been arrested and charged with a variety of public-order offences.

Fighting erupted during the match and police were forced to break up a large fight after several Cardiff fans managed to get into a section of the ground reserved for home supporters. They were evicted and taken into police custody before being released.

Police also went into the crowd after a banner bearing obscene slogans was set alight by rival fans during the first half.

Newport County will send Cardiff the bill for the damage to the £60,000 segregation fencing, which was installed only in time for Saturday's game. Many Cardiff City fans took wire-cutters to the game and cut the reinforced fence in several places. It is believed the damage will cost around £500 to repair.

However, Mr Clemo blamed the Newport club for the damage caused to the fencing. "As far as a bill is concerned we will look at that when it comes in, but as far as I am concerned Newport County are responsible for looking after their own ground," he said.

Mr Clemo said the club had

offered an open invitation for hooligans to wreck the fencing by publicising its cost and effectiveness and by their claims on how secure the ground would now be.

"They spent so much time advertising how good the fencing would be and how much it cost that these hooligans went out evidently with the sole thought of taking it down," he said.

"If they hadn't shouted out about the fencing this could have been avoided. They should have just kept quiet about it and the fans put in behind the fencing on the day.

"But they advertised everything in advance. To blame us for that is an absolute joke."

County chief executive Mr Ken James claimed before the game that not even a herd of wild elephants would be able to break through the segregating fencing.

Mr James said he wanted City fans at the match and did not foresee any trouble.

County directors declined to comment last night.

CARDIFF CITY'S so-called "supporters" are making the headlines again. Their antics both during and following the recent cup-tie against Peterborough, and at Saturday's League match against Newport County means that the City took a knock in the efforts to project a better image of the game and so attract more spectators to Ninian Park.

Following each of these unsavoury incidents, the question that is asked most often is, "Are these idiots really Cardiff City supporters and, if they are, what are they trying to achieve with such behaviour?"

The answer will probably remain a mystery since enlightenment can only come from the hooligans themselves — and their only form of communication seems to be limited to the use of the fist and the boot.

But it is possible to confirm that, whatever they are, they are not Cardiff City supporters in the accepted sense of the word "supporter." To call them supporters does a grave injustice to those few, and slowly diminishing, group of people who have followed the club through thick and thin, in all weather, and for most of their lives.

The differences between the regular supporter and the hooligan are quite marked. Many genuine fans are season-ticket holders at Ninian Park. Hooligans rarely buy a season-ticket.

Their allegiance to the club only goes as far as adopting its name and using it as an excuse to indulge in antics which are obviously more related to their personal hang-ups than the playing of professional football.

City fans go on yet another rampage

and, while they have their own opinion on how the club should be run, and how the team should achieve success, they don't behave like wild animals when things don't go the way the expect, or would like.

In fact, a hooligan's behavior seems to have little to do with the team-performance. Some of the worst bheaviour at recent matches has occurred when City have been winning handsomely — which goes to confirm that the game tiself is incidental to these people.

When Wolverhampton Wanderers visited Ninian Park last season, a group of supporters stood near a refreshment kiosk, which provided no view of the pitch, — for practically the entire match. When asked by the kiosk attendant, why they weren't interested in watching the game, they said, quite calmly, "We don't care about the football - we're only her for the aggro!"

The genuine Bluebirds supporters are ashamed and embarrassed by the hooligans' behaviour. They resent being tarred by the same hooligan-brush, doing everything they can to disassociate themselves from this scourge.

Chairman of Cardiff City Supporters Club Alwyn Evans has very strong views on hooligans at soccer games in general and Cardiff City's matches in particular, "These yobs are a pain in the neck. They make life unbearable for us at away matches.

"Travelling away our supporters clubs coaches are usually stopped by the police who herd us like cattle when we arrive and then keep us locked in the ground for up to a half an hour after the final whistle until the home crowd has dispersed.

"The ironic part is that the hooligans wouldn't be seen dead on an official supporters club coach. They always travel independently so that they can't be controlled, or identified before the game. That's why a ban on visiting supporters can't be effective. They'll pose as home fans until the time coes for them to cause trouble.

"Most of them never go to midweek matches because they can't make a day of it drinking and fighting. They like Saturday matches when they can destroy the enjoyment of the genuine football supporters.

Apart from their anti-social behaviour the very existence of hooligans does considerable damage to the game of professional soccer. It isn't only that their antics discourage many people from attending games — that's bad enough — but they project an unpalateable image of the sport which makes it difficult to attract commercial sponsors at a time when soccer most needs it.

The Football League have appointed a new Marketing Director who admits that his main problem is to convince business people that soccer is worth investing advertising money in.

Business people simply do not want their organisations to be linked with a sport that gets as much publicity from punch-ups on the terraces as they do play on the pitch. Hooliganism is also a major deterrent to a growing tend in sport — that of multi-purpose usage of a stadium.

Very soon, Cardiff City are going to instal a closed circuit television system. Many other clubs aleady have one. The photographing, arresting and conviction of hooligans might, soon, provide Ninian Park with the means to implement a system which will give Alwyn Evans his way.

The identification, on film, which provides the proof of bad behaviour, will lead to conviction of offenders which, in turn, will make soccer grounds a safer and more attractive place for people to attend. So watch out, hooligans, Big Brother is starting to watch you!

ANYONE WHO may have liked to believe that football hooliganism is a disease confined to the big English conurbations and not a significant problem in Wales should have been rudely disabused of such illusions by events at the weekend.

Fans on rampage

April 5th 1988.

Police escort Newport County fans back to the station after the match

NOVEMBER 28, 1987

● Helmetted police-men face the baying hooligans in the Newport County v Cardiff City match last weekend.

Hooligans

CARDIFF CITY'S so-called "supporters" are making the headlines again. Their antics both during and following the recent cup-tie against Peterborough, and at Saturday's League match against Newport County means that the City took a knock in the efforts to project a better image of the game and so attract more spectators to Ninian Park.

Following each of these unsavoury incidents, the question that is asked most often is, "Are these idiots really Cardiff City supporters and, if they are, what are they trying to achieve with such behaviour?"

SOCCER FANS STONE POLICE

By Paul Horton

A GANG of up to 200 soccer fans stoned police after last night's Cardiff City and Newport County derby.

Police today described it as a "totally unprovoked attack" as officers were escorting fans up Ninian Park Road.

Three windows in homes and a shop were smashed by the missiles but the uniformed police escaped unhurt.

"This one unnecessary incident spoilt an otherwise peaceful derby," a senior officer said today.

"The officers were dispersing the crowds on the way back to the station when between 100 and 200 fans started throwing the stones at the police.

"Luckily, no officers were hurt in what was a totally unprovoked attack by this gang. The crowds at the ground were otherwise well-behaved," he said.

The windows were smashed in Ninian Park Road and Craddock Street, Riverside, on the route from the ground into the city centre.

One man was arrested at the ground for an unrelated offence and is expected to appear in court later.

Chapter 9

THE GREAT OLD DAYS
By Mike Dye
ELY TRENDIES CCFC.

Its my old mate Dio, He's a lad and a half, as you will see he's a wanderer, always off in his small tight group, he never really liked going with the main group. Always said he had more fun in the 80's with his group, but if the other lads needed him he would be there before you could raise your voice. He's one great friend who you could always rely on and is one of my best mates to this day. Annis

After the success of Annis' first book and being asked to write in this one also, I was only too glad to share some of my exploits once again. I have known Annis now for nearly 25 years. We have travelled together many, many times and on the occasions we weren't able to travel together we always met up somewhere along the line.

We travelled to Düsseldorf in October 08 to follow Wales. Annis, Dan, Dave and myself lost the other 28 in our party and spent the whole of Wednesday drinking together and making our own way over to Munchengladbach. Funny thing about this little trip was on arrival at the airport, Pat of Chelsea had put Annis in touch with a mate of his called Dirk who supported Fortuna Düsseldorf. Dirk and his two henchmen said they could take 5 of us in their cars to the hotel. So Annis, Dave and Zedy jumped in with this lad Dirk, then me and Kaget jumped in the other, now one of these guys had tattoos on his knuckles, most people have love on one hand and hate on other, not this geezer he had hate on one hand and hate on the other! He told us a few tales of his own and how the previous Saturday Germany had played Russia and a meet was had in a field, 200 onto 200 he then told us how the Russians turned them over due to the Russians all being kick boxers an military trained, a different level I believe!, broken arms and legs etc and fight till you drop. Anyway, on getting to the hotel as I got out of the car I shook his hand and thanked him for the lift , his reply was in a groggy German accent "Ve have drink later then ve see vot happens, Ya?" I looked at Kaget and he looked at me, we were both gob smacked! I thought mate you can fuck off, you either drink with me or fight me you don't get both, as it happens they had a mob of about 50 or so that night, but the police had them contained and I believe later they chased them along the side of the Rhine and some were later locked up for the night. Can you believe then the following day they waned to have breakfast with us and show us the shops, you can't get weirder than that.

We were there for a good time, a drink and a laugh, those days abroad are long gone of running battles in the streets, then appearing on your local news, I think they realised in the end. Even our 6 spotters were laughing about it all.

Here are a few more of my many travels with a mob of lads who I grew to know from various area's of Cardiff as well as my trusted old Ely Trendie's!, The Mid 80's, what great days.

COLCHESTER Away (Mid 80's)

This match was played on a Friday night and we travelled by 'good old British Rail' - Little Colin, Annis, Pricey, Jerky, Reya (RIP), myself and about 25 others. We decided to meet in the Red Dragon pub which was situated next to Cardiff Railway Station (now Marks & Spencer's). We used to meet at this pub every home game due to its location, the problem with this bar, was on non match days it attracted mainly gay people. As we only used the pub once or maybe twice a week the landlord decided that the gay crowd brought in more custom and less trouble so therefore decided to more or less ban the football crowd in favour of the gays.

Whilst using this pub for approximately 6 months before we were 'banned' only one set of opposing supporters actually 'paid us a visit' and they didn't come out of the railway station…..they came from the Empire Pool end and that was the gypo's from up the road….Swansea.

Peter M had come running in the pub shouting "the Jacks are coming round the corner", no one thought anything of it and carried on drinking. But out of curiosity Rasper and myself popped our heads round the door and could see about 25-30 SWANSEA coming around the corner. Peter M was back outside but on the other side of the road. Rasper and myself walked towards these Jacks, we got within 10 yards of them ,when Peter M shouted "Dio, Dio old bill" and as I looked across to him "Fuck" a sly Jack bastard landed one right on my snozzer, with my blood spilling all over my C17 denim shirt. Within seconds our 20-30 lads from the pub fronted by Jammo, CC and a few of the other Ely boys then backed the Jacks off and run em back into the station'.

The police were quickly on the scene and looking to make arrests. Jammo and Rasper told me to go back to the pub and clean up as I was covered in blood and one of the boys lent me his jacket to cover this up and avoid arrest. Hats off to the Jacks though for their bold effort, even though we were playing them at home that day at least some of them made an effort.

The Red Dragon pub closed 6 months later, maybe if the landlord had chosen the football crowd over the gay crowd he could have made more money and stayed open because fuck me we used to down some pints in there!

Anyway, I digress, back to COLCHESTER….we boarded a train early in the afternoon. During this journey our little firm had a disagreement, about what, evades my head, so when we arrived at Paddington our group split into two, we crossed London to Liverpool Street Station using different routes, with both groups I expect saying "Fuck em, well go alone" etc. Looking back, how stupid were we, as we had to catch the same train anyway to Colchester! Thankfully by now our issue had been resolved and we were a group once again. Maybe that's what the problem has always been with Cardiff, we can never get on as a bigger group and that's why we've never really been organised.

Colchester is an army based town and we knew this could be a tricky one. On arriving at Layer Road we all decided to go on their end (hurray we all agree for once). On paying and entering the ground we grouped together near the back of the terrace, all keeping quiet and staying close together. As we looked over to where our supporters should be housed we noticed there wasn't a soul in sight. Heavy traffic had put paid to that, 2 coaches finally arrived at half time, thus missing the action on and off the pitch......Just as the match started a mob of Colchester arrived, including what looked like a few army lads. About 70 in all and they all came together walking below us on the terracing. They then all stood together on the same level as us, we were already sussed, They came running at us, as they got about 10 yards away from us they suddenly stopped, we adopted the fighting stance, but all Colchester could do at this moment was throw calling cards at us, these cards had the writing of the CRS (Colchester Riot Squad). We thought fuck it and got into them. They fought back and we were badly outnumbered. The fighting was fierce with punches being wildly thrown and kicks when it mattered, the fighting went on for what seemed like an age but was probably only a matter of minutes, eventually the old bill had the situation under control and most of us were either ejected or moved to the away end. My last vision before being ejected myself was little Colin, Annis and Pricey still fighting right by the dividing wall from the pitch side, not only were they fighting but rolling across the terraces, it was a sight to make me chuckle! The 3 of them done well and were eventually ejected themselves. In those days it wasn't unusual not to be arrested, simply separated and moved to your away section, unless you were very unlucky that is.

Staying with COLCHESTER, albeit 20 years later, I was back running coaches for this season with the odd train trip thrown in. As this trip was a night match on Friday December 22nd I decided to make this our Christmas piss up trip and on this particular occasion we went by train. Being so near to Christmas only 8 were able to make it, Penny, young Anthony, Gully, Justin, Squelchy, Wilkie, Arvo and myself. Our original plan was to go to the match and stop in Colchester on the lash for as long as possible before heading back to the smoke, where we would doss on Paddington Station and catch the first train back to Cardiff on Saturday morning.

After a lengthy journey and even lengthier drinking session, we got off at Colchester Station in high spirits. We saw the game out with glazed vision. I met Annis in the ground, he had driven up, and I spent most of the match speaking to him. On leaving the ground all the coach parties were turning right, not our suicidal 8, we ventured left, this was our Christmas party trip and we were stopping at Colchester with its bright lights, excellent night life, you name it.....Colchester aint got it!

As we were walking back to the town centre, we noticed behind us 2 policemen, one was the Colchester spotter, and one was our very own Simon Insole, they were tailing us about 200 yards behind. We were now becoming very spaced out in 1's and 2's, when a car carrying 4 lads passed us all shouting and giving it the large, we just laughed, raised our fingers and told them to fuck off. Within about 2 minutes the car returned yet again but this time slowed down, Penny was straight onto them, "what's up boys", they replied with "keep walking up this road and you will see a pub across a dual carriage way, our firm are in there and they are awaiting your arrival". Great we thought we've got the Dutch courage and although there were only 8 of us we were well up for it and marched on towards the pub which was in the direction we were heading anyway.

Now this road was never fucking ending, a pot of gold was surely waiting for us at the end....a pot of gold be fucked, more like a pub full of barmies! The pub was now in sight and we kept closer together, we could now see and hear their lads calling us on, the only thing standing in our was the very busy dual carriage way. Colchester were there beckoning us over, I said to our lot "Just get to the centre island and don't go any further, if you get across your fucked, let them come to us". With that I noticed our spotter, he started shouting at me "Mikey get them back," by now their lads were right opposite but not making any real effort to get across. I then heard our spotter Simon shouts to me yet again to get them back. We stood firm but listened, there was no point being collared now, the old bill had decided for our own safety to transport us back to the station where we caught the train back to London and enjoyed yet more ale, albeit in a gay bar for our sins! We then enjoyed a curry and a cold windy few hours at Paddington waiting for the first train home.

First I've got to say, Little Colchester have always had a warm welcome waiting for Cardiff and they always seem to have a firm of about 30 to 50 even today. As to Simon our main spotter, if you give him respect he is one of the straightest old bill you will meet as long as you don't cross that line in front of him, he will always give you a warning, not slyly nick you like some.

MILLWALL Cup Match 1987 at The Old Den

This was round 3 of the FA cup and the draw was on Monday at noon. We all eagerly anticipated this moment and wondered who we would be drawn against. We were young lads of 16 to 20 years of age and travelling regularly and we were really up for anybody.

I remember being on dinner at work and Radio Wales was on, the draw began, teams were coming out thick and fast, suddenly the number representing Millwall gets drawn, my stomach was churning and my brain was full of excitement, I was thinking we must be drawn soon there's not many left! Then another number, the commentator says "Cardiff City," well I leapt and bounced around, what a fucking draw! The adrenalin was running through my body. Fuck, how many will go? How will we get there? Will they be out for us? So many questions running through my head. That day in work seemed to last forever, finally home, shower and out. We all met up as usual outside Maggie's chippy, Ely Bridge. Full turnout Ely Trendy's for this one no doubt. The game was in 3 week or so. That evening all our lot were about, Annis pulled up in his car with Chrissy B, Darryl and Richard E. We decided on the 07.45 train to Paddington, straight across to Soho and drink there, we knew it was going to be the younger element of Cardiff going and a lot of older ones went on the special.

The day of the match finally arrived January 10th 1987 and my chosen attire consisted of a Fila BJ top, Lois jeans and a pair of red Adidas Munchen trainers. I knocked for CC, then Jammo and met the rest at the bus stop by Ely Legion. Caught the bus to Cardiff Station and about 60 of our lot (by our lot I mean our age group of 16 - 18). By the time of departure we had at least 100 - 120 all chomping at the bit, still virtually all the younger lads of Cardiff probably not more than 3 over 21 years old.

The "Smoke" was beckoning and we alighted the train. Some of our lot filled the air with

"Caarrdiff," "Caarrdiff," but we quickly told them to shut up. We got to Soho just in time for opening hours, we filled two pubs opposite each other and settled down for a few hours. Our young firm were ready for anything and anyone, but this somehow was different, it was the capital of football hooligans, and we were going to the most notorious of them all. At about 13.30 Rawlins got up on table and said "This is the big one, we're here for Millwall, let's fucking show em". With that the air filled with evil chanting and threatening songs which made the ball on my Fila BJ bounce! With this we left the pub and headed for the Tube which would take us to Kings Cross where fighting broke out with the old bill all over our youngest lad (15 yrs) not having a valid ticket, it actually towards the end of the year). Then it was off to London Bridge to change for Bermondsey.

On arrival at London Bridge the Met were everywhere, they gathered most of us up but Annis, Jerky, myself and a few others managed to slip through, so we headed to Bermondsey on our own without the police escort. When we finally got to Bermondsey our throats were dry and stomachs churned at the thought of what awaited us, how I wished I was in that escort right now! As we left the tube station we climbed the steps towards day light and the air was full of familiar chanting, low and behold it was only our boys in the escort being taken to the ground, so we hastily walked on the opposite side of the road to them and not a bushwhacker in sight, (I vaguely remember something going on at Millwall with regards to the way the club was being run or something and Millwall boycotting the game which could explain why there was no welcoming committee!).

During the game Annis and Little Collin had done a mad one and gone it their seats on the side by the away end, Millwall had soon sussed them and our spotter Jeff Richards (in them days) came to their rescue. I heard later that Little Collin hadn't given a fuck and had called it on.

The match passed off without any real incident until they tried to keep us in and in them days Cardiff would do the usual thing and try to wreck the ground to get out and a few pipes etc were thrown at the old bill holding the gates shut. Millwall that day and I mean that day were a let down, that's the only time they have never really turned out for us.

We arrived back at Paddington where the old bill were putting on special trains home....not us though, we didn't want safety on a special train and we broke out in song "We're the service, we're the service, Ninian Park" and our 90 or so went home in more comfort in one of those shit special trains. (A few lads never returned that day and were arrested and put on trial like Chelsea, Westham etc were in them days, like I say I will leave that for another book).

Personally for me season 83/84 was the best as we had just gained promotion and we were in a division that housed some of the greats in that time of Chelsea, Leeds and Birmingham followed by back to back trips to Man City, Pompey, Middlesbrough and Newcastle all coming later on in the season, this was also the year Cardiff were dressing rather smartly, to most this was the beginning of something that would take over our lives. Some of these trips mentioned above always had a good turn out for the train with anything from 100 on the train to Oldham and as many as 800 for Pompey. Here are few funny short stories from those memorable trips.

OLDHAM Away (Mid 80s) - We had 100 on the train and as we headed for the ground which we could see just across a large recreation field, the only thing in our way was a 4ft wall, as we gathered momentum and started to trot to this wall, the first few reached it and just went for gold and leapt over without giving it a second thought, next thing we heard was a lot of shouting and swearing so we looked over and saw the lads rolling around in pain, there was only a fucking 8 ft fucking drop on the other side! How no bones were not broken that day I don't know, but the sight of those lads rolling around was fucking hilarious!

CHELSEA Away (Mid 80s)- We had about 160 on train an it was chucking it down , whilst holed up in the dickens pub it was decided that we would get to Stamford bridge for about 15.20. I thought how stupid, we would miss part of game but I soon discovered why. Being a young whippersnapper back then I didn't realise it was unwise to arrive early, but we would turn up and make an entrance whether it be on the High Street or in the ground. As it was the Chelsea lads were all in the West and south stand and as we all walked in together they all rose an applauded us - were they applauding our arrival or taking piss out of our lateness?

MIDDLESBOROUGH Away (Mid 80s) - We caught the 04. 30 train Saturday morning and this was the day I first met Rawlings. 14 of us travelled including Zedy, Rayer, little Colin and myself. As we changed trains at Bristol Parkway I heard a voice from behind shout "Cardiff Trendies" I was dressed in a Patrick windsheeter which, we were wearing way back then .Rawlins linked up with us and on we went. We arrived at Darlington about 11am for yet another change and this was where we came across a "spotter" a spotter I thought, what the fuck is that all about, he was a Boro spotter checking how many we had. Anyway we boarded train and old bill were with us and he said to us "be careful up here boys, Leeds came out of station last week all 300 of them and were run back inside." Fuck we thought not much hope for our 14 then! The old bill saved us that day, with Boro trailing our every step.

NEWCASTLE UTD Away (Mid 80s) - Yet again the 04.30 train consisting of Peter M, Rawlins, Rayer (RIP) myself and not too many more. On arrival yet another welcoming committee, but also old bill and a welcome lift to St James' Park for the match. Whilst inside we got chatting to the NME and all was going well until a top Newcastle lad took exception to this and proceeded to squirt mustard at us through fences keeping us apart but only directly hitting Rawlins who was donning a white Tacchini tracksuit top, the man Rawlins went loopy and would have killed him if he had his way, we lost the game with that curly permed wanker Kevin Keegan scoring twice.

I would like to thank Annis for asking me to write again and also my wife Nathalie for assisting me and putting up with me whilst I've clung to the laptop for days! Also to all the lads I travel away with to this day and those that don't travel as much and my respect goes out to all the old Ely Trendies. Happy Reading!

Clampdown on fans pays off

WITH A CHANT of "We are Millwall haters" 500 followers of Cardiff City announced their arrival in London's docklands for the cup-tie between the two clubs.

And as thge Bluebirds entered the Lions' Den their welcome from the home supporters was a reassuring "We are evil." Such is the romance of modern football.

Four hours earlier, as the Cardiff fans arrived at the city's Central Station to board the 10.48 "Soccer Special" they had been greeted by a highly-visible police presence. For, behind crowd control at Saturday's match lay an operation that began the moment the third round draw spired Cardiff and Millwall, each club's followers enjoying a notorious reputation after past misdeeds by some of their numbers.

It was an operation involving four police forces, and hundreds of officers — on foot, on horseback and with dogs. Plain-clothes detectives mingled with fans aboard the soccer special as police in a "hoolivan" roamed the area of the football ground.

'Firm but fair' policy by police a success

Days before the the tie the South Wales division of the British Transport Police had sent a telex to forces between Cardiff and London. Ib read, "Cardiff City: One of the worst football teams in the country (needs constant supervision."

Plans were drawn up. All trains to London on Saturday were declared alcohol-free under the Sports Grounds Act, 1985. Fans carrying drink were asked to deposit it in station lockers. One supporter tkrned up at 10.30 am to find himself refused passage for being drunk and incapable.

"We aim to be firm but fair," said Chief Inspector Stephen Chapman, the man behind the operation. "If there is any trouble on the train we just stop the train

SATURDAY'S FA Cup t between Cardiff City and Millw saw unprecedented police mov to combat football hooliganis Reporter DAVID CORNOCK w aboard the Soccer Special London.

an put them off, but it is the way we deal with t before they board the train that sets the tone of journey."

Fans arriving at New Cross Gate station w filmed by officers using video equipment finance the Football Trust, and were given a mounted po escort to the ground. A Metropolitan Police sur lance helicopter hovered overhead, equipped long-range cameras.

Although 600 fans travelled aboard the speci a cut-price £10 fare, some 350 went by earlier ser trains, giving themselves a taste of London before game.

Collectively known as the "City Service Cr they comprise such groups as the Ely Trendies Barry Crew and the Under Fives — younger "fa who feel they have something to prove to their pe

No colours

"These are the regulars, the people we take a every other week," said Sergeant Gilroy Tyler as service travellers arrived at the South Lon station. "We know many of them by their names."

Many had spent up to four hours in the cap and had clearly availed themselves of lunchti opening hours. "They go to Paddington, then hop meet fans of other clubs as they make their across London," said one supporter on the ret journey.

It is often difficult to identify the object of t affection — they wear no club colours and canoni distinguished by their choice of designer clothing

Poied presence at the station had kept m Millwall fans away from the entrance. "They mus scared of us — they normally come and give u welcome." was the conclusion of one South W visitor.

City fans were locked in their enclosure after match before police gave them an escort to station, where a special underground train had b laid on to take the "Service Crew" to Paddington

The behaviour of the fans aboard the special praised by the Transport Police, who were pleas with the success of their operation, given pre-ma ffears about the meeting of such notorious s porters.

ID cards may not become matter of law

DOWNING Street sources were last night playing down claims that an identity card system could be imposed upon Football League clubs at a crunch meeting in two weeks'time.

Reports in a national newspaper at the weekend alleged that, if the Football League refuses a card system at that meeting. Ministers will force them to act by statute.

More likely is continued pressure from Government upon the clubs. The Prime Minis-

ter herself has made no secret of her support for schemes such as Luton Town's.

The weekend reports claimed that Sports Minister Mr Dick Tracey and Home Office Minister Mr Douglas Hogg have lost patience with clubs who fear a loss of income and trouble from excluded fans spilling over into streets surrounding grounds.

But a Downing Street source said at the weekend the situation remained as it had been before the Parliamentary recess, with Ministers preferring persuasion to force.

● Part of the police presence at Cardiff Central Station before the Soccer Special pulls in.

Extra police for City cup clash

1987.

HUNDREDS of extra police will be drafted in for tomorrow night's FA Cup replay between Cardiff City and Millwall at Ninian Park.

And police with dogs will be on board trains from London and at Cardiff Central Station in case of trouble from supporters.

Fans of both clubs have unenviable reputations as being among the worst behaved in the country

with a large hooligan element.

Chief Superintendent Alan Chadwick said "several hundred" officers would be drafted in from elsewhere in the South Wales Police area and other reserves would be at hand.

He said they had been in touch with the Metropolitan Police who had said Cardiff fans were not

well-behaved at The Den on Saturday and had required special policing.

Mr Chadwick said South Wales Police were skilled at dealing with such situations and they had already planned their operation in case Saturday's game had been drawn.

"Anyone who steps out of line will be dealt with fairly but firmly — we will

stamp on any hooliganism," he said.

Chief Inspector Stephen Chapman of the British Transport Police said their officers from London and South Wales would be involved.

"We will be taking special precautions with police and dogs on normal service trains and any football specials," he said.

He wanted to ensure the vast majority of supporters who were well-behaved that they would deal with any troublemakers or problems that might arise.

Cardiff fans in punch-up

1986.

CARDIFF CITY fans dragged their club's once-proud name through the dirt yet again yesterday.

There were ugly scenes throughout Cardiff's 2-0 defeat away to fellow strugglers Stockport County.

Trouble was not confined to the terraces. There were a succession of arrests as rival supporters battled it out in the main stand and the police used dogs to clear Cardiff followers from the pitch at the final whistle.

Just to rub salt in the wounds it was Stockport's first home win of the season and the result leaves Cardiff perilously close to the Division Four danger zone.

1987.

POLICE chiefs have warned that hooligan Cardiff City fans have resorted to new tactics in a bid to see their club's away games.

The thugs turn up at grounds without tickets in the belief they will be let in for fear of trouble being caused outside stadiums.

And police revealed that around 100 supporters got into the Leyton Orient ground on Saturday without tickets — directly against the orders of the football authorities.

In an attempt to avoid police detection it is thought that some hooligans joined London-bound trains at places like Swindon.

Activities

Inspector Dennis Tenporal, from British Transport Police force headquarters in London said: "They are trying to outwit us. They are using other means of transport and joining trains en route.

He added: "We have got to maximise police activities when they are travelling away." He added that although there were often long distances involved when City played away the transport police could still not expect many fans to stay at home. "We have got to expect them to travel by other means."

Insp Tenporal, who was one of those attending a football liaison meeting in Cardiff yesterday — along with the Football Association of Wales secretary, Mr Alun Evans — revealed that:

● About 100 fans without tickets were let in to the Leyton Orient ground — directly contravening the ticket-only rule on Cardiff City's games in England. He explained that the local police commander probably felt there weren't enough officers to look after the fans who were initially refused admission.

● Newport County supporters were identified as

By Adrian Colley

being among the visitors. Their side had played on Friday night.

● On the return journey, policemen noticed about 30 fans on one train got off at Swindon.

British Transport Chief Inspector Stephen Chapman based in South Wales said police concentration on the Wales-Scotland rugby international might have allowed some hooligans to slip out of Cardiff unnoticed.

Even so, groups of supporters leaving Cardiff had been monitored, and checks made on them at all stops between Cardiff and London.

Speaking about the incidents of violence after Saturday's game and the appeal for action from the British Transport Police, Cardiff City's managing director Mr Ron Jones said: "Cardiff City can hardly be held responsible for the scum of the earth who decide that they are going to hold society to ransom and use the name of Cardiff City.

"We only issue tickets to those people who we know will behave. There is nothing we can do about people who travel independently." He felt some hooligans may have obtained tickets for the game from contacts in London.

● British Rail suffered a financial loss of £4,950 after one of the their Inter-City trains was delayed after 43 minutes at Ealing Broadway due to hooliganism. This figure is calculated by using a formula taking into account the cost of delays to other services.

Clemo blasts Orient boss

CARDIFF City chairman Tony Clemo has hit back at Leyton Orient boss Frank Clark who controversially branded Bluebirds fans as "lunatics" and vowed to attempt to ban them from the London club's Brisbane Road ground in future, writes Robert Phillips.

Clemo was incensed after an unexpected outburst from the Orient chief who was angry at an invasion of the Leyton Stadium pitch by about 100 City supporters after the final whistle of Saturday's Fourth Division clash.

Facts

Clark blasted: "If we ever play them again I shall do my utmost to make sure there are no Cardiff supporters here at all. I don't know whether I can I don't know whether I have the power or authority to do it but I shall certainly endeavour to do that."

"We don't need the money that badly," said Clark, who described City's supporters as "lunatics" and "idiots."

But Clemo retorted: "I am flabbergasted. The fans went around the pitch, ran over the other side and then ran back. They would not have got on the pitch if it had not been for the inefficiency of their administration.

"I suggest Mr Clark gets on with managing his team and let other people get on with doing their things."

Clark said the City fans got onto the pitch because a gate was left open because of fire regulations and admitted his club would have to have "a thorough examination of our own organisation."

His broadside was a surprise because the game had been relatively trouble free. Indeed the most unsavoury incident was when two City supporters, in the Orient members' enclosure, were set upon by a score of home fans after the visitors had taken the lead.

City boss Frank Burrows said people should ensure they had their facts right before blaming Cardiff supporters.

"Everybody just jumps on the bandwagon," said Burrows who added: There are people coming here who may be not support either team."

He re-iterated his belief that football troublemakers were "hooligans of society." The game was supposed to be all ticket though some City supporters gained entry by paying at the gate.

Soccer thug 'recced' pit say support

SOCCER thugs sent out military-style scouts to "recce" Somerton Park before the violent Newport County derby, it is now claimed.

Six youths believed to be Cardiff City followers were discovered in the Newport ground five days before the game.

The scouting mission was alleged by Newport fan club organiser Mrs Pam Salway, who saw the six, aged about 19, around the ground.

Reputation

"They were looking around in the dark and we didn't know what they were doing. When they were asked they didn't reply at first," she said.

"But then they boasted that they were receeing the ground — and that they would wreck it on the Saturday.

"We just told them to go

and they went registration bl wish we coul who they are.

Genuine sup mit it is diffic spot the hoo are gaining a reputation for

The yobs proud of their colour to be pack. Jade gr in fashion th

The gangs cards from crew" which victims and send letter fights in the

Some of th been calling the "young but are like on a whim.

They oft vehicles th trips rather ficial, prop outings to a

True su rallying aro beat the take part in admit it battle.

Chapter 10

Three North East Firms In One Day
By Annis Abraham Jnr
CARDIFF CITY

At the end of the 1985/86 season, Cardiff City were relegated to the old Fourth Division for the first time in the club's history. As if that wasn't bad enough, it was almost like the Football League deliberately rubbed salt into the fans' wounds when the fixture list for the 1986/87 campaign was announced. They gave us a 600-mile round trip to HARTLEPOOL on the opening day of the season. What a way to welcome us to the dungeon that was.

The club was in a terrible state on and off the pitch at the time, and crowds at Ninian Park were down as low as 1,800 on occasions. Many so-called City supporters had turned their backs on the Bluebirds, although the young Soul Crew hadn't. Cardiff's away following was often tiny during the mid-Eighties, but we were among the small number of fans who stuck by the team regardless of what division they were in and what sort of results they were getting. Although the opening day of the 86/87 campaign was sure to be a very long one, we were all up for a journey to the North East.

Believe it or not, we had as much fun in those days travelling to places like Hartlepool, Scarborough and Darlington as we did when City were playing away to some of the bigger clubs. You never knew what to expect when you were turning up at a northern lower-division club for the first time and there was hardly any Old Bill on duty at some of the smaller grounds, so we usually had a laugh.

In the weeks before the Hartlepool game we sorted out a batch of cheap family rail cards. When we eventually caught the train there was about eighty of us, and most us were travelling on dodgy family tickets. The lads I was with included Viking, Jeff Lloyd, Richard E and Steve Kaged, Beer, Rhys, Rusty, Rawlings, Jonathan, Derek, Dowie and Steve from Llanrumney. Some of the Ely Trendies such as Dio(Mikey Dye), Jammo, Sissy and Jerky were along for the ride, as were a number of the Barry Casuals including Darryl, Kersey, Melvin, Bowcher and Staples. You could say we were one big happy family!

The night before the trip, forty of us had been over in Barry Island for the evening and we ended up staying out until the early hours of the morning. Our train was due to depart at around 5am, so it was pointless going home. Most of the lads were so drunk by the time we left South Wales they just wanted to sleep the beer off, but amazingly a few managed to stay awake for the whole journey.

As we were leaving Cardiff Central station we were apparently spotted by the police. They phoned ahead to Bristol Parkway, where we had to change trains, and told the local Old Bill to expect us. When we got to Parkway, two of Bristol's finest came over and told us they thought the Cardiff coppers were winding them up when they'd said eighty of us were heading their way so early in the morning. We assured them we wouldn't cause any problems and said all we wanted to do was sleep. Surprisingly, they let us board our train with no objections. I think they just wanted to go back to sleep themselves.

We arrived at Darlington station at about 10am. As we were waiting for our connection to Hartlepool, we noticed a load of local lads further down the platform. They were setting off to watch their team play a Third Division game in York, so Rawlings wandered over and began chatting to a group of them. They numbered around fifty in all, and they looked a decent little firm. Most of them were a good few years older than us and they were dressed in all the right gear. Jonathan, Viking, Darryl and I strolled over to where Rawlings was standing and listened to what was being said. Rawlings told us they were asking who we were and he said they were talking about how much they hated Hartlepool, but I sensed they were just weighing us up. Then this fat Darlo lad looked down his nose at us and sneered "you Welsh wankers won't be able to do anything in Hartlepool anyway. You're just a bunch of kids."

Having some chubby northerner taking the piss out of us was all the encouragement our boys needed. A roar went up and everyone was straight into them. Without going into too much detail, it's fair to say that the DARLINGTON lads came badly unstuck. There were bodies flying everywhere for a couple of minutes until the Old Bill flooded onto the platform and split us up. After things had calmed down we couldn't help laughing at the local boys. They had tried to belittle us but it backfired on them big time.

The transport police ushered us onto the next train, and about nine or ten officers followed us onboard. It was their intention to escort us straight to Hartlepool, but we had other ideas. This particular train was one of the local services that stopped at every station between Darlington and Hartlepool, so when it pulled into Stockton-On-Tees we jumped off and legged it out onto the streets. The coppers tried their best to stop us but as soon as we made it off the platforms they were powerless to do anything as we were out of their jurisdiction.

We managed to find ourselves a nice little pub within a few minutes walk of the station. I promised the landlord we'd fill up his tills and said we'd be the best-behaved football fans he'd ever encountered provided he didn't telephone the Old Bill and let them know where we were. He had no problem agreeing to such a deal and was as good as gold with us all lunchtime. We kept the doors firmly closed and made sure everyone stayed inside the pub in an effort to avoid detection. Either the police couldn't find us or they couldn't be bothered to look, as we managed to stay there for almost two hours without any interference from the local constabulary. When we were ready to move on, I asked the landlord to show us the best way to Hartlepool. He said a bus pulled up outside the pub every half hour and it went straight to the town centre, so that was that. Pretty soon, eighty pissed-up Soul Crew youngsters were on a double-decker bus heading for Hartlepool, and it was rocking. Literally rocking at times!

As the bus arrived in the middle of the town, one of the lads at the front of the top deck shouted that he could see a load of mods a bit further up the road. That was like a red rag to a bull for us.

Back then, mods had become an unhealthy obsession for our firm of young casuals. If we weren't fighting with other football fans we were fighting with mods, so the bus started emptying and half of our drunken loonies were staggering down the street chasing after them. To be honest, we must have looked a right bunch of clowns. We made so much racket that the mods were on their toes long before we got anywhere near them, but although we didn't manage to give them any grief, what we did do was alert the Old Bill to our arrival. The next thing I knew there were coppers everywhere and we were all running off in different directions. It didn't seem too bad at the time as we'd agreed beforehand that if we got spilt up we'd meet up later in Hartlepool's seats. Things didn't work out quite that way though.

Plenty went wrong before we got to the ground. Jammo's small group walked into the middle of a shopping square and stumbled upon fifty Hartlepool lads. By that stage he was pissed out of his brains, so with only a handful of boys behind him he just went for it and steamed straight into them. When we caught up with him later it was obvious he'd had a right kicking, and apparently he didn't get much in the way of back-up from those who were with him. The local lads had even nicked his shoes, which was out of order, although to be fair Jammo wasn't using them anyway as he could hardly stand up!

I was in a group of about twenty and we were involved in a few scuffles with the Hartlepool fans on the way to the Victoria Ground. I remember they were pretty game and never once took a backward step. The Old Bill had to get between us on several occasions before we got to the ground. When we eventually did arrive we went straight into the main grandstand as arranged, but we were disappointed to find the others hadn't managed to join us.

Nothing much happened for the first half an hour or so. Then we noticed the enclosure below the stand was suddenly starting to fill up, but the lads who were arriving weren't Hartlepool or Cardiff supporters. They were in fact MIDDLESBOROUGH fans. The situation was that Middlesbrough Football Club had gone into liquidation over debts of £2 million a few weeks earlier. As a result, the bailiffs had locked Ayresome Park and Boro were left with nowhere to play. A group of local businessmen were supposed to be putting a rescue package together, so the Football League allowed Boro play their opening Third Division game against Port Vale at Hartlepool's Victoria Ground. Bizarrely, instead of their match being played the following day, it was scheduled to kick off in the evening just a couple of hours after our match had finished.

As we approached half time there must have been a hundred and fifty Middlesbrough lads in the enclosure below the stand and they were making sure we knew they'd seen us. I felt like we were sitting ducks. During the interval some of them began making their way up the steps towards us, so a few of our lot ripped out a load of plastic seats and began hurling them at the advancing Boro contingent. From that moment onwards it was chaos. At first the Boro lads backed off and a few of them even spilled onto the pitch, but then they got themselves together and began charging up the stand towards us. More seats were thrown at them but they were returned with interest. For a couple of minutes the air was thick with missiles going in both directions. Meanwhile, a large percentage of the six hundred Cardiff fans in the away end were attempting to invade the pitch and come to our rescue. The Old Bill really had their hands full trying to keep the City mob under control. A few lads did make it onto the pitch and Dowie was one of them, but he was immediately bitten by a police dog, so he got himself back into the away end a bit sharpish.

It didn't take the Boro boys long to get decent numbers up into the stand and we had no chance against them. When they reached us we attempted to stand our ground for about thirty seconds but it was a pointless exercise, so we began to retreat. That gave Boro further encouragement, and they not only kicked us down the stairs but they battered us through the turnstiles as we were trying to get out. I took a fair few slaps, as did Beer, Kaged and Dio. Viking and Derek did their best to fight back, I could here Viking shouting to Derek by the turnstiles to to hit them as hard as he could and smash them like me,but they didn't last long before they had to clamber over the turnstiles and join the rest of us outside the ground. Luckily, nobody sustained anything more than minor cuts and bruises, which was amazing considering the punishment we took while we were trying to escape.

Beer was seriously pissed off with what had happened and demanded that we try to do something to get our own back, so we ran around to the stand's main entrance and tried to make our way down the players' tunnel. However, the Old Bill saw us and managed to stop us before we got very far. We told them we were only trying to find the away end and surprisingly they believed us, so they led us to the Cardiff section and let us join up with the rest of the lads. As soon as we got into the away end we began swapping tops with the boys who were already in there, just in case the coppers decided to come looking for those of us who had been involved in the battle with Boro in the grandstand.

The match ended in a 1-1 draw with striker Rob Turner scoring City's goal. Afterwards, the Old Bill had a nightmare job as they tried to escort hundreds of us back to the train. There were lots of Hartlepool lads about and there were plenty more Middlesbrough fans arriving for their game, so by the time we reached the station it had kicked off numerous times. No side could claim any sort of victory though, as the police were generally on top of things. Nevertheless, I should mention how impressive Boro's firm looked. Despite the fact that their club was at death's door and they weren't playing in their home town, they still had a large number of lads out. The transport police arranged a special train to take us back to Cardiff and at least a dozen officers joined us for the journey. Nobody was really bothered as most of us were knackered and just wanted to sleep after such a hectic day out, and that's hardly surprising under the circumstances.

When we got back home our phones were red hot. Bear in mind these were the days before mobiles and the internet, so information didn't travel anywhere near as fast. Those who hadn't been with us up in Hartlepool wanted to know what had happened as the trouble had made the national news on TV and radio. There was also plenty of press coverage over the following few days. The media seemed amazed that the first outbreak of violence of the new season had occurred at a Fourth Division match. The fact that the start of the second half had been delayed for fifteen minutes while the police tried to calm things down was the major talking point.

Cardiff City were destined to spend ten of the next fifteen years in the league's bottom division, but although the football was often rubbish, most of us stuck together and kept supporting the team all the same. The Eighties and Nineties are now considered by many fans to be the worst period in the City's history, and that's fair enough really. The club was often in turmoil back then, but the Soul Crew lads still managed to have plenty of good times. Having said that, the day we spent up in Hartlepool in August 1986 was definitely a one-off. After all, I can't remember any other occasion when we had to take on three rival mobs in one day!

City fans fined and told: 'Don't come back'

FIVE MEN who travelled as Cardiff City supporters for the club's first match in the Fourth Division on Saturday have been fined almost £2,000 for "terrorising innocent people."

And the chairman of the special sitting of Hartlepool magistrates has told them never to return to the North East of England.

But even people with convictions for causing trouble at football matches can not be stopped from travelling to matches outside official supporters club parties.

Children and pensioners had run terrified from the fights which erupted in the stand at the match in Hartlepool and several innocent bystanders were injured the court heard.

Damage

Michael Dow, aged 19, of Manorbier Crescent, Rumney, Cardiff; Stephen Bouchet, aged 20, of High Street, Barry, and Stephen Wood, aged 18, of Alexander Court, Caerphilly, all pleaded guilty to using threatening words and behaviour and were each fined £400 with £30 costs.

Sean Thomas, aged 19 of Plasturton Avenue, Canton, Cardiff, pleaded guilty to a breach of the peace and was bound over for 12 months in the sum of £200. He also admitted criminal damage and was fined £400 with £30 costs.

Four supporters from Hartlepool and two from Middlesborough, also after pleading to breaches of the peace.

Both Cardiff City Supporters' Club and Adar Glas Caerdydd take fans to away matches on alcohol-free, stewarded coaches and comply with the wishes of local police in the time they arrive and leve opponents' grounds.

Scuffles

Both clubs have stressed that no-one from the coaches they took to Hartlepool on Saturday was involved in the trouble. And anyone causing trouble is immediately banned from future trips.

About 150 people travelled with the clubs. But there were about 400 cardiff fans at the match, and about 50 of them travelled by train.

A British Transport Police spokesman said they left Cardiff just before 5am on Saturday. There were scuffles with Darlington supporters when fans from that town's team joined the train for their away match.

But the police are powerless to stop anyone travelling, although they can dictate on which trains fans travel to make policing easier, he said.

"It was an exceptionally violent disturbance in which several police officers suffered minor injuries."

90

SAD START ....

It was disappointing to l connected with ardiff City Football lub that the Club's eputation was damaged last Saturday's pening fixture at Hartlepool United by the action ' a small group of so-alled 'followers' who ere involved in incidants at half-time and lter the game. It brought s headlines of the rong kind on the pening day of the eason, and cast slur on ar genuine fans who ade the long journey in ood numbers, were ell-behaved, and gave ae team great support. A reat deal of hard work as gone on here to ebuild the Club, and we o not intend to see it poiled by trouble-nakers. We have aerefore decided to ban enceforth from Ninian ark, the following ersons who were dealt ith by a special magis-ates court:

............, f Manorbier Crescent,

Rumney, Cardiff;

............, aged 20, of High Street, Barry;

............, aged 18, of Alexander Court, Caerphilly, all of whom pleaded guilty to using threatening words and behaviour, and who were each fined £400 with £30 costs;

............, aged 17, of Blosse Road, Llandaff North, Cardiff, who admitted criminal damage, being fined £300 with £30 costs. He also pleaded guilty to breach of the peace, and was bound over for 12 months in the sum of £200;

.... Vaughan, aged 19, of Plasturton Avenue, Cardiff who admitted criminal damage and was fined £400 with £30 costs as well as admitting breach of the peace for which he was bound over for 12 months in the sum of £200.

If they are discovered attending our matches, we shall take legal proceedings against them.

City fans and that Hartlepool trouble

I could see it coming

THE violence at the Victoria Ground may have flared at half-time, but from the vantage point of the Press seats you could see it coming before the match had even kicked off.

A group of some 20 or more Cardiff City followers were seated in Hartlepool's main stand, separate from the 400 other South Wales supporters behind one goal, and free from the restriction of fences or police.

The small group made their presence felt by singing and chanting before the game started and yet the police made no attempt to remove them from the stand and escort them to the away supporters' enclosure.

Given the mentality of football hooligans it was inevitable that the Hartlepool "mob" would eventually attempt to get at this isolated group of City fans.

Sure enough, as the half time whistle blew a group of some 50 to 100 home supporters who have moved to the terrace directly underneath the City fans began trying to get up into the seats.

The City yobs responded by ripping out the plastic seats and hurling them at the Hartlepool fans and soon a bombardment of plastic, metal and coins was fly-

moved in quic the violence, managing t order and eje fans before th interval was c

Cardiff's shame as fans riot

OOLIGAN fans ahed Cardiff as ney kicked off their 'ourth Division sea-on with a fine 1 - 1 raw.

As the referee blew or half-time, with City goal down, the scores travelling fans erupted. They ripped up seats and hurled plastic and wood at innocent supporters below.

Police reinforcements had to be called in and several officers suffered minor injuries as up to a dozen arrests were made in the running battles. And there was more fighting outside the ground after the game.

On the field, City were under constant early pressure and could h........... as ea........... nth m........... Pool

Hartlepool 1 Cardiff 1

striker Alan Shoulder's 20 - yard drive was well saved by Graham Moseley.

The Welsh defence finally collapsed after 34 minutes when winger Nigel Walker's free kick found skipper Tony Smith, who headed home unchallenged from two yards.

After the break, Cardiff full back Andy Kerr was booked for a foul on Rob McKinnon. But City roared back into the game and Paul Wheeler saw a superb 25 - yard drive hit the bar.

Cardiff could have gone ahead when Hartlepool defender Tommy Sword miscued his clearance but saw the ball swept off the line by McKinnon.

The equaliser came in the 83rd minute when Rob Turner, born just ten miles up the road, volleyed home from yards.

Cardiff could have grabbed all three points in the last minute when Nigel Vaughan saw a shot flash inches wide.

SUNDAY BEST MAN: Wheeler (Cardiff).

Chapter 7

Seventeen
By Dave Sugarman CARDIFF CITY

Dave Sugarman, as you will see is not a hooligan, but if you supported Cardiff through the years, whether you liked it or not you would probably of got caught up in it. I wanted Dave's story in this book as I thought it would be different and it sure is as Dave is probably one of the best writers down the City and remembers everything, he's known as TLG on the City Message Boards. Annis

Seventeen. That's how old I was when it became painfully obvious that I wasn't cut out to be a football hooligan. My experiences during a six month period from March to September 1984 left me in no doubt that I was never going to make the grade as a member of the Soul Crew. If you're hoping this will be another collection of anecdotes from somebody who was one of Cardiff's top boys in the Eighties, you'll be disappointed. On the contrary, mine is a cautionary tale about a young lad who was drawn to football violence like a moth to a flame, but who soon learned that getting involved was more hassle than it was worth.

My father took me to my first Cardiff City game in March 1975 on the day before my eighth birthday. A trip to Ninian Park was his idea of a special treat. Sheffield Wednesday were Cardiff's opponents on that glorious occasion. The Owls were rock bottom of the Second Division table, while the Bluebirds were just one place above them. Predictably, the match ended in a goalless draw. The crowd jeered, slow hand clapped and chanted 'what a load of rubbish' at regular intervals throughout the ninety minutes. Midfielder George Smith ripped off his shirt and threw it at manager Jimmy Andrews after being substituted. His replacement, Johnny Vincent, missed a late penalty, and City were booed off the field following the final whistle. Both teams were relegated to the Third Division a month later. Happy days.

Although I'd been given a grim introduction to life as a Cardiff supporter, I was nevertheless bitten by the Bluebirds bug and became a City fanatic from that day forward. After my father had taken me to the remaining four home games of the 74/75 campaign, I pleaded with him to buy me a season ticket for 75/76, which he duly did. Our seats were situated in the back row of Block C of the Grandstand, directly in front of the old press box, and the view from up there was superb. I have lots of terrific memories from my first full season as a City fan, which was a very successful one for the club. The likes of Willie Anderson, Adrian Alston and Tony Evans played some brilliant football as they fired the Bluebirds to promotion to the Second Division, but it wasn't just the action on the pitch that kept me entertained. Back then, visiting supporters were usually housed in the enclosure, which was an area of terracing to the left of the Grange End. It was directly below our section of the Grandstand, so those of us in Block C had a clear view of what went on down there. In the mid-Seventies, the sight of rival fans smashing lumps out of each other in the enclosure was as common as the sound of fireworks on the Bob Bank during winter and the smell of cigars in the Grandstand at Christmas. Teams such as Crystal Palace,

From being a young boy watching I soon became a casual, one of the first from Riverside, my area near Ninian Park, mainly due to The Ely Trendies on Millbank Bridge who I became good friends with at the time. They were the smartest lads around, not for getting the Ferndale & Port Talbot and areas. I soon wanted to keep up with this new fashion craze Trim trabs – tacchini, Ellesse, Fila, Lacoste, Burberry, Pringle and Lyle & Scott. I could not wait for my Birthdays & Christmas to receive new gear and as a 13 year old so I had three Paper rounds and then worked a Sunday market.

Then I went on my first away trip to HUDDERSFIELD, with one of the smartest casuals around Mikey Dye. We set of from Cardiff Central Station, mostly casuals on the train but there was some ugly looking blokes that day with Cardiff. Being a bit weary of how loud they were drinking, smoking, playing cards I decided to stand in the corridor near the toilets. We arrived at Newport and more Cardiff lads boarded the train. Then we were off up north, when we finally arrived there, we walked out of the station into the main street and walked about 100 yards. This black guy in a green beanie hat started bouncing around and then, he started throwing punches, he was like a maniac. Then suddenly a large mob of Huddersfield appeared and they were armed with bottles and bricks, they were soon throwing bottles etc... at us, Cardiff had to retreat but were soon into them, when all they had left was their fists, it soon became a proper toe to toe. My heart was racing yes this was it, I was actually having my first fight and I was hooked.

After the game I was on the train on the way home, I was taking a lot of stick, mostly from an older guy who they called J Jack, as I was still on a high, I was having none of it, he may have been 10 years older than me, I thought so what, so we ended up having a row on the train to which I had the better of him, he soon took on board I was no mug. I was not your normal youngster that would keel over easy. Later into the years of following the City we then became good friends.

I wanted more and more of this new culture, I was growing up quick and loving it. I started to collect glasses in a well known nightclub, yes a night club at 13, so I could get money to travel and watch the city.

Then it was the family rail cards, me being the adult and taking four blokes all with moustaches as kids for a pound, this lasted for a while, but I got rumbled with Annis, Darryl, Collin, Beer and Co, when we went to a night match in Bury, there was a bit of a battle with the locals in Manchester Piccadilly and the Old Bill confiscated it from me when they checked our tickets, the main thing was we all got home that night.

So I then started taking Coaches to away games, I would only take the youth away and we would fill easily one coach, some times two, these lads were mainly Grange town, Whitchurch, Llanishen and Canton areas of Cardiff. They were all into the new culture of spending lots of money on their clothes, their appearance meant everything but they soon became wise that you didn't quite wear your best when it was game on, as the rips & tears in your gear was a gutter, especially when you didn't quite have the funds to replace all the expensive items. Respect to them all as they always travelled well, most of them still go to this day, they would row with any one, invade home stands and away teams pitches.

I would sell snide gear from Thailand – cord coats from Manchester, anything to make money to travel and watch City and Wales, as long as it was legal to do so and it made me fast money, so I was able to travel away.

We had many eventful trips, but the most disappointing ones would be at SWANSEA, as we would arrive at least three to four hours before the game, arrive at their leisure centre, leave the coaches and then walk into their town centre. We would get nothing from them and by time the train mob arrived, there would be thousands of Cardiff in Swansea. Many a time we would be roaming around the sea front, train station, the Queens pub(their old main pub), the Quadrant shopping centre, where they were supposed to hang around, they were just no where to be seen, until the game had started, then you would see loads of them mouthing behind the old bill. Many a time we would go in their stands and overtake their seats and all around the ground you would see other Cardiff lads, even on their North Bank end, we had about 40 strong lads all game for it. with a few hundred Jacks trying hard to kill you. Only once did that get naughty, when I got chucked out by the O.B and was led out through their end getting kicks and punches from all directions, then all they did was spit and throw plastic bottles at me, when I was on the outside, surely they should of left the ground, but hey you wont get a better feeling than standing in the North Bank Vetch, singing Cardiff, your adrenalin rushing through your body and your blood pumping.

I will let you in on a few of my past trips as a youngster ….. Bristol wurzels being my bogie trips.

17th December 82

With Annis, Darryl, C Beer, Richard E, being the youngest I always wanted to be the first in, to show I was brave enough to run with them and on one occasion at BRISTOL ROVERS, we were in their stand and as usual up I go, wanting to be first in, so straight in I went only to be confronted by a professional boxer. We were on the stairwell of their stand having a stand off, when he started to throw 20 or so punches a second, he just rained punches into my head and face. I didn't know where I was, he was a fucking hard man who knocked the shit out of me. Annis and Richard E got me quickly out of there and dragged me down the stairs, then we all walked along the pitch, back into the away end, to the usual clapping from the Cardiff fans for being in someone's end, I was soon washing my face up and I instantly had two black eyes for my troubles.

Another trip we were getting taken in a police escort from the train station, when I decided to break escort with a few lads, when we got further up along the river, we got onto a foot bridge where we ended up in a scuffle. All of a sudden I had blood pissing from my head, Matty(a lad from Cheltenham) dragged me away, I next remember waking up in an ambulance and Matty and some copper sat next to me. In the hospital I had stitches to my head I had been slashed, the Old bill wanted to take a statement from me, so me and Matty jumped out of the hospital window, stopped a car and told him to take us to the train station, we got on to the platform and I was swamped by O.B. I forgot I still had a fuck off bandage around my head, what a dead give away, me and Matty still laugh to this day. So the bullying episode did not exist, which has been said by someone(about Matty and myself), it was just that I did not accept outsiders, only the lads that we knew, end of, for the record.

Another day out in wurzel land, BRISTOL ROVERS, I got stuck in their seats with a lad called Palmer, when it went off just before the end of the game we ended up on the pitch rowing with the home fans, who had waited until they had grouped 5 times the number of us, we steamed into them and they backed off, when they re-grouped we had only one way out and that was onto the pitch. Then the police came steaming into us, there was no where to go, old bill or 100 plus home fans, the old bill option was taken and we both ended up getting nicked.

I travelled to many smaller grounds as did bigger clubs, I found that the smaller clubs were at their best for turning out for us, always get a meeting with the likes of Lincoln, Carlisle, Southend, Hereford, Gloucester, Hull, Plymouth and Wigan,

EXETER away, as I left a pub and went in to the car park with Dexy, Annis, Richard E, Darryl and co there was a scuffle, but outside the bar Dexy was having a toe to toe with some local, we all ran back and then some mad Irish man started trying to leather me with a shovel accusing us of walking through his newly laid concrete path, we ended up fighting with the builders on a site next door to the pub, that was a naughty day. There were all sorts of items landing on us, this was supposed to be about lads against lads, we don't know how that ended up happening. We ended up being escorted out of the area and all the way to the motorway.

There were many a day and night visit to NEWPORT, either football or dancing at Maskrals skating. One occasion I was left behind in the bus depot by Annis and Co, they some how had forgot me, I was stuck on my own for about an hour, the Newport lads Adams and Co were not to pleased with our arrival, they came out all tooled up but most of Cardiff were already gone, what a long walk back to the train station that night, dodging the scallys of Newport, hats off to the County they would always have a go and would come to Cardiff central station on many occasions and have a go at us.

BURNLEY about 16 years ago on Annis's coach we decided to get off in their Town Centre, well nine out of 53 of us got off, the rest stayed on. Annis and Lakey were walking ahead. As we walked towards the centre we heard a large roar, it was Burnley they had found us, yes they had found nine of us they must of thought it was Christmas. Annis and Lakey ran at them calling the rest of us on, what a mistake that turned out to be for us, we got kicked to fuck, we had to run for our lives, we were shouting at each other to stand but bricks, bottles and their numbers chasing us were far greater than us at least 40 odd of them, we were dropping like flies. I managed to get into halfords, I got cans of spray off the shelf, ran out and sprayed some of them who were giving Lakey a right kicking on the floor, he had gone down an alley on his own, he ended up looking like the elephant man. We all ended up getting a smack or two, Lakey ended up in hospital. The old bill said we were lucky to be alive as Burnley had been waiting all day for us and had wanted revenge for getting done in Cardiff earlier that year when they were dragged out of their transits and bricked in the away end.

CAMBRIDGE UNITED away in their Town Centre with Mac, we had been to several local boozers looking for their lads but they were either one step ahead of us or just not there. We were just about to leave the City Centre when we walked straight into a small mob of about 15, we ended up getting a right kicking, Mac got knocked down in a door way of a bookies only to get back up and go berserk, there was only 5 of us against 15 maybe more, then we seemed to re group and stick together. We eventually had them on their toes; they didn't think we had the bottle to stand up against them.

I have a lot of friends in the football world and in the know, I especially have a soft spot for EVERTON and SHEFF WED they both have very good firms, and I am very close with their lads Mr E Everton and Mr Sib Everton.

Mr N –scally Everton (he doesn't rate Cardiff to the maximum and thinks we have a bit of a rent a mob, because they come from all over Wales) each to their own but in fairness he's a character and a half. He rang me one night "alright fella, were in your town, do you fancy a beer?" I was in the house with my Mrs and daughter, "ok pal, you twisted my arm, I will be there in 30mins" we had a good few drinks with Andy and Co they were staying in a hotel by the airport. So on leaving the city centre in a taxi they decide to take me on a free trip to Serbia to watch Wales as one of their pals had dropped out.

I went into house to tell my Mrs the good news of a free trip to watch Wales abroad, but she was fast asleep, well at least I thought she was, I searched high and low for my passport and proceeded to pack an overnight bag. Then my Mrs woke up screaming "what do you think your doing", "I'm off to Serbia love on a free trip", "you what!", she hits me across the head as I'm dashing down the stairs, I've dropped my bag at the top, only got my passport and a pair of boxer shorts, I wasn't going back up for it and off we went to Serbia – few scuffles out there with the locals. On returning at the airport Mr N was skanking all the duty free fags for his mum to sell down the bingo, I bought my Mrs and daughter a jigsaw puzzle at the airport and got ripped by the lads, took me a week to get back into the big bed for my episode.

Wales's games, I've travelled like I do to City games, all the worst places you can think of.

Been deported several times   Italy 1995 – Belgium March 1991 – Germany 16th October 1991

Rimini I took a bad beating off the local police, Wales were playing in Bologna. We had arrived a day later than some Ely lads who were all pissing it up around the pool. I heard screaming from outside my room, it was my sister being attacked so they thought, Taylor (Ely lad) was trying to sneak into her room, I was stripped off, so I run out and not thinking just get straight into the owners and security of the hotel dragging them off Taylor, I knock a couple of them down the stairs, they must of thought I was bonkers rucking naked with them.

I go back to my room to try and get my belongings together, as it was obvious this was the end of our stay here, when the Miami vice come crashing through the door, I'm trying desperately to hang on to my bag, which I just packed, but they baton me across my arms which made me release my grip. I was arrested, bollock naked in the hotel room, it took 5 of them to get me down the stairs and into the police car.

Once in the cell every 10 to 15 mins, I would get a digging off them as they came into my cell. After a while, I thought enough is enough, when they came the next time I was ready, straight in

I went, throwing punches at them, so I thought. It was only the interrupter and solicitor, I was stitched right up, a very good friend of mine from N.Wales Mr E managed to get me released.

Another away trip with Wales in Russia Moscow, I was out there on crutches outside our hotel when about four hundred Russians attacked us, there must have been about 100 welsh fans in side the hotel, most of them were hiding or trying to slip onto the coaches on the side of the hotel. I can only remember Simon the spotter (old bill), S Wilson and the Viking being outside, the rest either stayed in side or got on coaches slyly, that were going to the game. I have to say the Viking saved me, when the Russians arrived and they fully charged at the hotel from the tube station there must have been at least 3-4 hundred bouncing off the front of the hotel and for his troubles Viking, he lost his Stone island parker or half of it as he stood up against them, must admit Viking, myself, Wilson & Simon (old bill) were lucky not to of got stabbed, as not one of us knew what had happened and the rest didn't want to know. The Russians have written in a book about The Viking standing up to them and getting hammered by them or shall we say his clothes torn off by them.

One of the better and classic ones was at Blackpool 21/09/85, after leaving the match it was going off all day and night with Bristol Rovers & Boro. For some reason they had large numbers in town, we ended up getting trapped in a side street and they even tried to run us down with their transit. Later on as we were being run once again, all of a sudden a telephone kiosk door opens Gethin (from London original Soul Crew) comes out stands in the middle of the road, starts screaming come on lets have it, we quickly re-grouped stayed close and fought toe to toe for what seemed forever, being showered by punches, this for me must have been one of the best rows I've had, how we survived this one was a miracle it seemed like every punch thrown, 20 more back we received, eventually we held our own and went to the Tower Lounge to clean up and have a few well deserved beers.

You will get stories of the West Ham (I CHUCK FRUIT) –Millwall (I do rate) – Man utd clashes yes they happened, but trust me the old days with the smaller clubs were far better than a large rent of a mob, Shouting at each other attracting attention.

I have lot of past history, but my Wife, kids, sister (Titch) mum and dad and family come first nowadays. Also about 10 years ago, Cardiff were at home and the referee was a nightmare giving penalties away for fun to Cambridge and then sending off City players. The referee was Barry knight, something sparked me off and I climbed down from the grandstand into the lower section and proceeded onto the pitch, I dodged the stewards and some angry players and ran straight up to the ref, as I was about to knock him out I was taken down by some Linford Christe type steward, then several stewards marched me off what was then to be shown on Welsh news for the next few days, the club were non to happy, as were the Welsh FA, a suspended 25k fine for the club and I was banned again.

I have been banned to many times and deported from many countries to get involved in anything, nowadays I just go with my Dad and want City to get to the premiership.

Would I change my past if given the chance, would I heck it was exciting and I have hundreds of friends who I now love, even though I have not been involved in anything for a decade, it's the best rush ever, the fear not knowing your fate being outnumbered and knowing your going to stand and get a result what ever the outcome.

I got caught up in something a year ago or so involving 8 police officers, I was supposed to off attacked after the game in the petrol station on Sloper road .All day it had been going off with BIRMINGHAM and there was a large police presences outside and inside the game, CCTV everywhere, there was an incident in the ground with the Zulus performing after the game. I preceeded down Sloper road with my sister Titch and my dad, the Zulus were behind us in a police bubble. We said our good byes to our father at the petrol station, when my sister gets pushed back by a police officer, "Alright mate were just cutting through to go down Virgil St", "no your not", replies the officer, with that my sister has taken a step forward and the officer viscously punches her to the chest, I raise my arm out to stop him and he draws his baton, with that split second I have caught him a treat and down he goes, then all hell breaks out, I've got about 6 or 7 officers trying to arrest me. I was having none of it, as it was the officer who had struck my sister and me first, so I end up rucking with the lot of them. I tried to explain to them it was robo cop P.C. K's fault, but they were all hyped up, honestly it took at least six, may be more to get me down, they strapped my legs, arms and chest along with tightened cuffs, they proceed to bang hell out of my face on the ground.

I managed to look up and my sister was going berserk due to witnessing my arrest, then they decide to arrest her, she ends up getting punched and kicked by the officers, which then drives me even more crazy, somehow I manage to pull my self up, now remember I'm cuffed and strapped, top and bottom. I dive into the officers with my head, I was then put into a police van, taken to Fairwater police station, processed and charged, whilst being locked up for some 15 hours or so I could here the Zulus begging to be released before their train leaves at about 9p.m. Some of the Zulus were charged and let out to catch their train home. 3a.m I got released, like I said it was all over nothing just P.C. K on some power buzz. That back fired for him, as we ended up on a three day trial which ended up going in our favour. I've been no angel in my life but can honestly say for the eight years my daughter has been born I've not been involved in any trouble but there was no way I was walking away from this officer as he started the whole thing in the first place.

I was on a ban for a year waiting for the trial, this crippled me as City were now starting to do well and with the new stadium due. Missing the City & Wales was a nightmare this time round, then I had a three day trial and justice was done I was back. You will never ban a City fan and my dancing days have long past.

R.I.P Dare Dare D FORD and M RAYER ELY TRENDY.

RESPECT TO ALL IN THE 80'S and 90'S HOME AND AWAY.

Chapter 12

Nine Miles Too Close
By Taffy Anton CARDIFF CITY

Taffy Anton he's another character had our little argument many years ago and have remained friends ever since, a good lad to be with years ago and hates the Jacks beyond, but who could blame him living so close to them. Annis

I would like to thank Annis for letting me tell a couple of stories of the old days involving the lads from my area.

I first met Annis when I was 19 years old, I had gone to Cardiff on a non football day to go shopping with two of my mates. I had got off the train and was walking by the side of the Prince Of Wales which was then called Caesars Nightclub which was situated in the main street in the City Centre. I noticed a few lads standing there watching us who I later found out to be Annis, Gregson, Darryl and Jerky. They soon started to follow us and for the next few minutes they stayed behind us until we got to a shop called Pavilion. By now I'd had enough so I turned around and said "what do you want?" with which Annis replied "who are you? And what you here for?", I said I was Cardiff to which he said he'd never seen me down there before so I reeled off a load of names Dai H, Terry Lounes, Alfie and Dave Jones etc… all older lads and who were well known in those days. From that second we soon found we had a lot in common and over the years we became good mates. I used to meet up with Annis and some of the lads in a Bar called Bar 11 and when Annis had his own bar called Brownhills that became a regular haunt for the lads from Neath and Port Talbot when they visited Cardiff.

I'm 41 now and I'm currently on a five year ban, I was actually born in an English town called Grimsby but moved to Port Talbot when I was 4yrs old. I've got four other brothers who all follow Cardiff and even though we only live 9 miles from the Jacks we never ever once thought of giving them our support.

My first game following the City was a 3-3 draw with CHELSEA at Ninian Park and what an eye opener, that was with one of the biggest battles seen at Ninian Park for years, with Chelsea trying to take the Bob Bank and Cardiff in their thousands defending it to the hilt. Terry Lounes was the lad who took me to my first game and from that day I was hooked. A year later I was soon with the PVM (Port Talbot's Firm) and the Neath Lads, we soon became like a family, we drank together some even worked together and of course come Saturday's we'd all go to watch Cardiff. During the week nights we would go down to Jack land and on the odd occasion the Jacks would visit us. Every Monday night I'd be down at Martha's Vineyard in the heart of Jack Land, it was Soul night, at least six of us would regularly go there and we'd meet up with all the Cardiff Dock's lads Santo's, Richard Cordell, Rusty, Annis etc… We used to take the place over and on rare occasions we would see the Jacks in their own city.

One night the Jack's did turn up 30 of them came in, I was in there with the usual 6 and just our luck none of the Cardiff lads had come down that night. Wallace one of their main lads came round the corner and grabbed me by the throat and said "Wallace is the name", with that the doormen flew between us and the Jacks started shouting "Jack Army, Jack Army" and "c'mon lets do the bouncers as well", some of the Jacks surrounded Aiden and said "your one of Anton's lot", "yes, he's my brother" and with that Aiden head butted him to the floor, at that time the Jacks called themselves the mini angels, well it was flattened angel that night. The doormen managed to back the Jacks out of the club and eventually the police were called to the front, if only the Cardiff lot had been here then.

I will put my hand up from the beginning and say yes, I've been run and done and the two occasions which stand out in my mind, one with NEWPORT, I got run well over a mile by them in their Town Centre after a good scuffle with them, fair do's to them they've got a good little firm.

The other one that stands out MILLWALL away in the FA Cup January 1987, at the end of the game I came out of the ground of the Old Den and five of us were walking back to the car, one of the lads with me that day was Terry Lounes and he shouted to us all to run, run, as Millwall came flying out of all the bushes and these weren't kids that came flying out of the bushes, these were dozens of men charging at us like lunatics and we just had to run for our lives ,we were virtually falling over each other as we probably beat Linford Christies 100 metre record.

So I don't intend to make out I'm invincible as at some stage in our lives if we were all honest, we've all been done somewhere but I can quite honestly say I've never been done by the Jack scum and even they admit that one about me. In those day's I was going out with a bird from Jack land and the hassle she got for going out with me became so unbearable that it didn't last long, but I've got to admit their lads might be gippos but they've got some tasty fit birds down there.

One of my best experiences of the 80's was PETERBOROUGH away in the FA Cup 3rd round, we left Port Talbot in a van about 8am with some of the rest of the PVM following us, there was a solid twenty of us, Vince, Guff, Nigel H etc…We got to Posh about 12 noon and as we walked over the bridge by the ground towards the town, we bumped into about 20 of their lads and we had a bit of a stand off with them but nothing really to write home about as the old bill did the usual thing. Through the town wherever we walked Cardiff were everywhere, pubs were packed full of lads from all over South Wales, near kick off we all made our way to the ground bumping into quite a few of the lads who had now moved to London. The match started like a cup atmosphere and as usual Cardiff letting their massive support down, when we were loosing 2-1 with about 5mins to go I decided to leave the terrace, as I got to the turnstile to go out I pushed it and found that the doors opened with that I rushed back in and shouted to the boys "come on the gates are open", with that a good 50 of us left and bowled around to the home supporters side terrace, we were soon on the side of the terrace by the side of the pitch, but can you believe it, we weren't attacked by their lads, we actually got attacked by old men with their umbrella's and shirties shouting abuse at us to get out and before we knew it a few of us were actually injured by fists, boots and umbrella's, I can even remember Darryl being knocked to the floor, fair play, in their younger day's they must have been good lads.

Eventually we stormed onto the pitch and ran towards the main home end goading the posh lads behind the goal and I'll give them their due they climbed over the fence and confronted us head on the pitch where we fought a running battle for a good 5 minutes, what a buzz!! They were game as fuck.

Little was I to know that two weeks later I'd get a dawn raid from the posh police, me Nigel H, Jammo, Mikey Dye, Billy and some of the original Soul Crew Gethin etc… all ended up nicked for it. I ended up with a 1 year ban, in them days that was a lot and 60 hours community service, he! he! I miss the good old days.

Another game that sticks in my mind was BRENTFORD away when well over 5,000 City fans turned up, we were really doing well then, on one of our rare occasions. Well what a turn out from the PVM and the Neath lads we had a good 50, all dressers in them days from Armani to Lacoste. Amongst the lads with us was Neath Punk (Simon), Huw, Guff, Vince, Aiden (Bro), Fulman and many more.

We arrived at Brentford about 11am and went straight into The Bricklayers Arms, it was already packed with Brentford lads (probably half of them being CHELSEA). Well here goes, I was playing pool with one of the lads while the rest of the boys were outside drinking in the sun and with that a load of Cockneys started to be abusive to my mate and I calling us Taffy wankers, with that all hell broke loose and I just lost it and went steaming straight in and all the boys outside piled in as well, you had pool balls, glasses everything flying around and as the battle went on we were backed up by the docks boys, this battle continued into the street where quite a few Brentford got cut badly. Eventually the old bill arrived and over 30 Cardiff got nicked including my bro, I managed to make a quick escape and got myself to the ground.

It was unbelievable outside the ground thousands of Cardiff were locked out and so hundreds were making their way into the home end, I managed to get myself in the ground, Cardiff were on all sides of the ground. Whilst the match was going on apparently hundreds of Cardiff were steaming the turnstiles and gates to get in, with eventually one of the gates being smashed through, so in some areas of the ground it was well and truly rammed. Also scuffles were breaking out in the home end all the way through the game, our support that day had well and truly surprised the old bill.

But my joy was short lived in the ground as I was pulled out by the police on suspicion of a serious assault, I pleaded my innocence and had said that I didn't know anything about it all and eventually I was let go when the game had finished. After the game we headed back to the police station to get the boys out, one by one they were released but with no sign of my bro so I waited there and some three hours later he came out and a big cheer went up and I gave him a big hug as he was now a fully fledged hooligan. What was unbelievable was that everyone of the 30 lads were let off.

I've got to bring this subject up living only 9 miles from the scum, the swim away episode they keep bringing up, I've got to rectify it once and for all, that day down in Jack land the Jack scum seemed to forget that we had been over SWANSEA for over two hours before the game running them all over the Sanfields area of Jack land. We even knocked a couple of their boy's houses doors but to no avail, well anyway back to the swim away. The scums only claim to fame, chasing a bunch of 15-17 yr olds into the sea including my youngest brother who was 15, against no more than a dozen young Cardiff and over 80 Jacks so well done scum, I can see your still proud of it.

Along the way I've made some great friends Viking, Jonathan, Pepper, Pablo P, the Author of this book and many many more.

CAN YOU NAME HIM?

Wanted for questioning

Thursday October 23 2003

■ FAMILIAR LOOK? South Wales Police want to question this man. *TAFFY ANTON.*

Steve Edwards
Chief Reporter
steve.edwards@wme.co.uk

THIS man is wanted for questioning by police investigating a violent disturbance involving Cardiff City football fans.

Detectives from the South Wales Police football intelligence unit have already made a number of arrests relating to trouble that took place in Cardiff city centre before the Bluebirds' match against West Ham on September 23.

Three men aged 25, 29 and 31 appeared at Cardiff Magistrates' Court last week charged with violent disorder.

The men, who are all from the Cardiff area, were bailed to appear before the court again on Thursday, November 28.

A fourth man from Ynyshir, Porth, has also been charged with violent disorder and will appear before magistrates this week.

A spokesman from South Wales Police said: "We are investigating disturbances before the Cardiff City – West Ham Carling Cup match on September 23 and are issuing a further appeal for information.

"Officers would like to speak to the man pictured as inquiries continue into incidents relating to that match."

He added: "Police are urging anyone with information to contact Crime- stoppers in confidence."

If you are this man or yo know who he is ca Crimestoppers anonym ously on freephone 08(555111.

Chapter 13

THE ZULUS
By Joe Cardiff City

Joe is a few years younger than me and so came on the scene quite a few years later; we became friends through the football scene and have since become good friends away from football. Annis

I am from the Northern City suburbs of Cardiff and started following Cardiff City in 1983, when I was a young teenager, back then we were in the old Division 2. I would look forward to games against the likes of Man City, Newcastle & Chelsea as they always brought large away support and contributed to an amazing atmosphere at Ninian Park, we would often see our attendances double in size with these sought after games.

I initially attended every home league game with my uncle and my beloved City scarf, I would stand in the cold Bob Bank terraces and can often remember watching a section of support in the Canton stand, which would usually be between 150 & 200 young Casuals (I later found out that they were the young Soul Crew), I was intrigued by their behavior, fashion and whitty songs.

The first incident that affected me was against LEEDS UTD in September 1984, when my uncle's car had its windows smashed, ironically it was not the away fans but the home fans who contributed and the sole reason was because his car had a Leeds number plate. From that moment on, the other side of football intrigued me more.

As I grew older I slowly started to go to Ninian with my friends, Julian, Popeye, Paddy, Dog and Jacko leaving the City scarf at home. I had become more aware of the terrace culture and fashions and wanted to get more involved with these cultures.

A few games clearly stick in my mind, however, being a young unimpressionable lad I was oblivious to trouble at these games and just thought it was high spirits and nothing too sinister.

Towards the end of the 83/84 season, I started to attend away games with friends, my first away game was against Swansea on a warm Easter Bank Holiday, I can remember wondering why we left Cardiff on the 9am train when the game didn't kick off till 3. I soon found out why, as when we arrived at Swansea there was constant fighting in the hours leading up to kick off between City and Swansea fans. I wasn't really involved but watching the fighting and scuffling got me excited and I knew then I wanted to become part of the City crowd and the alternative side to football.

Over the next few seasons I gradually became more involved with the trouble associated to Cardiff City while still following my beloved Bluebirds.

Being in the Young Soul Crew

After several seasons of attending many City away games I became part of the Under 5's, the numbers of our firm was very small, approaching 150 on a good day, we were a close knit outfit ranging from 16 to 25 years.

We would share similar interest and fashion sense. I would make regular trips to London to ensure I had the best looking clobber anything from Cecil Gee and Swank were a must, I always found prices were quite often 50% cheaper than overpriced Cardiff.

When wearing this gear it gave you a new found confidence where you thought you were untouchable and you could easily make new friends and acquaintances.

We became a notorious following and were emulating the older guys from what is now well known as the Cardiff City Soul Crew, so much so that we even arranged our own coaches to away games and drank/and socialised together outside of football, our favourite watering hole was Brownhills, many a good drunken night was had.

Trouble back then was often sporadic and unplanned not like today's pre-arranged "flappy armed" bullshit.

One of the most memorable trips that our firm organised was Birmingham City away in October 1989.

Birmingham City (The ZULUS) - 14th October 1989

Annis and Mojo arranged two coaches for the Birmingham City away game, one leaving was filled with guys from Docks and the other with Cardiff, Valley and Barry boys. Although, I arrived early for that evening's game, the coaches didn't leave till 6pm because of internal strife, mainly City fans refusing to pay on Mojos coach. Annis s coach was all up and running, lads paid and driver happy. Where as everyone on Mojos coach seemed to want to take the piss out of him. Mojos come a long way since then as he now represents the lads in court as a criminal solicitor and as even become a Football FIFA Agent and has a lot of Cardiff players, amongst other players on his books.. Getting back to the coach, Annis had to come on Mojos coach and in the end everyone paid , happy days we were off and running.

We travelled up in eager, yet nervous anticipation as we all knew Birmingham had a fearsome reputation both on and off the field and would be more of a match for our relatively young firm.

One of my mates, Brummie (Steven), knew the area very well as he was originally from Birmingham, he directed our 2 coaches to Digbeth, For anyone who hasn't seen this part of Birmingham, it's run down and just behind the Bull Ring. It's been through a period of neglect and many of the buildings were derelict. However, some of the city's oldest establishments and pubs can be found in this part of the city. The whole area was extremely dark, dreary and industrialised this only added to the tension and anticipation of the possible events that's evening.

As kick off was fastly approaching, 100 of us decided to park in Digbeth and walk the 1.5miles through the cold dreary back Street of old Birmingham to St Andrews Stadium, home to **Birmingham City.**

On the way we encountered small groups of Birmingham fans but they were easily chased off and did not put up much resistance.

As we approached the ground the game had already kicked off and a few of the main lads suggested we should attempt to enter the Spion Kop stand, a large terraced area for the home fans, we thought this suicide mission was a good idea and would only enhance our growing reputation if we managed to get a result against such a fearsome firm.

We made our way across the gravelled façade arming ourselves with bricks and debris ready for the inevitable confrontation. Viking, Annis, Jonathan, Little Collin and a couple of other lads were going through their turnstiles, when if I'm honest a lot of other Cardiff didn't seem up for it and stood well back singing, were the famous football hooligans and Cardiff City songs, which not only brought the attention of The Zulus but also let the old bill know we were there. The few who were already in the turnstiles were then attacked by dozens of Birmingham and had no other choice but to retreat from the turnstiles.

We charged across the façade throwing various items at the Birmingham mob, to help the lads by the turnstiles, who had managed to catch the Brums of guard, they quickly retreated back into the home section and only a few blows were thrown between the rival fans. Rapidly we were gaining confidence but not to be outdone, it didn't take the Zulu's long to realise we were low on numbers in comparison. They quickly began to fight back and again several blows were exchanged, almost as quickly as the event unfolded it died down as the police baton charged people back, a few of our guys sustained injuries, but in the scheme of things we were lucky, but felt given our numbers we had obtained a result and again our reputation was on the up, but in all honesty the mass numbers the Brums had, that had gone down to the turnstiles would have eventually done us. We were starting to feel that we were not a firm to be messed with, as we had gained the upper on other occasions seeing off firms such as Wolves, Bolton Wanderers and Exeter.

We thought the night's events were over especially as the police were aware of our presence, but both us and the police were very wrong. During the match, attended by 600 City fans, twelve of our group decided to leave the ground about five minutes from the end of the game and look for the notorious Birmingham Zulu firm, they were not to be disappointed. Some of 12 if I remember right consisted of Little Collin, Jamo, Annis, Jelly Head, Brummie, C Beer and Darryl. We all tried to follow them but were soon stopped by the old bill.

When the game finished and they let us out, we all turned left and said to the old bill our transport was down there, We could here shouting in the distance and with that Brummie(Steven), came running back saying our lot needed help and were taking a bit of a pasting. We all tried to force our way through the old bill but to no avail, but we were soon able to get down to ours, when a lot of the old bill left us to rush down and stop the fighting. As we got down to the other side of the stadium our small group were surrounded by old bill, but they weren't being arrested they were being helped back. The area was now completely under control by the old bill and our lot looked like they had just done General Custers last stand.

Our small group sustained many injuries, but one guy who sticks out in my mind was Little Collin, both eyes were pumping blood out, and apparently when about 60 Zulus had charged at our 12 he ran on his own straight into the middle of them. Annis and Jellyhead had gone into help him, but Collin by this time had fought about 6 of them on his own and had taken some right punishment for his madness, Jammo and Jellyhead had been knocked to the floor and stamped on, all of them had sustained injuries. , They had been done, but they were all laughing about it when we all finally managed to re-group. The lads wanted revenge and on our walk back to Digbeth, on any occasion the lads saw any Brums they flew through the police escort and had a couple of Brums on their toes.

When we got down to Digbeth, the Zulus were standing around all over the place, our lot got smacked back a number of times by the old bill, with the Zulus smiling and laughing at us, which got us more wound up and a few charges and roars went up with the Viking going mental as he was fuming he hadn't been there earlier and he in particular wanted revenge for his mates. Eventually the police managed to gain complete control of the situation, we were ordered back to our coaches and escorted back the 100 miles to South Wales.

The feelings on the coaches were ones of relief and exhilaration, we knew deep down the Zulus had won the night, but they can never say we never took it to them and we felt our reputation was enhanced once more,

Chapter 14

The Dirty 30 (Docks Boys)
By Jonathan Evans Cardiff City.

Like I said in my previous book, your not going to get a much better lad than Jonathan in any ones firm. He wont bullshit and wont bounce around, he's straight in no matter what the numbers are, Forest can testify on that account and make sure your not on the receiving end of any of his punches. You will see by his following stories, he can't stand Muppets who have to make up a story that never happened Annis.

After writing a few stories for Annis's last book whilst in prison, I felt I had to draft more material for the latest book. After I had read a proper blag account of Swansea's Football crew, especially how there telling everyone, who'll listen how they've never been run or done, also the best part is how fucking hard and tough there main mouth piece's are, they make out there all like the Spartan's, well to be honest, I bet half these Spartans have never had a proper straightner in there lives, and in there heart of hearts they know they really can't cut it against us, these cunts are probably the one's at the back pushing everyone else forward. Because lets get one thing straight they have never and never will do anything against our lot, and they know it, the one and only time we have ever met head on they got fucking leathered, end off.

Dirty 30

Annis back in the late 80's had Brownhills pub and Hotel, situated right next to central station, it was the ideal spot for us to hang out in.

It was a really tough ole place. (It was no Hilton I can tell you), but it was our HQ at the time and we were always there, for a few years it got to see some pretty naughty thing's happen, plus also some pretty funny time's too, especially when Jellyhead got stabbed in the back, he's screaming he'd been cut, so we were all worried about how bad it was, until we saw it for ourselves, well lets just say we used a plaster to cover it.

The hardcore of our crew was about 30 strong hence the name Dirty 30, we were mainly Docks and Grangetown boys, but had a few other lads from all over Cardiff, but mainly preferred our areas.

With Brownhills so close to the City Centre and with our number's, we hit Cardiff's Nightclub and Football scene with a bang, like I said we were a good 30 odd strong and a fucking hand full.

We had a crew of some of the top and most maddest boys you could ever meet, added with this, we also had some of the toughest lads in the city. Who today are all sadly touching 40 and over, but from the late 80s, we were boys and boy didn't we learn to grow up fast, fighting blokes twice our age.

Through that period we've had to battle out of town gangs, for the control of the doors of our City Centre, which at that time you then had the Rave Scene in full swing, (where there was big money to be made), which like all over Britain exploded in Cardiff.

This was all Pre Mac days before he had control of most of the Door's in Cardiff, so the togetherness of us outside of football, was a tight bond and therefore made us stick together at the football, them days we were a very close knit firm.

The Viking was our front man, any big steroid head doorman, who faced us, the Viking was always the one who stepped forward. At one stage when battling the doorman, it nearly got to the stage of an all out war, it came to a head one night, when over 30 of our lot destroyed there main venue in town(The Ritzy), the whole club was shut down as the doormen got battered and run out of the club, leaving it to a Manager and DJ to Run a club that held over 2,000.They were never seen again.

"Going on someone else's manor."
Swansea v Panathinaikos 27th September 1989.

So the Dirty 30 became another part of Cardiff's Soul crew at football matches, I suppose it's like a bit like Man Utd's mob, with the cockney reds in London and Utd's firm in Manny that's a bit like ours, you've got Cardiff's main firm, then you've got the Valley Commandoes, who do there own thing, but for big games its just one firm together.

A dark mid-week game in Jackland, think of any big Derby game, your Utd v Liverpool, Newcastle v Sunderland or any big London Derby, well Cardiff v Swansea is no different, proper evil on occasions, plus you don't give a fuck about getting nicked for this one game.

So picture the scene 24 of our lot Myself, Viking, Santos, Annis, Cocoon. Little Digger, Brummie, Jeff Lloyd, Darren, Jellyhead, Rusty ect, plus Muffy from Leeds, 25 of us going into our most hated rivals city and ground and we were not even playing. I'll just try to explain a little about what we were going to do, because believe me if this went wrong we were in big fucking trouble, but that's the buzz of it.

Imagine 25 manc's going to Liverpool after the scouser's had been stabbed and attacked out in Rome by the I'ties the scouser's are going to be out for revenge in the returning game aren't they?

Well the Jacks had just been out to Panathinaikos in Greece and had been battered, some put in hospital, some in jail, so in their return game, their whole City is out for revenge, so into this melting pot we arrive, we know it could really get bad, but we still go, anyway we go straight into the home end, no police nothing were in, but were in with about 3,000 Jacks, the whole end, fuck it! We take the high ground, were all tightly packed together, but there's quite a few blocks, so trust me we stick out.

At first were ok, there's a few nudges and glance's but nothing to heavy to worry about, so I decided to go and get some grub, I walk about ten steps and the Jacks surround me, "oi butt, where you from?" well I know I don't look fucking Greek, so Cardiff, I say, just as its coming out of my mouth, he's stuck the head on me, as I go back, I think, right, if I go down mate so are you and try to bite on to his face, with that I here that roar Ca rdiff Card iff from our little firm, Santos and Muffy came flying down the terrace, and steam straight into the Jacks, there off, in fact the whole fucking end is off, all pushing and shoving each other out the way, they all push to get on to the pitch, thats the element of surprise.

This is great! Well however great it was, it didn't last to long, as the Jacks start to realize there's only a handful of us and about 400 turn and charge back up towards us, were fending them off now, as hundreds steam forward, blows and kicks are flying everywhere, Santos and Cocoon are both big black guys and it seems the Jacks are not going into them, so it's proper backs against the wall time for the rest of us, this is what the 70's must be like, madness, were fighting, a fighting retreat all the way down the back stairs as Jack baddies fly past us, its such a tight space, there numbers aren't counting for much, We eventually all get out with Santos and Cocoon the last to leave and keeping them at bay for a few seconds, Were out and I cant believe we've only come out with minor cuts and bruises, we eventually get rounded up by the old bill just outside their end, so basically we've had to fend off hundreds of fuming hole filled gypo's for a long fucking time.

They're shocked, as 25 Cardiff cunts have just had the fucking cheek to try and pull something like that off, we're ecstatic though, we've just had a nice little lunch, 25 gone over to there game, taken the piss, whacked a few, run half an end, no bad injuries and only Santos nicked, a good nights work by all I think, but do you for a second think they'd try something like that at our place? Neither do I lads.

THE Zulus v West Ham 19th September 1989 (League cup 2nd rd)

When Cardiff weren't playing we would sometimes turn up at other games, not always a wise move, especially when your only 15 strong, but why I don't know, we turned up at this Birmingham v West Ham game, god only knows, because on this occasion it didn't really work out to plan, anyway we reached Brum and there Zulu's are everywhere. Oh I forgot to say we picked up a hitch hiker, but forgot to drop him off, so he was with us in the back of the transit, not really knowing what was going on. We drove past a mob of 40 Zulus on a corner and we got checked, they were shouting "West Ham get out the fuckng van if you want it", we did shout back "were fucking Cardiff you mugs". So we drove a bit further up the road, "stop the van" we all said and Annis, C Beer (the driver) and me get out to face the Brummies, who are now charging up the road mobbed up, were still game though as I go to the back of the van to open the door's, but there locked shut, can't open them at all, either there broke or some cunt is holding them shut. (I had my suspicion) either way its bang on top now, we manage to get back to the van but there all over it.

They are now at the passenger side window trying to slash us, so I'm leaning to get out of the way, so I've leant on Annis who in turn is nearly on Beers lap, who can't get the van into gear, their Zulus are now trying to slash Annis and me and turn the van over, the boy's in the back are in bits, finally we get the van to go and were off.

With the Brummies in hot pursuit I check for injuries but because luckily for Annis and me the Zulu who was doing the slashing had arm's the size of yoda's, the force was with us that day I think. Were stopped up the road by the old bill, who we then say "look at the state of our van", it was dented from top to bottom, with no wing mirrors left, we were lucky it was a transit with hardly any windows. The old bills reply was "teaches you a lesson for jumping out and offering people out"., they had watched the whole thing.

Fulham (plus Chelsea) v Cardiff 1993.

A typical day out in London for us, especially in any type of firm, is rounded up escorted to the game and then sent packing home again to the sheep, this day we travelled to Fulham, who don't really expect to much trouble, we got there 22, of us in all and there were Cardiff everywhere that day, don't know why but we decided to go into their seats, it kicked off straight away. They had a go, but hundreds more Cardiff invaded the pitch and put an end to Fulham's expenses.

After the game we're driving slowly along the road, and we clocked a mob of about 50 strong coming over to our van, the first one bounced over telling us were Chelsea "come on", and kicks the passenger door!! Come on Cardiff were Chelsea again boys' so we ask for there autograph's cos they are Chelsea!

Anyway Farrah and the Viking jump out, Farrah has ousted the first 2 bang, the rest see the star war's bar emptying out of the back of the van (and a car load of ours) and they are backing off leaving the second KO's behind, but as they are going back, they back straight into the Barry boys who had been in a boozer behind them, game over for them, they've got a bit of a leathering. Serves them right for being so pig headed and thinking they're it.

There's been plenty more exploits to be told next time around and I'll tell you about our battles with West Ham, Bristol City, Newport and Wrexham, maybe not big hitters in the thug world, but put up some good performances, and off the night the on going battle with Newport's firm, one night which lead to the petrol bombing off the Docks police station. Plus our tours on the MARCH in Europe.

Dirty 30 role call, Viking, Farrah (Thomas Hearns) Toddy, Luddy, C Beer, Jellyhead, Rusty, Pepper, Bullet, Hicksy, DEDA (R.I.P), G Walton, Robbie, Porta, Wella, Buster, Frankie, Greckson, Pigga, Big foot, Brumble fish, Princy, Starship, Carthy, Kieron, Spudd, (Long Lartin Crew) Faison, Cocoon, Shitty Darren, Brownie, Jason, Cookie (Break it up).

Break it up Cookie, now that's a name that sums up this person perfectly, he's a good mate not really football but was the joker of our crew, well were all in Peterborough one time we got all our firm there, been a few little off's here and there, there not a mob you need to really worry about so no one is really thinking about them , well I'm in a shopping centre with about 5-10 others and we get steamed by their crew, I take a whack to the eye which fucking hurt bad, my eye is fucked, ballooned up and shut straight way, I automatically cover up, I try to swing punches back, but to be honest this big hairy cunt aged about 35 (I was about 18 at the time) was whacking fuck out of me, I'm thinking where the fuck are our boys, are here they come, it's Cookie, but instead of smashing this cunt over his head or something, he gets in between us, shouting break it up, break it up, can you believe it, break it fucking up, I'm in agony with a toffee apple for an eye, and he's trying to play school teacher by pulling us apart, can't buy time like that

CCFC Docks Boys

Chapter 15

"ARRIVING LATE BUT WE WERE WELL UP FOR IT"
By Neil C.S.F. (City Service Firm)
BRISTOL CITY

I was given the following lad Neil his number, by a Bristol lad called Marc (which is a long story but, I've got a lot of respect for him), Marc said Neil was a really good lad and wanted to give an account of one of his trips to Cardiff. Neil seemed a decent lad and straight talking and was about during the late 80s. Annis

Following Bristol City started for me in the 80's. Now our main rivals as everybody knows are Rovers, but we know when we play Cardiff or Millwall it's always going to go off and these are probably two of the main teams we always look forward to. Swansea are a bit like Rovers a waste of space, all mouth no bottle. I personally have always found Everton have always given us a good battle and have always turned out for us.

Now the early 80's weren't good for us and after 3 straight Relegations, things in Bristol were quite, you had the odd ruck, but that was about it. Then in 1984 the Reading riots were the turning point, that day everyone lost the plot and the game was held up for about 15 mins. I knew then this was for me, as the excitement and adrenalin, plus then getting promotion topped it all. The 84/85 season there was also a lot of trouble, but it wasn't until the 89/90 season that things changed for me as we had Cardiff City away on the 16th September.

We all met up at Temple Meads, there seemed loads of lads waiting outside, on the platform and in the bar. I'm no good at figures, but people tell me there were hundreds, all I knew was that this was a mob anyone would have been proud off. Now at home games we were not that organised as everyone had their own little mobs, but away we seem to stick together more and we usually all end up going as one and I think this game got us going more as one mob.

The train before ours, the lads on that one had stopped in Newport, so we all got off to join up with them. The earlier mob had got off at Newport as they thought their numbers wouldn't off been enough to go straight into Cardiff with. This is now why this game sticks out to me as we were all together, our mob was fucking massive and we knew we were ready for it. This mob was buzzing, we all knew Cardiff would be waiting for us. The problem was the police were on to us, big time, we tried to loose them but this wasn't happening. At one stage we all got on buses in Newport, thinking we could just drive off, no chance, we were going no where.

We wanted the row and everyone was up for it, so it was now back to going on the train, We finally got to Cardiff, more police were there, but it was now late, about 20 mins before kick off. We wanted to get to Ninian Park before kick off and nothing was going to stop us. We didn't know if Cardiff had thought we had given it a miss, as were late arriving. As we came out the station, opposite at the time was a bus station and everyone was now streaming out and pushing through the police. Then we saw a few Cardiff, calling us to come towards the City centre, but that wasn't happening as everyone just went fucking mad, fists were flying people running everywhere, it was mental, by now the police were trying to whack us back and show us who's in charge or so they think. The 30 odd Cardiff were still calling us on, game on about 150 of our lot had gone through the police and straight into the group of Cardiff, they stood for a second or so but it was game over, they were run. We run some up into a big building, which was like some kind of pool place, I think it was called The Empire pool. I admit by now it was about 15 mins to kick off and most of Cardiff's lads must have given up on us and what Cardiff had then was only a small group.

We finally got to the game, with the same old thing, Cardiff telling us how much they hate us and coins and bottles flying back and for. We won the game 3 nil and were happy as far as the result went. The police once again tried to hold us in, so we smashed the gates through and poured out onto the road. Cardiff were waiting, hundreds of them in the park outside, it looked like the police had driven them back. So we just went straight into the park and a full on battle took place, both mobs went for each other, neither backing off. The police took well over 5 mins to get it under control. Fair play to both sides, as both went for it big time. Then all the way back to the train station, Cardiff tried to get at us with the police only just keeping both mobs apart. All in all, a good day was had.

When Cardiff came to us that season, it was game on all day, with them wrecking our turnstiles, walls and us trying to steam down from the Dolman stand to get in their end during the game and them breaking through the gates. We also battled after the game with the police to come around the Cardiff end. There were so many battles that day it was unreal.

As the season came to a head, it was May 2nd 1990 we needed to beat BRISTOL ROVERS to win the league .We got to Bath at 12 o'clock, 8 hours before kick off, everyone was buzzing. We met up with the usual lads as the game got nearer, Bristol City fans(us) were everywhere fighting with Rovers, its hard at the best of times because they are a no-show usually and the mob we had that day done City proud. As we got to the ground, the old bill were nicking people for anything, but this didn't stop City from taking the piss just knocking the Rovers lads out for the fun of it. The game started and as usual Rovers start taunting us, then they went 1-0 up, that's to much for some City. We then tried to get in Rovers end, but as usual Rovers ran back, fighting with old bill then started. They started getting a bit heavy, but they had the sense not to come in our end.

While all this was going on, the second half had already started, and before you know it Rovers were 3-0 up and City fans had lost the plot. They were smashing everything up, We were now ripping all the signs and hording boards off the walls and throwing them at the Rovers fans. Fighting them was hard as they just backed off. I do admit we were mental. At the final whistle we just carried on into the night trying to do Rovers, police were nicking people everywhere and it started to come on top as the night was ending. I made my way with the lads to the train station still buzzing from the last ten hours, then a police van pulls up in front of us and stops us. Which

I thought was a routine stop and its only the old bill that I've tried to have a go at in the away when it all kicked off and that was the end of the night for me a fine and a football ban from the club I Love.

Fans' riot 'worst for years'

SEPTEMBER 18 1989

By YORK MEMBERY

CARDIFF CITY fans went on the rampage at the weekend in the worst outbreak of soccer violence seen in South Wales for three years, say police.

The trouble flared after City fans saw their side go down to a crushing 3-0 defeat at Ninian Park, leaving Cardiff stuck at the bottom of Division Three with just one point.

As the crowd left the ground angry groups of youths started pelting rival Bristol City fans with stones and coins, and hurling abuse.

Police battled to keep the supporters apart, and had to issue a call for all available officers in Cardiff to converge on the football ground.

Chief Inspector Alan Chadwick, who commanded the police operation at Ninian Park on Saturday, said, "It was the worst incident of disorder at the ground for a long time.

"The Cardiff hooligan element were very frustrated and bitter about the result of the match.

"They hung around outside the ground after the game waiting for the Bristol City fans, and started throwing stones at them."

Police tried to hold back the Bristol fans to avoid trouble between rival supporters but a cordon was unable to hold back the 1,400-strong English crowd.

A thin blue line of officers was sandwiched between the two sides, desperately trying to keep them apart.

Chief Insp Chadwick said, "The police operation managed to contain the disorder, but it was a hairy situation.

"We expected a lot of Bristol supporters and had double the normal number of police officers at the match, but we still had to put out an appeal for all available policemen to attend the game in order to contain the trouble."

A special train picked up some Bristol fans at the Ninian Park halt, but police had to escort the rest of the visitors to Cardiff Central station to protect them from local football yobs.

Nine home supporters were arrested for public order offences and drunkenness, and one youth has been bailed and ordered to appear before a Cardiff juvenile court on October 2.

Afterwards Mr Chadwick spoke of his sadness at the violence. He said, "I am dismayed that Cardiff soccer fans don't seem to have learnt anything from recent football tragedies like the Heysel stadium and Hillsborough disasters."

And he made an appeal to the law-abiding majority of fans. He said, "We need supporters to co-operate fully with our requests if we're to prevent a repeat of Saturday's violence.

"Our aim is to keep away-supporters inside the stadium while we clear the area of home supporters. This is the only way to avoid confrontation between rival fans."

113

September 2008 at the Liberty Stadium - Carling Cup 3rd Round.

Just one of many different mobs of Cardiff City.
Ant Hill Mob - Caerphilly Mob

Gwyn Davies (Valley Rams), Chris and Guto at Ninian Park.

Bristol City Lads in Cardiff Central Station 2000

*A few of the lads in Portugal on tour Summer (July 08) with Cardiff
Happy Days - our spotter Simon & Wayne (a Portuguese spotter) relaxing for once.*

Cardiff hooligans trying to get at Leeds

Simon (Neath Punk)

Cardiff 2 - Wolves 0 16/02/08
Wolves Fans at Cardiff F.A. Cup. - We totally outplayed them, so I think they got a little upset

Standard Liege fans looking for Cardiff fans in Belgium

Liege 1993

The Police draw their batons against Cardiff Fans at Bramall Lane
Sheffield united 2005

The police line in Sheffield 2005
no way past for Cardiff Fans

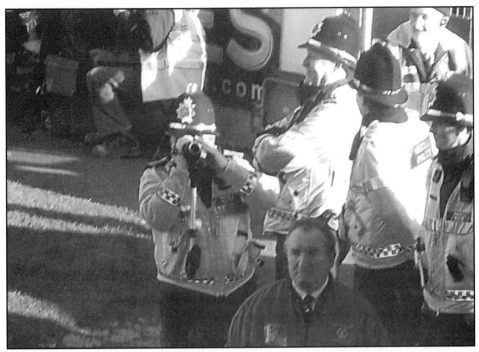

Ninian Park - our 4 main spotters & behind them Jeff, now a steward, but the main spotter in the 80's
Being filmed again, but all quiet at Ninian Park

Some of the original Soul Crew in the 80's
Gethin, Glen, Worzel & Barry lads

The 80's
Myself, Darryl, James, Jock (Tim) and Barry Lads

Viking (Nils) and Jonathan at Vikings Wedding 2008

Welsh Cup Final 1987 - Newport County v Merthyr at Ninian Park
Newport on Bob Bank getting surrounded by City (Cardiff)

Blackpool Away 1988
Holyhead Lads and Cardiff Lads together

The 80's at Newport
Young Cardiff would invade Newport

Away at Newport in the 80's
Cardiff Young Soul Crew being escorted from Somerton Park

Ely Trendies at barnsley away
Zeddy, Peter M, Myself and Mike Dye

Guff and Steve(Palmer)
Wales game

Simo, Mallo and Mac - Swallow Hotel, Mansfield away
Sam Hamman's Champagne Party 2001

Swansea fans taunting Cardiff at Swansea
Sept 23rd 2008

The Bridgend Lads and Myself 5 hours before going to Jackland Set 23rd 2008
Just 1 of 30 coach loads

Sept 23rd - 3 miles from Swansea Stadium, 30 coaches of Cardiff kept in an empty industrial estate
for over an hour, just sitting there while the Old Bill watch over us

Cardiff Fans at Swansea
Sept 23rd 2008

Swansea Fans half heartedly call Cardiff Fans
on Sept 23rd 2008

The Old Bill push Cardiff Fans back after the match
at Swansea 23rd Sept 2008

No way through, Cardiff Fans try to get to Swansea after the match
at Swansea Sept 23rd 2008

Cardiff Fans invade "The North Bank" Swansea in the 80's

1984

Cardiff Lads messing around at Ninian Park before the Front Cover Shoot to this book

Big Sam as usual on his phone to an away game

The Docks Boys at Vikings wedding
Cardiff City

City fans throw planks, bricks

Bristol City fans — police were trying to move them away from the ground

Cardiff City fans kept inside the Bristol ground to prevent trouble between them and the Bristol fans

Police take shelter as planks of wood and pieces of masonry are thrown over the gate

1989

Cardiff fans at Ashton gate 1989

Away on Dib's Tours
(The Bridgend lads)

CCFC The 80's
Conrad, Daryl, Simon (Neath Punk) and Jammo (Ely Trendy)

The 80's
Guff, Wilburs and other Cardiff Lads

Police move in after being attacked on Bob Bank during the match between Cardiff City and Swansea City

Police make arrests after being attacked on Bob Bank during the match between Cardiff City and Swansea City

Gabbidon (Cardiff player)
Matty, Stu, Morris, Gus Yuan, Neath Punk (Simon) - The Cardiff Lads in th 80's

Stu, Simon (Neath), Myself and Graham Kavanagh (CCFC)

Cardiff, one of the first clubs in the country to introduce the membership due to the violence at Ninian Park (70's)

Mallo, Family Rail Cards in the 80's

Viking and Little Pete Cardiff City - Wembley 2008

Wolves away 2004

Wolves away 2004

Wolves away 2004

A True Bluebird!

Sloper Road Ninian Park

Cardiff Fans outside Molineux after a riot with Wolves fans in 2004

Police face Cardiff Fans at Wolves (Molineux after trouble between the police and Cardiff Fans Game delayed for 15 minutes in 2006

Police split Cardiff Fans down the middle after a battle between Wolves Police and Cardiff Fans at half time
11th March 2006

Cardiff Lads and Myself in Denmark with Wales

Welsh and German Police watch over us in Dusseldorf, Germany
14th October 2008

The Lads and Myself at our hotel in Dusseldorf, Germany
14th October 2008

The Cardiff Lads and Myself with Robbie Savage in Denmark celebrating after a Welsh Victory on Danish soil

Bristol City's Lads in Germany

W.B.A. Firm 2008

Bristol City Lads in Germany 2001

Darren Purse (Our Club Captain) & myself at Ninian Park

Chapter 16

I LOVED EVERY MINUTE OF IT
BY Simon Neads (Neath Punk) CCFC

Simon, well what can I say about him probably a million and one things, He's probably one of the biggest characters you will ever meet at the football, He's mad ,no I will rephrase that, he's stark raving mad, with no fear and will at the same time be one of the funniest lads around. Known as the Grave Digger for a while (don't ask) and also Neath Punk. I've known him now for a long time and through the good and bad times, and we've had many a good time a long the way. His stories you might find different than anyone else's, but everyone will be true. Annis

After no deliberation I am finally putting a few lines together, for a good friend of mine Annis, he has been a mate of mine for more than 20 years and like most mates we have had our disagreements, but they are always patched up quickly, as the next row could be around the corner and as we all know good mates are needed at football and that is one thing we have at Cardiff.

I am not going to go on about me and Annis together at football matches, because I haven't got the time or that big a memory to recall them all and also that would be a book on its own in the 80s.I could tell you stories of Blackpool, Gloucester, Tenby, Bradford and many others, which is nothing to do with football on a Saturday afternoon. I've chosen one which was Western Super-Mare, which as usual turned out to be, fighting and a good laugh thrown in with it.

Before I tell some stories of the past, I thought I would tell you a bit about myself. Most of Cardiff know me as Simon from Neath (Neath Punk), but the truth is I am a Valley boy and proud of it. I was born in Tredegar and I lived there until I was 15(I spent my first 9 mouths, in a place called Cwm near a good lad Called Rotter, a very game lad too). As with most lads I was first taken down the City by my Dad when I was 9 years old. These were memorable days, which will never leave me and I can't believe this will be our last season at Ninian Park. I thought only a life ban would have ever stopped me from going there and I've had 2 of them from the club. No a new ground next year thanks to Ridsdale and co.

Back to my Tredegar days, my first match on my own was against MAN UTD in 74, I went on an old Charlie Hills bus from Tredegar Town centre. Thanks to a lad called Coco who was a legend in my eyes and many older lads from Tredegar who went on the bus that day to see Cardiff v MAN UTD, I became a hooligan on that day especially. Talk about having a laugh, I was chased back to our bus, thrown around like used chip packet in Caroline street and given a few boots up my arse for good measure. Why oh why did I have 2 scarves tied around my wrists, that day totally bewilders me. I may as well said, go on you Big Manc twat , spin a 12 year old around like a whirling Deruish you 18 year old bully. I hope you rot in hell you over grown twat. From that day I've always hated United.

I carried on going on the bus with these Tredegar lads, others who I remember called Porpoise and the strangely called Bible Eyes, well to be honest he use to put the fear of God into me at the best of times. Not many games stuck in my mind until 1977 FA Cup run and I nicked my first scarf of an EVERTON fan on the Bob Bank and boy Everton didn't half get a pasting in the ground that day. That sadly was my last days of being a Commando, as In 78, I moved to the land of the White Shite Neath, but boy did Neath Blues and myself soon turn that around.

Now lets get something straight I was first and foremost a football hooligan, I am not ashamed of my past and I will take those pleasures with me to the grave, as you have just read the minute, I went to a match on my own to see Cardiff play, I was in love with the fighting side of it, but lets be honest the 70s and 80s were known for that and the majority of lads or even fans got caught up in it at some time or other.

I have been arrested 15 times at football matches, 3 of those times I have been abroad, once I've been deported. 2 life bans from Cardiff City and 3 bans from the courts. 6 months in 88, 1 year in 91 and 3 years in 2002. At no time have I thought of giving up the path of which I chose at the time to follow. I have been involved in literally over 100 football related fights and in March 1984 alone I've had over 17 against the pebble dash kids (SWANSEA Jack filth) alone. I have given more than I've received, yes I've had my ribs broken by PLYMOUTH, had a fractured cheekbone, and nose broken, by other firms. I've also had 12 stitches in my head (from a machete) from the Gypo Jacks and even been run over by them. Been gassed by the old bill and other firms , you might think , I might have been put off by this , wrong, I will give up when I choose too and I feel I cant take it no more. Like I say I've given more than I've received and whoever said its better to give than receive is spot on. As long as those scruffy Gypo twats are living next door to THE PRIDE OF WEST GLAMORGAN, WHO ARE NEATH AND PORT TALBOT BLUES and 150 STRONG. You Muppets you will never get past us to even take on Cardiff's other firms.

NEATH BLUES

My introduction to the pride of West Glamorgan, started on a Monday night in Neath Town Centre, where my band the Auschwitch Ashmen were playing in a bar called the Full Moon. We were in my eyes a hard core punk band, hence my nick name in several books Neath Punk. Thank fuck I hadn't been a New Romantic, it hasn't got the same ring really. In the crowd watching us that night was a lad called Gareth Jones, after chatting to him and Gareth telling me that tomorrow night he was off to see Cardiff v Swansea in the Welsh cup (1982), I was back into football. Since I had moved down to Neath, I hadn't been to football for 5 years. So off we went on the 5.40pm train, we got there at about 6.30pm and I was nicked at 7.30pm, fined £300, and the rest is history.

Over the next decade we held our own and came out on top time and time again, as Toozey the author of the Jack book told me, a lot of their book was tongue and cheek stuff. I would like to meet any 2 Jacks who in them days can say they slapped me or Fulman (probably the best lad we had down this way) for good measure, so please step forward I only live 3 miles from you and some of you have got my phone number. There were only 2 SWANSEA lads who would have been able to have had a go at Fulman and they worked with him anyway and they will admit that. With Fulman you get no change in a row with the guy, I've been with him in at least 30-40 rows and we've only ever come unstuck due to the severity of the numbers stacked against us at the time. This was on 2 occasions, one when he stood at Swansea Guild hall and just faced a mass of them and the other when we tried to take EXETERS end. A couple of us were left on there and we just fought till we were fucked and there's photos to prove it. I don't mind saying and admitting I got a right old slap off them. I'm not ashamed to admit, unlike most of the Jacks, who say they've never been run or done, who are they kidding.

NEATH Lads and PVM (Port Talbot Lads)

At about Easter 1984, when after taking the piss out of the Jacks all day in SWANSEA, we then marched down to the East terrace at the Vetch Field. We were 200 strong, all dressers and all laughing and celebrating that we had just run the Scum absolutely everywhere before the game. As we got to the ground a copper asked us where we were all from, I showed him my Neath Punk tattoo and that was it we were off. 200 now on their end, we had taken the piss all day and now the best was to come, We all ran on the pitch towards their other end as this end was shit in here(when we had scored), but We were soon driven back by dogs etc. The second goal came and this time we had other plans as when we scored it, we ran to the half way line and then faced the North Bank and called them on (photos to prove it), we hadn't even done anything and they were running away. I got right to the fence and without a second thought, I climbed the fence and ran straight in, to my left was a lad called Ginger from Pencoed. The scum were everywhere, they had all scattered, to my amusement.

I then saw Ginger climbing back over the fence and the other 198 gingerly walking back to the away end. Did I look for sympathy, did I fuck. This is all fact and no Swansea modern day myth story, well the whole inbred family steamed me, I then ran into the corner of the North bank and the East Terrace, where I was trapped in the corner, I remember seeing a load of Jack hero's steaming towards me, I thought to myself, fairplay, they've come straight from work to the game, well why else were they wearing steel toe caps and donkey jackets, I was soon to find out that they were their notorious Town Hill Crack Commando Squad, but I swear one of them didn't have a moustache or in Neath we call individually a mush with a tush.

Well I got cornered by about 30 of the muppets, fairplay I'd just run the North Bank in ½ a minute on my own and I pulled out a blade or was it my William Hill bookies pen and couldn't believe they backed off from 4 inch of blue plastic. I got to the emergency gate, tried to crawl under the fucker and got a bit of a slap but thanks to the special copper who pulled me from under the gate, I was then taken to the rest of Cardiff to be given a hero's welcome. Well if any Jack has climbed over the Grange End fence, run in the Family Stand never mind the Bob Bank and lived to tell the tale, I'll put him in my book when I can be arsed to write it.

My second true story is about the FA Cup saga of 1991 at the Vetch for starters the Neath lads were in your seats and running all your top jacks out of their seats during the game and you can see this on you tube along with you bastards doing the Canton mile being legged by 9 Cardiff lads outside the exchange in Canton.

Back to 91, we had one of our biggest mobs out for years and we met up with the Cardiff lads in the Bear pub in Neath, we had 40 good lads just from Neath alone, it would be like the Jacks having 40 lads living 3 miles from Cardiff, in their dreams! We all made our way to the railway station a good few hundred lads, that day Cardiff had over 5000 fans at Swansea with no restrictions, hooray for the good old days. In total that day we had over 1000 lads and if you twats don't admit it then your lying to yourselves. Your town was run ragged and even the police have said that we were out of control that day, we had so many mobs out that day that we kept bumping into each other, each time praying it was you lot, you must have gone to the Rugby for the day. 2-0 to me I think.

My third story, lets get this straight from the start, I'm going to finish with" THE GREATEST NON EVENT OF THE 80's" (swim away), I'm referring to the gippo jacks only self proclaimed victory over Port Talbot, not Cardiff by the way. I'm talking 12 people in total, 9 Port Talbot lads age 15 - 19 and 3 Dinas Powys lads, let's also get it straight there was only one old head present that day and that was Kersy from Barry (Dinas) who was 19 at the time, the other lads were Tongy and Bazza two 17 year old, from Port Talbot, 16 year old Lee Webber, Aiden (Taffy Anton's brother) who was 15. The only wrong and backward step that they took that day was going back to their cars about 300 yards from the Retch Field, also remember these boys parked up only 3 minutes from all your pubs and had the nerve to march around Swansea and give it to whoever they could find. At this time Swansea's oldest trick was to stay in their pubs until Cardiff had been safely escorted back to the train station and the coaches. So then Swansea would then pick off the one's and two's and then their full mob would attack anything up to three cars full of kids. So fairplay when there's 200 onto 12 like there was that day, I don't think Swansea will even get done, when those numbers occur, so in their favour of 18-1 I'll take my hat off to them. So the Jack steamed down on them and steamed them onto the beach and then the kiddy fiddler's swarmed all over them. So yes the 12 lads took only one option and jumped in the shit filled Swansea Bay. I would have rather stayed and fought than be unlucky enough to swallow a floating turd from the land of the unwashed which is Townhill, you gippo scum. It was dark by this time so imagine what it must have been like with syringe's floating around and a load of bricks raining down on them, young Lee Webber was shouting "come and join us over here" so why didn't they go in their shitty water or was it they couldn't swim.

Luckily enough for the boys, a few old bill turned up and told Swansea to fuck off and thankfully they did, apparently the boys came out like drowned rats, a couple of car loads had come back for them, but when they saw the state of them they said your not coming in the car like that boys. Anyway, result you may have had and to this day this has been your biggest result to date.

You do have some top lads, the ones I have respect for, Stacko in particular has saved my arse on more than one occasion and a couple of other lads Boxer, Alan and Laddy. Personally I know he has upset a lot of people with his book Mr Tooze but he has never given it the big un to me or Fulman, so respect where it's due.

Mystery Trip To Western Super-Mare

It was in the summer of 1989 and we were all woken by the call of Angel's or was it the DHSS, tramps coughing and pukeing outside my room in Brownhill's hotel. This wasn't a football day it was one of Annis's mystery trips, he got one of is paying guest's called Nigel a WEST BROM fan and a coach driver to take us all on a trip to Western Super-Mare. Now Nigel in my opinion was a few sandwich's short of a picnic, he told us he was a bus driver and he told me his wife was Olive, I would have believed him and he also said he was a bricky, I asked him who for, "fucking Lego", this was totally over his head as he said "no, I work fro Wimpy", there was no beating this guy! But to be honest he turned out to be a real gem.

It turned out he had a 33 seater bus and he let us fill it with full of lads and one girl called Helen from Lisvane. We filled the bus up with booze from the bar before Annis got there (he! he!), (you bastards! From Annis), cause contrary to belief he's not tighter than Asthma. So off we went to shop lifters paradise of Aust services Bristol. Why the leather jacket shop man decided to go back to his van at 11am to get more stock (which he later needed) it beggars belief, because rather than the usual stuff of pasties and crisps and the latest top shelf magazine, the next thing I was seeing was a couple of our 18 year old lads wearing full length leather jackets in the middle of July, marching past the guy looking like a couple of SS stalwarts, it still tickles me to this day.

We arrived mid morning and I swear the driver was more pissed than me. He finally parked up and probably hitting two cars at the same time and with this Annis, Darryl, Myself, Martin (Cheltenham), Little Collin, Brownie, Chrissie Bear, Helen and various other beaut's got off. We had only gone a few yards to the first pub, when we set eyes on a big mob and can you believe it WEST BROM fans about 50 in total, we found out later that they were on their main lad's stag do.

Well being a WEST BROM fan yourself i.e. the driver, the first thing you'd do was to steam straight into them saying "come on you Baggie bastards" wouldn't you. Well our deranged driver, who rendered himself insane by this time with whatever he was on, did exactly that! We all steamed straight into them and never mind "boing, boing", we bounced them all down to the beach. They, I kid you not were running faster than the donkey's. They tried standing to give them their dues but it was a lost cause, especially when you are being steamed by one of your own. I dropped a lad on the beach and I was just about to give him a good wellying, when I though fuck it and walked away, just as well as the old bill arrived 5 seconds later, thank fuck because all the lads were loosing all sense of rhythm and reason and it was getting unnecessarily heavy, so we all scuttled off except the driver who thankfully got nicked.

While walking back into town Little Collin was approached by a couple of kids and they said "did you see the fighting Uncle Collin?" with which he replied "wasn't it great, did you see me, I was the first in" (priceless). No but in all honesty Collin worship's his nephew's and Nieces and he gave them a couple of quid and told them to go and enjoy themselves. We all then went on a jolly, I've got to admit, we felt invincible in our own eyes, it sort of felt like a football day.

Later on that day we asked a couple of old bill what time they were letting our driver out, they said he would soon be dropped back by our bus and they didn't give a fuck who was driving, as long as we all fucked off back to Wales, as apparently half of our group had just had a fight with

118

a load of Worzels from Bristol City scattering the carrot cruncher's everywhere.

In all my times of walking half a mile to a bus, nothing could prepare me for what was about to happen. We were all on a high anyway, so what better than to nick a service bus and drive it back to our own bus. What happened next goes with me to the grave in my top ten laughs. There was a bus parked outside W.S.M depot, I'll never forget it was one of those mini town riders and the keys were in the ignition with the doors open. It looked like rain and a good 2 minute walk to our bus, so of course we were going to nick it.

So one of our lads Chrissy B who had stolen a bus before, jumped in, with this everyone except 4 of us got on. He then drove off while shouting "fare's please" with immaculate maneuvering. A moment later the driver came sprinting out of the depot shouting "they've nicked my fucking bus and it's my first week in the job". To see what at that time to us a grown man running up the road after his pride and joy and in all probability his livelihood disappearing before his very eyes and almost crying was fucking hilarious.

I have this picture in my mind still of us all singing "we're all going on a summers holiday", whilst banging on the bus windows. At first we didn't pick anyone up until our crazy fucking driver Chrissy stopped and picked up this old geezer, well he wasn't amused when we took a roundabout at 60mph with a police car up our arses, he was thrown from pillar to post as there was no where to sit, well at least we didn't charge the fucker. To be honest I wished him well as he staggered eventually off the bus (I've always been a sarcastic bastard).

How those highly trained motorway cops kept up with us I'll never know because everyone knows, you're a much better driver when you've had a few. When we finally grounded to a halt, we were out of every possible exit, well two, guess what the old bill only caught one, poor 16year old Helen. Once we got back to the bus, through about 30 people's gardens, we were met by the old bill and our real driver and who by now had a face like Hitler's gas bill. We were then escorted over the Severn Bridge.

I hear you shouting please let there be more and if you're sitting comfortable there is more. Well we decided to go to NEWPORT, to smash Tutty, Adam's and co but firstly I must point out that Annis, Toddy, Darryl were not allowed in NEWPORT because of a pending court case. We stopped off in Newport Town Centre the above mentioned and the driver stayed on the bus, while rest of us planned a surprise attack on their main pub on a Saturday night, knowing that all their main faces would be on show. The plan was to send two of our lads Martin and Browny into their pub, offer them out and then get chased back to where we were waiting at the bottom of the pedestrian walk ways in the bus station. Well it happened and we waited for about ten minutes and NEWPORT COUNTY didn't disappoint, about 40 in all turned up chasing our two over the bridge as planned, down the ramp and into our open loving arms, but the reason they had taken so long was the two stupid twats had stood there and virtually let them get at them, but in a way maybe this helped bring them all down to us. We were straight into Newport's finest, we were like fucking mad men, then I noticed that two of our lot were trying to hold these fuckers back armed with a shopping trolley, we eventually finally got down to it, those were the days of no CCTV. I got hit in my leg with a big brick, forget the nonsense of being in the wrong place at the wrong time, I was in the right place at the right time and fucking loving it, unlike most rows this was confined in a subway, confined, loud and no place for the weak, it was every man for himself.

I have no regrets whatsoever that day, because I done to those what they were hoping to do to me, the first County fucker who came within punching distance felt a brick right in the mush, what a connection, I've only made the same once since twice, it was good night Vienna and good night Newport and a very good night from me, and then seeing a few of their mates horizontal soon had the rest of them running and the night was ours.

The last 12 miles were great all the lads on the bus who missed it wanted to know every detail and cursed Jerky for getting them banned from the Town Centre and missing a tear up with County. When we finally got back to our beloved Brownhill's there was a bit of good news, Annis asked us all to pay a pound so that we could pay for Helen to come back by train from Western Super-Mare, it wasn't a problem, she took the wrap, had 9 points off her licence, which she hadn't even applied for yet and when she arrived home at 12pm in the bar, she was given a hero's welcome because she was one of us.

● **Injured constable Jeff Richards leading a youth from the Bob Bank.**

Soccer thugs clash

Police blamed for failing to prevent violence

By DAVID CORNOCK
and KARL WOODWARD

VIOLENCE AT the weekend soccer derby match between Swansea City and Cardiff City could have been prevented by police at the game, the Cardiff club's chairman claimed last night.

But South Wales Police said the violence that led to 15 arrests and four policemen being injured was preplanned, with the large hooligan element among the 6,000 supporters attending the game intent on causing trouble.

Two officers were attacked and had a substance believed to be CS gas sprayed in their faces.

The fans were arrested before and during Saturday's game at Ninian Park, Cardiff, as scuffles broke out and later charged with public order offences. Two police officers were assaulted, while the other two needed hospital treatment after the spraying incident.

A police spokesman last night condemned the spray attack as "a very dangerous prac-

tice." Traffic officers Malcolm Dean and Andrew Stephens were treated at Cardiff Royal Infirmary for irritation to the face, eyes and mouth. Neither was seriously hurt and both were back on duty yesterday.

Pc Jeff Richards was kicked and punched to the ground and sustained a cut eye and a bruised back. Pc Peter King sustained bruising to the right of his face when he was punched as he went to Pc Richards's aid.

Police officers were forced to draw their truncheons to defend themselves as the violence erupted, only days after similar scenes at the ground after a cup match between Cardiff and neighbours Newport County.

On Saturday, a metal crutch was thrown on to the pitch from the Swansea supporters' end after they had a goal disallowed, and rival fans stoned each other as the crowd dispersed at the end of the match.

Violence also flared on the field, where Swansea striker Joe Allon was sent off for elbo-

wing Cardiff captain Terry Boyle in the face. Cardiff won the match 1-0.

Mr Clemo said last night that had there been enough police controlling the Cardiff fans the violence would have been stopped.

But a South Wales Police spokesman said 120 extra officers were drafted in to control the crowd for the match, with Cardiff City only meeting a small proportion of the cost.

"The number of officers on duty is carefully calculated in regard to the nature of the match, the number of supporters anticipated to attend, and the history of previous crowd behaviour. We are confident that there were sufficient numbers of officers on duty."

Mr Clemo said segregation of rival fans at Ninian Park was very good. "This is the first trouble we have had inside the ground for a very long time," he said.

Closed-circuit television would be in operation at the ground within two months in an attempt to identify trouble-makers, he said.

Ninian Park's crowd control will be put to the test again next Saturday when club are at home to Wolves in an all-ticket match, the restriction imposed by the Football League after crowd trouble caused by Wolves fans on the opening day of the season.

"I don't know what the answer to hooliganism is. It is something better brains than I have deliberated on and we still have the problem," said Mr Clemo.

Cardiff City's managing director, Mr Ron Jones, could not be reached for comment last night, but writing in his regular *Western Mail* column today he says, "The problem will only be solved by more rigid and thorough policing by the host organisation at those events which might have crowd trouble."

Welsh FA secretary Alun Evans was at the derby clash and witnessed the ugly crowd scenes — but he guaranteed the safety of fans at next week's Wales versus Denmark match, expected to attract a 30,000-plus crowd.

"Whatever the case on Saturday, there is no question that Denmark's match will be safe and secure. That is one guarantee we can give fans of both nations." Up to 10,000 Danish fans are expected in Cardiff for the crucial European championship clash. Closed-circuit television will be in operation for that game, and known troublemakers will be banned.

SOCCER POLICE HIT BY CS GAS

Violence flares before City-Swansea derby

FIGHTING RIVAL soccer fans let off a canister of CS gas at a police patrol before the start of the Cardiff City clash with Swansea this afternoon.

And there was more trouble inside Ninian Park when around 200 Cardiff supporters surged towards the Swansea fans.

Missiles rained down on dozens of police who desperately tried to keep the two factions apart.

Community Constable Jeff Richards was kicked to the ground and had to be rescued by a colleague.

Police dog handlers then moved in to clear the fighting fans and Pc Richards was treated by a police doctor.

Two policemen were taken to hospital and one man was arrested following the gas incident at the junction of Leckwith Road and Wellington Street.

Fans were searched as they entered the ground and close by officers dis-covered a gruesome weapon of a klaxon doctored to spray what was thought to be ammonia.

The policemen were taken to Cardiff Royal Infirmary for treatment to streaming eyes. They were later released.

At half-time the situation inside the ground was so tense that the officer in charge of police operations called in reinforcement units to prevent further possible confrontation.

An estimated 3,000 Swansea supporters travelled to the game and British Transport Police had earlier had trouble on a train from Swansea and another from Barry.

● **Fourth Division EXETER** have banned CARDIFF fans after Saturday's 0—0 draw was marred by crowd trouble.

Play was held up when fighting on the terraces forced fans to spill on to the pitch and, after the game, police dogs were called in.

Video move — eight arrests

EIGHT people have been arrested by West Mercia police in South Wales for alleged offences during the Cardiff City versus Shrewsbury cup-tie.

The arrests follow a squad of detectives bringing a video of violence on the Shrewsbury terraces down to Cardiff for examination by local police.

All eight people were arrested by the West Mercia officers on charges of assault, criminal damage and public order offences.

They have all been released on police bail and are due to appear in court in Shrewsbury next month, said Detective Chief Inspector Chris Thurber today.

Inquiries

"We are satisfied with the operation so far. Our men are back in Shrewsbury today for discussions about the investigation," said Mr Thurber, head of the Cardiff operation.

"But we will return on a later date to follow up other inquiries with the five officers who have been working in Cardiff," he said.

It is the first time in South Wales that a video of scenes on the terraces has been used in a police investigation by another force, as reported in Saturday's Echo.

The West Mercia men have called on several homes and public-houses in South Wales during their investigation and also attended Cardiff's game with Aldershot at Ninian Park on Saturday.

Echo men forced to flee

THREE Echo reporters were caught up in last night's violence — and had to flee in the running battle between police and thugs.

After leaving the match at Ninian Park, Echo men Jeremy Bacon, Jim Clarke and Paul Horton were trapped in the middle of the warring soccer fans.

"Suddenly a roar went up of 'They're out' as Newport fans were allowed from the ground, and the City fans ran back up Sloper Road," said Mr Bacon.

"We saw the mob clash with the police and the air was full of bottles and bricks. It was horrific."

Frightening

After a few minutes, the mob broke up and ran as police counter-attacked onto a garage forecourt, forcing the crowd down side streets.

Police used dogs to disperse the crowd and the three Echo men found themselves in the mob with a snarling police alsation at their heels.

"It was frightening because we knew that the dog could not tell the difference between the thugs and innocent passers-by," said Mr Clarke.

A police wagon was forced to do a violent U-turn, sending a fire extinguisher into the road. It was recovered by the Echo men and returned to police.

"It had been a good clean game — this sort of mindless violence will kill football," said Mr Bacon.

Chapter 17

MY TALES
By Mac CCFC

Well I've known Mac for well over 20 odd years and he's probably one of the best known lads we have and rightly so, but he's not just one of our top lads, he's a fan as well. I've been with him to places like Carlisle and Chester on cold wintry Tuesday nights, where all these so anorak supporters don't bother to go, they only appear at places like Swindon or Reading on a Saturday afternoon. Macs been there with people like Big Sam and Myself when Cardiff have had no more than 50 away fans during the early 90's. Mac could probably write a book or 2 himself, but here's a couple of his short stories. Annis

Before I start to tell you a few tales of my years following Cardiff , I've got a short story to tell first.
One day in about the mid 80's I was standing on the Bob Bank watching the same old shit as usual, so I got chatting to the person next to me for the next half hour or so, what else was there to do in them days as City were shit, it was either that or fuck off home, no seriously in them days half the time was either spent chatting to fellow City fans and the other half of the time you were usually fighting the opposing fan if he bothered to come down to Ninian Park in them days, we might not off had big crowds but virtually everyone down the City in them days was a game lad. I was a Cougar in them days and if I wasn't watching the City I was always going on Scooter rallies all around the country, most the boys I was hanging around with then were into The Jam and The Clash, I still play all that music now on the way to away games. At the same time as those scooter days, you had the mods as well,who in them days were fighting the trendies and Casuals from Cardiff, in the City centre on non match days. Now for the next year or so all I kept hearing about was the Trendies did this and Trendies attacked us here etc. One name that kept coming up was Annis s and a lot of people were stirring between us both, but some how we never met and never even new what we both looked like.

Going back to that day on the Bob Bank, when the match finished the person I had been chatting to said good bye and as he was leaving introduced himself and I did the same, we both looked gob smacked at each other and then burst out laughing as we both shook each others hands. From that day we have been friends ever since and on many occasions we've gone on many a trip together and had some right old laughs.

I went to my first match with my dad in 1970 when Cardiff were in the old second division and for the first few seasons I regularly attended with my old man but then by the 1974/75 season, I started going to games with my younger brother. One of the most frightening times was when I was about 10 and MAN UTD came down to Cardiff with about 10,000, it was mental and I was shitting myself , to this day I've never seen anything like it, both sets of fans fought for the whole 90 mins of the game.

After I left school I trained as a butcher, which was handy for me because the terrace fashion at that time was white butchers coats, I think MILLWALL set that trend going. We had a lad called Frankie Humphries in them days who was the Cardiff leader, he was a legend and the fans used to sing songs about him. He was the gamest I've ever seen at football but at the same time a real gentleman with it.

One game that brings back some good memories was the FA Cup game at Ninian Pak in 1977, I was actually in the enclosure standing on the other side of the pitch with my Dad. Everton were the team and they had been given half of our home end on The Bob Bank, the match hadn't even started and it had kicked right off and within in minutes Cardiff were chasing Everton back and I then suddenly saw EVERTON not only being chased but they were chased totally out of the ground, what a sight to see and I was still only a kid.

On the football side in 1977 we had a player called Robin Friday for about half of the season, honestly, he was fucking brilliant but at the same time he was as mad as a hatter. He looked like a Gypsy, a real scruffy bastard, but had so much talent, he was a genuine gifted player. Then he just disappeared and later on in life he sadly died at a young age, but what a privilege it was to have just seen him play in the flesh.

By the 80s I was going to football suited up and I remember being on the pitch at Loftus road against QPR in a cup game having a row in my Armani suit. I personally like the classic labels Boss, Prada and Lacoste, some of the fake stuff and the shell suits the scourers wear is fucking awful. While were on the subject of QPR I remember going there in 1990, there was a massive queue to get into the away fans end, so two of my mates and myself walked around to the other side of the ground and went in the QPR end. As soon as we got in there we let them know who we were and we backed a load of them off and with that a big gap opened up around us and some how we managed to stay in there till half-time, unbelievable when you think of it , just three of us. We then jumped over the wall and walked down to the Cardiff end, where all the Cardiff fans started applauding us.

WOLVES Away in 1988, it was the old forth division, they were top and we were second, and we won 4-1. I was sitting that day in the front of a minibus with about 15 of us and we were stuck in traffic waiting to pull out of a car park. Before the game we had had a bit of a result as we had run a mob of Wolves outside the ground, so perhaps we were a little confident or complacent after the game and guess what about 200 of them spotted us and surrounded the van. The next thing the windows were all smashed and they were using scaffolding polls and planks of wood, fuck me it was frightening. Then I really thought I was going to die as a breeze block came crashing through the front window and hit me full on, I virtually collapsed in my seat, and went faint and the pain was beyond, my ribs felt totally broken.

The driver managed to mount the curb and speed of along the path and we just about managed to escape. As we were nearly half way home I shouted to the driver to stop and an ambulance was called to me out on the motorway, but I refused to go and said just get me back to Cardiff no matter what, they did and I was then rushed into the emergency ward where within minutes I was being operated on. I was told later by the doctors that I had been so near to death as I had internal bleeding, a ruptured spleen, several broken ribs and other internal organs were damaged. That day turned out to be the most frightening day of my football life.

One of the greatest days was taking the town over of our rivals the JACKS, in the FA Cup in 1991, that day will live with me forever, well over a 1,000 lads from Cardiff went and not only did we do what we wanted, but also the old bill couldn't stop us, they had to just keep up with us. At first there was about 300 of us and up ahead in the main shopping streets we saw a mob of about 400 and we charged only to find out they were Cardiff as well and then we bumped into a few more hundred Cardiff. The Jacks were non existent that day, it seemed that every window in every pub and shop was smashed to pieces, maybe they did turn up, as the cleaners the following morning to clean it all up.

MILLWALL, first game of the season at our place in August 1999 was another day to remember, we were massive that day, probably one of the biggest turn outs since the 70's, anything between a 1,000 to 1,500 lads. We had been trying to get at them all day as the old bill had stopped and even banned us from drinking in our own town. There had been a small mob of about 30 Millwall in a pub at 11am,there was no real toe to toe as a mob of Cardiff got to them and wiped them out.

Then when about 300 Millwall arrived and plotted up in Sam's bar in Mill lane, the shout went up a mile away in Grange town and over 600 lads ran up Penarth road, two police motorcycles rode through the crowd of Cardiff and one was dragged from his bike, the police on horses were attacked by the Cardiff fans and at one stage a police helicopter landed in a park about ¼ mile from the ground, it actually hovered between us and Millwall to keep us apart. So you could say before the game it was a bit of a non event between us and Millwall.

After the final whistle well over 1000 lads were waiting outside the ground and the old bill tried and tried to move us and during that time, some Millwall managed to beak out but the minute we saw them we steamed straight into them and totally hammered them back into the ground. It was so bad they were fighting one another to get back inside, but I've got total respect for them, they had brought the fight to us and not many firms do that.

Later on that season when we played Millwall at their place we had a mob of well over 700 and some of the faces out that day I hadn't seen for years, we were awesome that day and I heard Millwall were good to, but the old bill won as they had wall to wall police where ever we went through the tubes, we couldn't go left or right and it ended up as a non event.

In my opinion Millwall are one of the top firms of all time, first because I've got personal experience of them and second I've got total respect for them, in the old Den you've got to say it was a nasty place to visit.

WOLVES they are a top firm to match anyone on their day.

STOKE they can pull the numbers and are game.

PORTSMOUTH I've got respect for them as when ever we have played them they have been well game.

BARNSLEY and HULL have both come to our place and gone looking for it.
Barnsley, Cardiff had it with them and they were as game as fuck, they held their own at our place. Hull we weren't out the night they came, but that's not their fault 120 Good lads from Hull came to Cardiff on a Friday night, not many firms can say they have done that.

BORO they came to Cardiff shocked us at 11am, we tried our best but they run us, on that day in 1994.

I've got a lot of respect for CHELSEA and they use to come to ours big time in the 80s and we always gave them a run for their money.

A lot of smaller clubs such as Chesterfield, Huddersfield, Burnley and Darlington all tough northern towns, they might not travel down to us, but up there never underestimate them.

Just to finish off, If Cardiff loose it fucks up my whole week and even my wife looks out for the score, then she knows what mood to expect me in.

Chapter 18

A FOREIGN PRISON WAS ENOUGH
BY Tony Ridgeway CCFC
(Guff PVM Port Talbot).

I've known the Port Talbot lads for well over 20 years and for them to be only about 9 miles from Jack land and be firm Cardiff fans, has always been greeted in Cardiff with a lot of respect. I knew Guff from the Brownhills pub days and he and the other lads from Port Talbot always use to pop in for a drink and a chat. They were really good lads in the late 80's and when we all went to an away game as one, Cardiff were then probably in any ones top 5. Annis

I was born and bred in Port Talbot in 1968, I've followed Cardiff since 1984 and still do, even though I now live in London and have settled down and married. I had brilliant parents who were always there for me and took a keen interest in me regarding sport. I played rugby but to be honest, it bored me and having it forced on you in school, made me eventually give it up.

The casual scene arrived into Port Talbot, due to following Cardiff City and the music, loyalty with your mates, the travelling away soon took a grip of me and I was wanting to go more and more with the lads. You had many a tale told you from the older Port Talbot lads from the Sandsfield areas of Port Talbot, a right tough old place, The Jacks would never venture there. Many of my mates then had the same concept, we want more of this. These lads remain close friends of mine, till this day, Steve, Nigel, Huey, Stavvy, Taffy Anton, Wayne, Vince, PT Scouse etc etc.

We soon began to make good friends with the lads from a Town Called Neath, even closer to Jack land (4 miles away), Simon (Neath Punk) and Gareth etc. Regular trips to Neath for nights out and then trouble with the Jacks when they were returning home from their away games. We soon realised we were becoming a close knit bunch, the more trips away with Cardiff the more our numbers grew.

For a laugh one day, we came up with the name PVM, we never thought it would get around so quick and all over West and South Wales, lads knew of us. The problem was every young adult in Port Talbot became linked with these 3 letters and every crime, we were soon blamed for. We were just football lads nothing else and every Saturday we would look for an off. The home games in Cardiff were followed by a good drinking session in a well known pub called Brownhills, owned and run by the Author of this book Annis. We would then sometimes stop off in Bridgend on the way home from an away game and always end up in bother. We would go to the away games usually all crammed into a transit from Port Talbot, on the big ones we would join up with Neath and maybe have a coach. In the transit we would have a right laugh, setting off really early, plenty of beer, Huey at the wheel, trying to keep his eye on the road, while there was mayhem in the back, it was the good old days. I bet every lad up and down the country remembers those days.

There were some great days with The Soul Crew from Cardiff, we would sometimes go on their coaches to places like Blackpool, Peterborough, Rotherham and the famous Tranmere trip then on to Blackpool. We made some really good mates with lads from all over and the friendships are still strong today. The Ely Trendies, Barry lads, Docks boys, Taff's Well lads, Bangor and North Wales lads they were all the same as us, up for it.

ENFIELD FACUP 1988 Away (SPURS)

Recalling the FACup game away to Enfield on a rainy Sunday, boy I miss those trips, still to this day. On the Saturday I hired the transit, how I ever got it, after the state, we use to return them in, is a puzzle, always full of used cans, fag ends and the old mattress in the back, for this trip to London the same old faces were up for it. Huey, Vince, Taffy Anton, Stavvy, Webber (only just turned 16 at the time, but would always be game for it, sadly no longer with us RIP), Steve, Nigel, Kenny, Aidan, the Charles brothers, and a few others, about 15 of us in total. Small in numbers, but they were all up for it, no fear whatsoever.
We all thought no doubt one of the London firms will show, it might be little Enfield, but that's where the surprises usually happen. We did think it will probably be SPURS and with them in mind, the idea of getting tooled up came about. One of the lads worked where they made windows and so he got small iron bars, about 18 inches thick, just in case it came totally on top.

We got to London and then headed to North London, we got to Enfield and Cardiff had a fair old following there already. After parking up in some terraced street, all of us did the usual thing and meet all the lads who had travelled up. Once in the ground, the usual heavy police were present and, not much really happened. We all decided at the end of the game we would all go off on our own, and would probably bump into SPURS, if they have bothered to show up. As soon as the final whistle went and with a 4-1 win behind us, we were off and got back in our van and sat there for a while, we watched the train mob being escorted and finally the old bill were gone as well.

We then drove off, but within a min or so we spotted about 20 lads in a side street, this was our chance we all said. We parked up in the next street, but no sooner had we parked the mob had noticed us, the only problem now was the mob had grown to about 50 odd lads. We were already out of the van and out numbered yes but there was no way back now, so we just stood in the middle of the street, waiting for the now charging mob, who were heading straight at us, it went into the usual toe to toe. But soon they were waiving Stanley's at us, they were shouting "Yids Yids" and were really going to fuck us. One of our lads managed to open the van door and got our bars out, oh no ,could you believe it, the old bill turn up in mass at our end and Spurs fuck off, leaving us by the van. We couldn't believe it, we had just held out against such numbers and were just about to defend ourselves and were nicked.

All handcuffed there and then, I think about 12 got nabbed, given the usual few head slaps like they use to in those days and off we were to the local police station. Webber was taken on his own (juvenile), the rest of us were kept in a room together, over the next hour, we must have had at least a dozen police look in at us. Then each one of us were lead out, myself like 7 others were released on to the streets of London, while the others were kept and charged including the driver.

We had to dash across London to make the last train home. The others were eventually let go and were back up in court on the Tuesday. It looked like they charged whoever's face didn't fit or they disliked. That's the only thing we could think off.

In court Stavvy said that the bars were all in there, as he was making rabbit hutches for his sister, that statement made the evening Standard. The following home game, we were all slated in the match programme for the trouble, they said it marred the day ant that the club had nothing to do with this extra match entertainment. The fact remains in my opinion, 90% of the fans in that ground that day were lads.

A few weeks later, a well known Spurs lad from Port Talbot invited 2 of the lads on a Spurs coach to Bradford away in the cup. They were all of Spurs lads and guess what on the coach were the lads we had it with in Enfield. On this trip they said to our lad's fair play, your lads stood against us when you were totally outnumbered. Our 2 lads were well looked after by them, that's why being a lad at football is a funny old game. As one min you want to batter each other, next week you're drinking together.

WALES 1989 (Germany away)

I loved these days, even though the team was doing shit , a bit like our club side, and with Neath Punk(Simon) by your side, you were always guaranteed a great, mad day and a good laugh with it. In 1988, I made my first trip away with Wales and from then I was hooked. The 1989 Wales game in Germany will always stand out in my mind, running the Germans full on and no Jacks with Wales. Seeing the Bangor lads throwing Harley Davidson's into the Rhine, our base was in Amsterdam and on the day we just caught the train in. I would say Wales had a top firm that day one of the best I've seen at an away game with Wales.

The JACKS

Getting back to our neighbours, the Jacks of course everyone knows theres no love lost between us, but, we would have at least some respect for them if they were more truthful, about the 80s and 90s. They found it a hard enough battle just fighting Port Talbot and Neath lads, so how they ever thought they could do Cardiff on the whole, when Cardiff had ten times as many lads as them. Don't get me wrong our firm from this area has taken some beatings from them and vice versa, but like I say that's us, not Cardiff as a whole. I will tell a couple of tales of us and them and honest accounts, no bull shit.

In and around March 1987, I was aged 19, 16 of us went over to Jackland on a Saturday when Cardiff didn't have a game, at that time we had no worries, nerves etc, when I think about it now it was suicidal, even today our lads laugh about it, when we talk about it, Taffy Anton, Clunis , Stavvy and some others arrived in SWANSEA around 2.45pm.We made our way down the high street, after already being clocked at the train station when we had got off, so there was no going back now. The Jacks were playing home and word had spread all the way down to the Vetch. We were now down the Quadrant, which is famous for where they hang out, about 30 odd Jacks were there, the same ones who we regularly have trouble with either on our own turf or in Neath during the nights. Crazy how it seems now ,but as soon as we saw them we ran straight at them, everyone a mirror image of each other, and yes we ran them back into their own shopping centre. This was happening on a sunny spring Saturday afternoon and in full view of all the Swansea shoppers. We then hung around for a while, until we heard sirens and then went back via all the side streets to avoid being arrested.

Back at the train station we all stood outside, waiting to see if they would come back, we were wishing if only our other lads back home had been here today to witness this. As we were going into the foyer of the train station one of our lads looked back and said there here, not thinking myself and the others went straight back outside only to see the road totally full of them ,it looked like half the North Bank had left the ground to come and find us. We were now in the middle of the station car park and were virtually surrounded by all sides, we had to show bottle, so we called the ones on at the front, we slowly moved towards them knowing we had no chance. Punches were thrown between the front line of them and us, then I was hit straight into the side of the face, by a temp bus stop sign , by now we had being going totally backwards and were being attacked by a load angry wolves from all sides now, this was vicious. We were still trying to fight back, but were knackered and relieved to hear sirens once again. The old bill came from every where, to our relief. The Jacks were gone and all that was left was us and the old bill, we quickly went to board our train back to Port Talbot. The old bill must have been pissed off with us by now. We were on our train and we couldn't believe the old bill had gone on to another platform and were checking another train out, carriage by carriage, we spread out on ours , not to look like we were on this one, we spread out amongst the normal passengers.

The train left and all we could think about was, that we had held our own and gone down to their area on a match day, kicked some arse and then stood and took what they had to offer in such numbers. We had once again gone down to our local enemy and had a good day's entertainment and now we were going to hit the pubs in Port Talbot and enjoy the evening thinking about them.

We had many battles with them over the years, Mumbles road, the swim away incident, we have been hurt by them, but always out numbered and we've held our own. They have never come into Port Talbot's drinking area and tried to take us on, in our own backyard.

LIEGE 1993 (away) "THE NIGHTMARE".

After a nightmare trip the year before to Vienna to Watch City in ECW Cup, we had stayed 7 hours away in the Tryol, then on a coach trip full of pensioners etc So we decided to go this time with the rest of the lads on the ferry as we knew City would take loads .
Leaving Port Talbot on the Monday late afternoon, myself Phil, Thugsy, and Darren were going to meet the rest of the lads up in Victoria (London), so they set off earlier in the day to have a few drinks in Cardiff. Those lads being Neath Punk (Simon), Huey, Tongy, Palmer and a few other older lads from Llanelli. We met up with these lads in the Shakespeare pub just outside of Victoria station before boarding the train to Dover. Palmer already seemed on his way to being pissed, something which would play a major part in the tale later on .The train was packed and everyone was looking forward to this trip .At Dover we met up with Kevin -Bangor and Ger who had been drinking in Dover all day.

Everyone carried on drinking throughout the crossing and once arriving on foreign soil, everyone was carrying some mighty hangovers. Ger had pulled a girl on her way to visit her boyfriend in a Belgian prison for drugs, so Kev stayed with us to look for accommodation etc. Once we arrived in Liege after another train journey , we all split up with the intention of finding digs for 2 nights, soon found digs ,after a short taxi ride just outside the city ,chucked our bags in ,showered then we were back out .Myself, Kev and a few others found a small Belgian pub, where all of us and the owner sampled all the local beers and what a landlord he turned out to be, as he later drove us to the City Centre, whilst no doubt like us with a merry head, all of us cramped into his car {7 in a 5 sweater }.

All the City lads had gathered outside a small bar opposite the train station, nearby we settled down for a few drinks, where we bumped into Palmer, who was on his own. After the other Port Talbot lads had gone just over the border to Holland to get a few hours of the local coffee shops etc .Therefore Palmer hung around with us all afternoon.

Early evening outside the train station there was a lot of stories going around that there had already been some trouble during the day with their mob -HELL SIDE...Soon this mob began to gather not so far away from the pub where the majority of City had gathered .The Belgians looked the typical Belgian look of the day, shell suits, mullets etc.

Myself and a few others walked into the bar where there was a few of them who were drinking, when we entered there was a total silence from them .They knew we were City without a doubt, they continued to stare the other way .Shortly after leaving the bar a few plastic tables and chairs were being thrown threw the entrance to the bar. Then the Belgians just started giving the usual 'come on 'behind the windows of the Bar which eventually got put threw by us.

We returned to the original pub opposite the train station ,which was packed full of City including the Neath lads and where by now Palmer was very much worse for wear and because of his Love of the whole punk scene stood out from the rest of the City mob . Suddenly threw the doors came the local cavalry all padded up and most looked like they had a love of the local steroids -euro robo cops .A few of us were dragged outside, and then they grabbed Palmer for no reason .the only thing he had done all day was drink like a fish .Seeing this I decided to have a few 'words 'with this local old bill. After the short distance walk from our seats to the other end where Palmer was now under cuffs, I started to try and explain to them that he had done nothing wrong etc. With a very sly side whack from a baton wielding steroid spotty twat to the side of my head, I was dragged outside and handcuffed to a waiting van where a line of muzzled police dogs were stood. They were stood guarding the doors of the police vans .The van was already full of Cardiff lads, some trying to get rid of their powder etc from their back pockets and one youngster getting stressed out, as this was his first time he had ever been arrested .Inside the pub you could see Neath punk etc really giving the police a hard time .Wish full thinking by me as I just thought we would just get deported in the morning just like others from Belgian 3 years earlier with Wales in Brussels.

We were driven at a fairly high speed through Liege, we were then met at the Police station by a line of baton wielding police, with each City lad then being dragged out of the van and then beaten as they made their way through this police 'tunnel'. Myself and Palmer were to be the last out and we seemed to receive the best, till last, we had a right pasting. Then we were placed face down on a stone cold floor and threatened to be hosed down if we did not shut up from the abuse. Some how we were separated from the others, there was around 9 of us in total, then they decided to put us in a cage, no blanket nothing. As you can expect we had to piss in this cage as well. ..

What must have been the early hours by now, we were soon to meet our local friends the Police from South Wales. Mr Jeff Richards and a WPC .asked us the usual questions got ticket for the game etc ,we were then made to sign some forms, , (stupid thing to do) ,but we just thought we would be deported at the worst.

With a massive headache and a severe black eye from the baton the night before myself Palmer and a guy from Barry (hedgehog) were now being taken to what we were told was the local court. My mouth was so dry as we did not receive a drink at all, but just kept in tiny cells where you could only stand or sit (like you see in those prison of war camps in the 40s). There we were kept for around 6 hours before finally seeing the local judge who would decide the next step of our lives. But this turned out to be a pointless exercise as there was no translator, from what we could gather he was saying etc.

They then forced us to sign more forms without an explanation, they kept pointing sign here, sign here, we thought the Judge might be letting us out. Around about 5 o'clock all 3 of us were put into another van which also included a few locals .It was at this time we found out, there was no homeward bound journey for us, but a stay in the local jail -LANTIN {about 30 minutes from Liege). All 3 of us said to each other whatever happens we must stick together .I Must admit this was the first time I had a feeling of true fear without the buzz .Finally there we were put in a holding cell and then one by one we were asked to strip and change into the clothes of our Belgian friends .Blue shirt, grey track bottoms with a thick blue strip down the leg ,not something which you could get in Woodies at the time .Once all 3 of us had seen the doctor ,Palmer told him he was an addict as he knew the medication for this would make him sleep ,Mark and I knew nothing about this scam as this was our first time inside .Palmer had done a small bit of time regarding non payments of fines or something like that.

We were then placed in a lift to what was the 4th floor we arrived on .The centre of the floor was the control room and on either side of the corridors were our cells .At the time all the prisoners were out in the corridors and the sight of us drew them to the cage which separated them and us .Fuck me all this was becoming a night mare of night mares, I would rather face a hundred Jacks on my own than stay in here.

Mark was taken to one side and myself and Palmer were taken to the opposite corridor, at least I would not be sharing with these Belgian twats, I thought to myself, but we both feared a bit for Mark . We were then placed straight into a cell, there were continual stares through the small cell window (size of a letter box). .The night was one of my longest, just getting used to the sounds and noises as well as the smell .Toilet in the cell had no screen, not until our 2nd week, no razors -fear of suicide etc .But there was pen and paper with 2 stamps .So I started to put pen to paper and write home.

Next morning was the start of the beginning of the usual shit ,first hassle of the screws ,then we had to meet the governor .We did not have a clue what he said to us, but he looked a horrible little twat .During the day I somehow managed to have a chance to use a phone and I phoned a mate from Port Talbot who then told me that, we had been on both the national news and the local .Front page of the western mail and evening post .Shit I thought ,my parents must be worried sick .Later I found out ,they had been told firstly by the press who had been going around the local pubs i.e. Sker pub for a story etc ,Thankfully a friend of mine Lyndi who used to work in one of the pubs and was a Cardiff steward and he told them where to go . I will always be grateful to him for this, as there were plenty of locals who would have slagged both of us off.

The days just continued not knowing what was going to happen. Overall we went to court around 7 times, that was the only time we were let out of our cell, Then we finally got let out of the cell after around 2 weeks, for a bit of exercise in the yard, where we played football something which Palmer took a little bit too far with his tackles etc .No way would we make any friends in this place. The 3 of us would share our cigarettes and we always looked out for each other .The trips to court were a long day, with the screws always looking for us to return their little digs or kicks, whilst being led down to the holding cell before boarding the van to court. We got assigned a free lawyer but she must have been younger than us ,and could hardly speak English. Each time we would return from court and we would be a bit more down, without knowing anything about a trial date or release date .

I soon started getting letters from both family and friends, friends sent City posters and poppies for us to wear .We wore these poppies just to prove that we were all proud of who we were ,Welsh and City . We started to get stronger and believing there had to be an end to this. We joked about an escape plan and I read a book about Colditz .Crazy ideas I know, but it broke up the boredom etc .Strange book though to have in English in the prison library, along with their French novels etc. The food wasn't too bad, steak, chips, meatballs but some how we were always last to be served and always on Wednesday and Saturdays the last for the showers .They were always playing mind games with us, our cell being turned over around 4 in the mornings for a search .I Wrote on our cell the amount of days I had been here and I decorated it as well with City and Wales, small flags etc -sent over, plus our own artwork .

After 4 weeks, and still here, we got a black and white TV which could receive BBC1 and MTV, we were landed, life looked up a bit .I remember watching songs of praise on a Sunday and being originally from the Rhondda it did bring a tear to my eye, crazy but true. .

Finally after around 6 weeks, we were told of a trial date and it would then be another 2 weeks after that, where we would receive a sentence .Pre trial, Palmer went to see the Lawyer on a visit to the jail, I could not be bothered any more, I thought what a waste of time, she had been shit so far. She told him with our charges we could receive 10 years i.e. AFFRAY, 3 ASSAULTS ON POLICE OFFICERS, CRIMINAL DAMAGE. Palmer also had a charge of holding a bottle with threats to use it .When he told me about this, I did shit myself a bit but promised myself if it did happen, we would only serve a third of that but I would learn French to improve our time . I had become tougher don't know why, you just go one way or the other. Each night he would receive his 'medication ' which sometimes he would save up for a big one the next night .Once he took the liquid he would be out cold till the next morning .I just would write letters or watch the TV .The thing which did help our release was that Arsenal drew Liege after they beat Cardiff. We were told they feared we would return with them and they still had this hang up about Heysel in the 80's with Liverpool, they really hated Brits in Belgium.

Finally after 8 weeks we got our sentence, me and Palmer got some form of conditional discharge and Mark had everything dropped , what a relief the night mare was finally over. It was then we all had a real buzz, time to go home after 8 weeks. We were given a free ticket (THANKS FOR NOTHING) to Dover and we were then told to get out of the country quickly. We all got drunk in Ostend and on the ferry, Palmer somehow managed to steal his trousers from jail and he changed into them on the ferry, not a wise thing to do....

Both with anger and the odd nightmare I will always remember this time. Neath punk was the first to phone me when I got back home and the other Port Talbot lads and North Wales lads I will always be thank full for their letters etc......Must admit it has calmed me down, so there was some positive out of it...... I kept the letters for a while but threw them out to try and put away the whole nightmare .The local press were shit ,trying to stir things up ,hassling my parents and their neighbours ....I Still try not to drink Stella etc because I hate those Belgian twats to this day ,but it has made me even more support the City ,great bunch of lads through out ,true friends.....

After Liege, I admit I took a back seat as such, it was a mind thing from a foreign prison, the rest of the lads continued going looking for it , including new younger lads Trev, Miffy, Petty, Webber (RIP) AND WITH Steve and Huey still making their mark. Today like many other older heads, I just look forward to the game instead. I cannot afford to throw away what I have now, a great wife Sharon and a nice life style. But the friendship remains strong and the memories of Brownhills, sleeping in the reception the night before an away game with about 20 other lads, those were the days... I'm still addicted to watching Wales and the City BLUEBIRDS.

City fans on rampage — 150 seized

Liege.
1993.

WESTERN MAIL 🌺

It's forthright, it's frank
It's a pile of old wank

By GREG SWIFT and JONATHAN CALVERT

MORE THAN 150 Cardiff City football fans were arrested by Belgian police last night after violent clashes with rival supporters in Liege.

The fans waged a number of pitched battles throughout the day in the run-up to Cardiff's first round European Cup-Winners Cup tie against Standard Liege at the Sclessin Stadium, which Cardiff lost 5-2.

Belgian police reported that more than 200 of Cardiff's travelling band of 1,000 fans — some armed with baseball bats and bottles — fought with locals in one incident outside a city bar.

Some of the rampaging Cardiff supporters were arrested

for smashing up a police car as the violence escalated.

Water cannon were mobilised and riot police were forced to escort hundreds of fans to the ground.

A police spokeswoman in Liege said that no one was seriously injured in the clashes, but she confirmed that 150 Cardiff supporters had been detained.

Yesterday's bursts of violence came less than 24 hours after nine Cardiff fans were arrested when 50 supporters clashed with

Belgians at a train station cafe causing damage estimated at £4,000. One fan is alleged to have been found with heroin.

Six were immediately deported, but three fans were being held in Belgium's Lantin prison last night.

Two were named by Belgian police as Stephen Palmer, aged 27, of Bywass Street, Margam, and Anthony Ridgeway, aged 25, of Groeswen Lane, Margam. The third was a 30-year-old from Barry. A judge will decide today whether to charge or release them.

Anthony Ridgeway's retired parents Lionel and Barbara said last night that their son was a fervent Cardiff City fan but had never been involved in any violence.

"Anthony has been unemployed for six weeks and he used up his savings to make the trip to Belgium," they said.

ENJOY THAT DID YOU, YAH LITTLE FUCKERS?

ABOVE PAPER CUTTING FROM
WEDNESDAY 15th SEPT 93 FROM
THE WESTERN MAIL, TELLING
A LOAD OF BULLSHIT OF HOW I
GOT ARRESTED IN LIEGE.

THE E
GOT H

Guff

Apex

Class	Ticket type	Adult	Child	
STD	APEX RETURN	ONE	NIL	OUT
	Date	Number		
	13·SEP·93A	77550 246663899W98		
From		Valid		Price
PORT TALBOT PAY		AS ADVERTISED		£24·00M
To		Route		
LONDON BRIT RAIL AP SLOUGH			1513	
Date 13/9	Train 1650	Coach/Seat Reserved 1 09 F		

adidas

Liege 93.

Chapter 19

A DAY IN EUROPE
By John Simmonds CCFC

I rang the General, as I usually call him, a bit of a joke between us, I remembered he had told me that he had taken his own coach to Standard Liege in Belgium in 1993, where as most of the lads I had gone with stayed over in Brussels for a night or two. So I asked him if he wanted to tell his tale of their events. I call Pam (his wife) his Lieutenant as in the 80's and 90's, Pam was probably more game than half the lads. Their two sons Lee and Jamaime have followed well in their foot steps and are well respected by the rest of Cardiff. Annis

Annis asked me if I wanted to tell my tale, I know Annis and many other lads went over there, in fact over 1,200 fans went including about 500 lads and they all probably have a tale to tell, as so much went on over there, especially in the town of Liege.

On the day of the game we all met up at a about 3am at the Forresters pub in Canton Cardiff, the game was a midweek night game in Belgium and we knew we had a long journey a head of us. So by 4am we were off, 50 Good lads, Beechie, Dolphy(RIP), Freddy(RIP), Ely Trendies, The Canton lads and of course my wife Pam and my two lads Lee and Jamaime who were only young teenagers then.

It was 2 o'clock in the afternoon by the time we arrived in Liege, some of the lads were well pissed up but not pissed enough to not want go to the first pub we saw, not far from the ground. We found a pub on a corner of the road to the ground and we made camp there. The lads gave the barmaids ayatollah t-shirts to wear and the banners with Cardiff City on were put straight up. There was no problems for the first couple of hours, everyone was having a smoke and a dozen or more beers, we had heard rumours that a couple of miles away in the town there had been some right battles, which we were to later hear about including over 200 Cardiff, had been deported. We were all as sound as a pound in our corner pub, no old bill and we even had the barmaids having a right laugh with us and they seemed to know their football. To top it all, some of the players who weren't playing on the night popped in, Nicky Richardson and Thomo.

Then a couple of locals started coming in, one had Hell Siders on his back, no one said anything at first, but then more piled in, including a couple who started on Tomo because he was black. Beechie came over to me and Pam and said you better get your boys out of here, but they wanted to go no where even though they were still teenagers. One of our lads then saw the double headed barmaids pass some knives to the Liege lads, that and the business with Tomo sent our lads to go steaming right into them. More and more came piling in, the next one who went past me had a full pint over his head, what a fucking waste. Eventually we were all battling outside and each side were given as good as they got, until the Soul Crew cry went up and we got that little extra go in us and had them going back towards the stadium.

Old bill came from every where loads and I mean loads, Liege made a stand then and as I went towards them I got punched in the head by a copper and he started chasing me with his baton, Pam was having none of that and she was soon steaming into him and whacking him, she hasn't half got a good right on her, it was fucking mad. This went all the way down the road into a big car park, where the Liege lads just seemed to Vanish. We walked all around the stadium looking for them, no such luck, just old bill who eventually had had enough and put all of us in the ground

By kick off all the lads except the two hundred who were deported were all telling there tales to us. In Brussels the night before Cardiff, had had a right off in the square with the local Turks, who pulled carving knives etc on them. Also last night in Liege, Cardiff had smashed The Hell Siders pub up and run about 40 of their lads out of their own pub. This afternoon the Docks Boys had fought the old bill for over an hour by the main train station and a water canon was eventually used to calm it down, Fucking hell every one had a story.

As to the match we got hammered 5-2, even though at first we were leading. It was totally peaceful in the ground, just Riot police facing us for the whole of the game.

There were no pubs open after the game and the old bill put hundreds of lads on buses and straight onto the trains and out of Belgium. We had a bit of an off on the bridge but the police soon had us on our bus and out of there. When Liege came to us they brought over a hundred lads but our owner Rick Wright put them all up for the day in his Barry Butlins camp for the day, so we never saw them till they were in the ground. Liege had Arsenal in the next round and I heard Liege made mince meat of them when Arsenal went over there. As to us we had the long journey home and we were going to Blackpool on Friday to see City play there on Saturday, another long journey for the Battle Bus.

Chapter 20

WEVE GOT RESPECT FOR EACH OTHER
By Danny PLYMOUTH(Central Element)

I've been to Plymouth probably a dozen times and you always know something will happen down there. Meeting Danny in Brussels was the first time I'd actually spoken to one of their lads before on a friendly basis, We were made welcome that day by Danny and his mate and talked about previous encounters, Danny has turned out to be a genuine and honest lad and there is respect from both sides. Annis

I'm Danny, born in Plymouth in 1977, now 30 years old. I have spent my whole life living in Plymouth. From the early age of 4. I soon had an affection for my local team and started attending every week. I have just finished my 3rd ban and been part of the scene in Plymouth for about 14 years. It was during the early 90's that I took an interest into what was happening off the pitch and by 1994 I started drinking with known local faces and attending home games with them.

I met Annis in Brussels during the Euro 2000 championships outside a pub in the main square. There were about 30 Plymouth lads in Belgium at the time but at this point it was just me and my mate Chris. I remember getting into conversation with a group of lads who turned out to be from Cardiff. Most clubs were represented and there were quite a few other small groups of Cardiff over there too. The ones we met were Annis, Dai Thomas, Mojo Flynny and another lad named Harvey, they had a Welsh flag up, with Cardiff City on . Through our previous encounters with Cardiff I had heard of Annis but never had a face to put to the name. We stayed together for much of what turned out to be an eventful day and ended up in the same military prison as a couple of them before being deported. We kept in slight contact after this and came across each other at a couple of Plymouth v Cardiff games since then. In October 2008 I contacted Annis and as we were chatting he asked me if I would be happy to give an account for his new book, I was happy to accept this request.

During the 1994 season, like I said, I started turning out for all the big home games and my first away game with the Element was at Exeter that season. One game that occurred that season was a home fixture with Cardiff. I have asked a very close friend of mine who has clear memories of that day and was a lot more active than me at the time to give the Plymouth account of what happened.

CARDIFF HOME 1994

My name is Nick and I have been part of the Central Element since its coming together in 1985 / 86 and after 23 years, several bans, arrests and subsequent penalties that go with it, I am still involved in the scene in Plymouth.

Back to February 1994, Cardiff City were the visitors along with members of their much talked about Soul Crew, who were highly regarded and respected within the football hooligan scene. There were no many mobile phones back then, but people who worked away from Plymouth and various lads in the know, made sure that our firm, The Central Element, were aware that we were expecting a visit. Cardiff always bring a mob to Plymouth and this day would certainly confirm this and cement our rivalry with them. We met early, as usual, and I remember being impressed with our numbers and "up for it" attitude. Our mob numbered about 150, made up of lads of all ages and we were spread between the Britannia Pub and the Social club across the road. These two venues were where we had been meeting since the days of drinking in the city centre had gone. They were very well sited due to the proximity of our ground, Home Park, and the fact that any visiting lads would always pass by them or near to them. Going between the 2 pubs and getting the info on Soul Crew sightings, led us to believe that they were in a city centre pub called the Noah's Ark and that they numbered about 40. The Noah's Ark pub use to be our main meeting place, what a pity we had not decided to go back and meet there on this occasion. A car full of our lads had agreed to drive down there and review the situation and let the Cardiff lads know where we were drinking and the best way to get there undetected. If our mob that was spread over the two pubs had tried to go into the city centre, old bill and cctv would have been all over us and it would have been game over. The car left but returned back to the pub no more than 15 minutes later. I remember seeing the car speed up to our pub and judging by the condition of it and lack of windows, we knew something had happened. The news went round that Cardiff were defiantly in the Noah's Ark pub and more so definitely up for it. It turned out that a few Cardiff were outside the pub having a drink as the car had pulled up, they clocked each other and within seconds the pub emptied and bottles and glasses were directed towards it.

I remember looking around our pub at this time and thinking all our main lads were out and even more up for it than ever. We needed to know when Cardiff were going to leave the city centre and start making there way towards the ground. A few of our lads were sent out scouting and made there way to the train station and some to the near by park ,all prepared to report back on any sightings. At 2pm, word went round that Cardiff were on their way and they had been sighted half way up Alma road, the main road to the ground, still with no police presence. At this stage Cardiff had two routes they could have taken, one was through the park, the other was directly to the pubs. Due to this, a mob of ours, about 30, made there way into the park and the other 120 stayed in the pubs incase they arrived there. Within minutes, I remember looking out the window and seeing Cardiff 200 yards away and steaming towards us in the pub. The shout goes up that they are here and things start to get serious. Bottles and glasses started flying from the pub into the nearing Cardiff mob and there was a slight stand off when we were about 50 yards apart. There was only about 2 / 3 coppers around and by the look on their faces they were not prepared to get involved until backup had arrived. At the front of our mob were some very game lads in their 30's and they went straight into the soul crew, who in return were steaming into us punching and kicking everything around. The traffic stopped and normal fans were staring at the brawl erupting around them, shouts of "keep it together" and smashing glass could be heard by all.

The first impressions of the Welsh were that they were certainly up for it and I mean every single one of them. Plymouth were now all around the group of soul crew and everyone were trading punches, the 40 visiting lads are doing very well bearing in mind they are heavily outnumbered and at one stage they are even backing us off. There were a number of bodies from both sides dropping to the floor but getting straight back up and into it again. The fighting just went on and on and I remember thinking that this was one of the best offs that I had ever witnessed or been involved in. All of a sudden both firms seem to split and a gap appears, give Cardiff there due they had us at full stretch. The shout goes up "We are Central Element" and at this point across the park came the 30 other Plymouth who had broken off before Cardiff had arrived. At this point we steamed straight back into them from one side and the 30 from another. Cardiff were now well and truly on the back foot. The old bill, who are still short of numbers were seen running around randomly hitting people with there bats. There had been lads getting out of cars in the traffic, leaving their kids and steaming in to have a go. Eventually, sirens in the distance could be heard approaching and both mobs backed off. Coppers pile out of riot vans on mass and within seconds the boys in blue are everywhere. Only a few lunatics from both sides are left fighting. Cardiff backed off into the park now as the old bill were pulling anyone they could get there hands on. Plymouth re grouped and tried one last attack but by this time it was game over. Fighting stopped and the verbal's started over the police lines. The Central Element mob, which now must have stood at about 200 lads certainly knew that they had been in a battle. Both mobs started to clap and applaud each other, a sign of respect, as they were escorted away. The police could not understand that mentality and they looked puzzled by this.

That was about it, we all made our way to the game. On reflection I would say that honours were even that afternoon. One of the other Soul Crew books tells their version of the incident and now we have had the opportunity to tell ours. A number of lads from both sides had been arrested that afternoon, and when the Cardiff lads came back to Plymouth for court hearings, a few of our lads turned up and took them out for a drink as a sign of respect. Cheers Cardiff, a top row and one that is still talked about amongst older heads to this day. Nick

The following season came my first proper experience at football, the eye opener, the game that will stay with you forever and it just happened to be the return fixture, away at Cardiff. Although certain points of the day stand out, and probably will do for many years to come, many parts of the day are still a blur. After speaking with some of our other lads and finding that there memories of the day were slightly clearer, I felt it was better to once again ask one of them to give their account.

CARDIFF AWAY 1996

Cardiff has always been one of my top games. For some reason there's always been a mutual respect between the two of us. For a start after Bristol City, even though its about a 300 mile round trip, geographically they've usually been the nearest team to us with a firm worth bothering about. Exeter City can bang on all they like, but they've never been up to anything so far as I've ever made out, and as for Torquay, well.......

Another thing with Cardiff, which they have similar with us, is that they make an effort. Like us, we get somewhere, usually without getting picked up and then have a scout around. It always amazes me when lads make the effort to go somewhere and then just sit in a pub until the police turn up. We've never been like that and neither have Cardiff. So I think another reason we rate each other is that we do what we can to make something happen. Although in the last 5 – 6 years its got harder with camera's and informants.

I've met a few of their lads over the years and they're pretty good. One thing that has pissed me off slightly though is the way in their books they've put a couple of meetings with us across, so its nice to be asked about a trip we made up to them to get the story from our point of view.

One of my favourite trips there was in 1996. We took 2 vans up, so around 30 of us, and got there a couple of hours before the kick off. Old Bill were there but we parked up and had a plan to get in the Ninian Park pub. The Ninian's not their main boozer, their firm tend to drink in the city centre or Canton, its where their shirts and scarfers go and the odd lad having a beer before the game, but it's the nearest pub to the ground. The plan was to get in there, have a few beers, and get something on when they made it down that way to the game. Though most people know that Cardiff have got more than their share of civvies who'll have a row when it comes to it, and the pub had plenty of likely opponents if it went off.

What's quite funny about this is that back then hardly anybody had mobiles, so we were going off instinct and things that we'd learnt and remembered from going up there before.

Anyway, after being there for a while, a few Soul Crew wandered in. One of them blatantly stands there counting heads, while the other 2 are just basically there as back up.

I remember one of our lads, (DK), ask who the fuck they were. "Soul Crew mate. Is this all you've brought?" DK looked at me, and I have to say I had to give these 3 respect, but anyway, DK took exception and gave him a tidy right hand and put him down.

Obviously it went off pretty quick. A lot of our lads got into having it with door staff and scarfers, and about 10 of us actually got outside. When we did we realised we weren't going to get a result. I've heard all sorts of estimates about how many they had up the road, but it was at least 80 – 100, maybe more. They were into us pretty quick. To be fair we were backing off right away. You hear stories about 10 lads standing against that kind of number and giving it to them, and if you've been there and done that, fair enough, but I've never witnessed it working against quality opposition in 25 years of going to games.

In my opinion you do what you can to save a bit of face, but make sure you're fit enough to make a better show later in the day. During all the mayhem of flying bottles and kicks and punches, I'm sure both sides all stopped for a bit to let a mum get by with her pram, before it went off again. One of our boys, (SM), got knocked over by a car, (I don't know to this day if it was done on purpose or not).

Anyway, we backed off down the road and under the railway bridge, turning every now and then to exchange a couple of blows, and as I said, save a bit of face. It died off then, because you get to the corner and turn down to the ground and I think the fact that the police were about and realising what was happening, Cardiff made their way back to the Ninian, where it was still going off with the rest of our lads. To be honest I think the ones who got stuck in the pub came off worse than the ones who got out. We all have a laugh now about this because everyone's got their own version of events. My brother and a couple of other lads even ended up on the railway lines making their escape.

Anyway, we all got together again in the ground and we had a chat about what to do. It was agreed we couldn't just make our way home and pretend nothing had happened, so we did the old trick of leaving after the game, giving it 30 minutes and getting back into the town to hit one of their pubs.

We did a bit of checking and found out we'd lost a couple of our lads to the hospital and the cells, but most of us were fine and up for a bit of revenge.

Back then, like I said earlier, you couldn't just call Lakey, or your "Soul Crew" contact number out of your mobile phonebook to find out where they were, so we decided to drive back into the city centre, get a lad to stick his head in the pub doors and see if any Cardiff were in.

We found one pretty quick, so we drove the vans down a street behind the pub, left 2 lads in the driving seat with the doors left open, and went to work!

Basically we just did as you'd expect. Straight through the front doors and into whoever was there. It was just one of those mad few minutes of high jinks. Punches thrown, tables and chairs turned over, a few glasses and bottles flying around. It was just a quick in and out, to let them know we weren't just taking what had happened earlier. We also take a lot of pride in putting one over on the police. There they are with all their "intelligence", manpower and resources, and we've still had 2 good offs without them anywhere to be seen!

Anyway, you know when its like that, and in a major city centre high street, that it can't carry on too long, or those blue lights and resources are going to turn up. So we start to make it back to the vans, and get out of there, job done!

Everyone piles into the vans, and we start to head out of town. We're all laughing and buzzing with the adrenaline and feeling that we've done a nice job, then suddenly the van in front pulled over and they're waving us in.

DK got out of the front van and makes his way back to ours. "Is PO on your van?" Quick checks reveal he's not. Obviously we've got to go back and see if he's around and make sure he's ok.

We turned around and drove to a car park which was close enough to the pub we'd just hit, so that a few of us could walk down and see if P was around.
Me, my brother J, a friend SH, (who some of Cardiff know as Pinky) and a couple others walked a couple hundred yards down a sort of narrow back street, which brought us out more or less opposite the pub. Unfortunately, during this last 10 - 20 minutes, Cardiff have had time to get the message out about what had happened, and they're mobbing up around the pub. We had a quick look about to see if we could see P anywhere. He wasn't, and in the meantime we got spotted by a few of their lads.

We started to walk back up the street to the car park, but pretty soon these few lads had put it about that we were back, and their firm are coming after us.

To be fair to them, it was nowhere near as many as they'd had earlier, probably around 30 to 40 lads. I told J, my younger brother to run on and get the lads ready, and to get the vans out of the car park. My feeling was that this was a pretty fair potential row. The   numbers were near enough the same, the big problem was confusion.

Most of ours were sat in, or stood around the vans, just having a can or smoking a fag, chatting about whatever, and I just think that when J raced around the corner and starts barking instructions the message got lost. Instead of just the drivers getting the vans moved, and the rest of us getting into them, everyone starts getting into the vans.

If we could have just got back down the street it would have been a good toe to toe. Even if we were a bit outnumbered the street was narrow enough that it wouldn't have made a difference. But it didn't happen, and it was the one part of the day when I think we let ourselves down.

Within seconds Soul Crew were on the scene. The car park was on loose stony ground. A couple of us did try to make a go of it. I threw a few punches, caught a few back, and managed to get away up the road. The lads in the vans, tried to drive out of the car park the wrong way, so had to turn around and come back past their firm. By now they were all tooled up with rocks and stones, and as the vans came past they let loose. Every single side window and back window on both vans was put through. The drivers just had to keep their foot down and get away. Apparently it was a bit mad, although everyone says they remember laughing as they raced off down the road. There were a few cut up with flying glass, but nothing too serious.

I was stuck there now on my own. I decided to walk out of Cardiff on the main road so that if our lot came back I'd get spotted, but I didn't have to go far, because after a few minutes I saw them up ahead on the road.

Me and a couple others had not got into either van, so they'd stopped, thinking they'd have to come back again, and a police car had pulled over to see what was going on. Needless to say, when he clocked the lads, and the state of the vans he was calling for back-up. They sorted a couple of bikes and squad cars, and escorted us as far as the other side of the Severn Bridge to make sure we weren't coming back.

The 3 lads missing had all made their way to Cardiff station and got a train to Bristol and then on to Plymouth. It was good later, meeting up at home and finding out they were ok.

We had a couple of good moments on the way back. At one point we were in a traffic jam by Gordano Services near Bristol and a few Bristol City lads in a car asked what the fuck had happened. One of our main lads, PW, said, "We've been in Wales fighting the Welsh for England, where the fuck were you!" Even the City lads saw the funny side!

We all chipped the extra money in to cover the deposits on the vans and dropped them back at the rental place and went out for the Saturday night. On the Monday morning at about 8, I got a call, and get this shrieking voice down the line, "What happened to the vans???". "I don't *know," I said, "What's up?" "All the windows are smashed!!" came the reply. "Well they were ok when I left them there," I said, and hung up. I don't know if he believed me but he never bothered calling back.*

There's a story Lakey tells in the Soul Crew book about seeing us the following week in Manchester. A few of us went to the Oasis gig at Maine Road, and bumped into him and a few mates at Old Trafford earlier in the day, (I think United were at home to Forest). Anyway, Lakey's a fair guy, but in the book he says we thanked them for not using weapons. To put the record straight time has probably clouded his memory, because that wasn't said. What they had done was let a couple of our lads out of the Ninian when they could have hammered them, and we said Ta for that.

All in all though it was some more good memories of a day out in South Wales.

As the 90's came to an end our mob was losing numbers, many of the older lads had stopped going for one reason or another and a new generation was coming through. We might not have had the biggest numbers but the lads that were going could all be trusted. As a mob we would not only go to football together but we were drinking together on Saturday nights and you could feel a real bond. We also started going to more England games home and away because Plymouth Argyle were in the bottom division going nowhere. One trip I remember well was the away match at Cardiff in 2001, it was evidence that we might not have had many but we were all up for it and ready to keep the name of The Central Element firmly within the hooligan scene.

CARDIFF AWAY 2001

We all decided that the Cardiff game was a must. At first we had the usual "yeah I will come", off everyone but numbers dropped for one reason or another as the fixture came closer. So when the day arrived, and all we had was a 17 seater mini bus and 1 car, we knew we were set for an interesting day. Despite us only having 22 lads it was a good set of lads and we knew we could all rely on each other. One of the lads that came along, Les, I had only met him 8 hours before in a Plymouth nightclub. He seemed like a good lad who wanted to get involved in the scene and so he also travelled with us on the mini bus. Les turned out to be one of my very best friends and still is to this day.

The plan was to park the car and the van at Bristol Parkway Train Station and get the train in. The car arrived in Bristol probably 30 mins before the van. They phoned us to say they arrived and that they were going to wait on the platform for us. As we were coming into Bristol on the mini bus, we received another call from our 5 lads in the car. They were shouting down the phone "Hurry up, it's going off". It turned out that when the went on the platform where there was another mob already there, numbering about 25 - 30, sly as they were they turned on our lads. Its believed they were Rovers waiting for a train to arrive, cant remember who they were playing that day. Our van arrived just as this 30 were jumping in cabs but that did not stop us chasing off a few tail enders. You could tell by the look on their faces they were not expecting us 17 to turn up. The van had been parked next to a skip full of bricks, metal poles and wood and so you could imagine the array of weapons we had. Fancy 30 lads turning on 5, no one likes bullies. It was then decided that rather than hang around the train station, where the old bill were likely to turn up at any minute, we would get out of Bristol as fast as we could and cross the bridge to Wales by road.

We took the mini bus straight into Cardiff and went for a drink in an area called Tiger bay. This is were we stayed until about 2.15. We were getting calls from some of the Cardiff lads asking where we were but due to the lack of numbers we were in no position to be marching around the city centre. Not only were they saying they had hundreds out but there numbers were boosted by about 10 of Aston Villas lads including Steven Fowler. We parked the mini bus and car just behind the main car park and then the 22 of us made the walk to the ground. As we were getting nearer to the turnstiles we could see large numbers of Cardiff queuing to get into the ground. They were probably numbering 100 if you added them all up but on top of that were unknown numbers of Welsh who might not be lads but hate the English and are happy to take you on. We made the decision that we were not going to sneak into the ground unseen and so we steamed straight into them. To be fair they never seen us coming and a few Cardiff were floored before they even knew what was going on. Its what you might call the Element of Surprise. Before they could re group and come back at us, the old bill turned up and surrounded us with horses, dogs and riot shields. Cardiff were appearing from everywhere as our unannounced visit spread around. My banning order file, suggest that 300 - 500 known Cardiff hooligans were congregated in the area. The old bill put us straight into the away end. Although heavily out numbered, our attack on them was not taken well and you could feel the hostile atmosphere coming from the stand on the left throughout the game. I cant remember much of the game as we were all a bit intoxicated but I can remember various objects being thrown at our stand by Cardiff supporters. I think its funny how the stewards looked to scared to even ask them to stop.

About 70 mins into the game a Welsh copper with a fair few stripes on his arms congregated our 22 lads. He explained that if we did not leave the game now, they could not guarantee our safety, or our vehicles. Half the lads told him to fuck off and no matter what, we were staying to the end and we would deal with the consequences. The other half had more realistic thoughts and were happy to leave. I remember the coppers telling a few of us that what had happened before the game was seen as a piss take by a lot of people, your not talking about a group of 50 or 60, we are talking hundreds if not a thousand. In the end as the game neared its end we were forcefully removed by the police to the disappointment of some and the relief of others. As they escorted us across the car park half the fucking home stand must had tried leaving as well. I remember seeing the riot police fighting back Cardiff lads at three separate exit gates, once again my banning order suggested they had 500. That was it for our day, on the vans and a police escort back to England. It was a different experience to my first visit but could quite easily have turned out differently. I imagine many other mobs of 20 would have taken the easy option and kept their heads down, at least we made our stand. They day ended with a trip to Dawlish where we were greeted by some of our rivals from Exeter and members of the Dawlish rugby team, another interesting event.

From 2001 the team started picking up results on the pitch and the numbers of lads regularly attending home and away games started to swell quite heavily. We had achieved promotion and as we started climbing the leagues the fixtures became more interesting. During the 2002 / 03 season it was once again decided that Cardiff away was a must.

CARDIFF AWAY 2003

It was a Friday night game and we decide to make a show for this. It turned out to be Cardiff's next home game following the visit they had from Barnsley. After our previous poor turnout of 22 lads we managed to book and fill a 52 seater coach, add to that some cars and a few on the train and we managed to number 70. Not bad for a Friday night, if it had been a Saturday you could have added another 30 - 50 to this number. We decided to do what we had planned on our previous trip which was to park in Bristol and get the train to Cardiff central. We were greeted in Bristol Temple Meads train station by a couple of CSF who we reckon were scouting for Cardiff. They also promised us a reception on our return later that night. We boarded the train and got off at Newport for a drink whilst we waited for a couple more of ours to arrive. The drink was flowing around the pub nicely and add to that most lads on the sniff, there was a good positive vibe coming from within the group.

The train we took eventually arrived in Cardiff Central at about 4pm. We had the usual welcoming committee from the Police but they seemed to just let us go where we want. We came out the station and headed straight towards the Prince of Wales Pub. It was a busy Friday afternoon and there was a busy feel to the main street. All eyes were on us from the general public as a group of 70 males walking around is not the norm. We still had some old bill with us but not many. As we approached the Prince of Wales we saw a few lads stood outside on the phones and all the lads at the front of our mob steamed right in. The lads at the door went back into the pub before any punches were exchanged and the law managed to put a line between us. Then no more than a handful of Cardiff attacked our mob from the rear, the lads at the back of our mob turned round and a small ruck took place. A couple of ours got nicked and a few on each side took slaps but nothing to much. We then had the usual bubble from the police to contain us. To be honest I though Cardiff would have made more of an effort to come out the pub, we were told they had 40 in there but fair play to the 5 who attacked on their own at the rear. Whilst in the police bubble I remember looking around and just feeling a hate from all the locals. Not just lads but everyone. There were lads on a building site opposite giving it the big one, taxi drivers, even some of the police. You certainly got the feeling that we were not welcome.

The police quickly escorted us to an area adjacent to the railway station car park where we were held for what seemed like ages. It was still three and a half hours before kick off. We were kept there for an hour or so before being escorted to the ground. It's a fair walk to the ground but even still, we arrived about 2 hours before kick off, we were the only one's in the ground which was a bit weird. I normally get to the games a minute or two before they start, not 120 minutes. As the ground started to fill up the usual atmosphere started to form from the stands on both our left and right. It was obvious that Cardiff were not happy with what we had done earlier in the day. I also imagine that there was a bit of a bad taste left in them from the recent visit of Barnsley just a fortnight before.

After the game we were kept behind for about 30 mins, for what we were told was our own safety. We attempted to break through the barriers a couple of times but to no success, just a few sore heads from police batons. You could see all the riot police and hear all the sirens outside of the ground so it was clear Cardiff were up to something. After 30 mins we did eventually get let out but all the streets seemed pretty quiet. However there was still a lot of sirens going on in the distance, you got the feeling that Cardiff were keeping the police very occupied not to far away. We were taken back to Cardiff Central where a specially organised train had been organised for us. There was a little skirmish with a few Cardiff in the station which led to 4 of ours being arrested. That was it, back to Bristol, where the CSF reception failed to materialise, and then back on the coach to Plymouth.

Most games with Cardiff always attract large mobs from both sides. Another game that stood out was our home fixture during the 2003 / 2004 season.

CARDIFF HOME 2003

I remember Cardiff bringing good numbers for a Tuesday night. Before the game we had met in a pub and we were numbering about 80 and as we made our way to the ground. On the way we had a couple of skirmishes with the law but turned up in the ground without seeing many Cardiff. As it happened Cardiff were being escorted in last minute by the police to avoid trouble. A few of us managed to get out the ground and had a small battle with them on the grass by the mayflower end. Our mob of 15 - 20 was mainly younger lads and there mob that just got off a coach numbered about 40. Hands up, they backed us off before the law ran in and separated it. Shame the bulk of our mob could not get out of the ground as this would have made things much fairer. After this there seemed to be lots of fighting between twos' and three's all over the place. It was fairly dark at the time and know one seemed to know who was who as everyone had split up. I heard afterwards of a couple of incidents where Plymouth lads had mistaken each other for Cardiff and ended up fighting.

After the game we had numbers of 200+ but the old bill had this well under control. Both mobs were kept apart by one off the heaviest police presence I have ever witnessed.

I was going to leave the story at this point but me and a few of the other lads have just seen an account of a Cardiff v Plymouth game in the "Diary of the Real Soul Crew" book. It describes a very recent incident that occurred in Plymouth during the 2007/08 season. Some of the lads that were there just wanted to give their opinion on what happened that day. As this incident occurred within the last 12 months names are going to be disguised. Also it has just been found out that one of the young lads who had been getting more and more active was a paid informer for the law and so we just need to be a bit careful. Here is Mr S to tell you about the incident as he seen it.

CARDIFF HOME 2007

One of my best mates had just been found dead the week before and so we had a wake in "Jumping Jacks", a pub we use in the city centre. The lad was a really close friend, we use to travel around the country doing unlicensed boxing together. Because of his death and the fact we were playing Cardiff we had a good 120+ older lads out. We had a couple of phone calls from Cardiff telling us they were in different pubs in the town centre but both times turned out to be false when our scouts turned up. I have personally had a couple of incidents with Cardiff over the years and always found them to be game and always have good numbers. However the problem in Plymouth now is the old bill are so on top, nearly every one of them has a hand held camera and you don't even have to do much to get a banning order.

Anyway my mate got a call just before 2pm to say there were a mob of Cardiff lads in a pub on the outskirts of the city, in Plympton. Plympton is one of the nicer suburbs about 6 miles from the town centre, although there would be limited police and cctv there. A few of the lads were up for getting a couple car loads to drive out and have a look. Mr "G" asked me if I fancied it, at first I said no as I was not prepared to waste anymore time looking round for them but the game was still an hour or so away and so 5 of us drove up in a car. We had the rest of the pub on standby, outside of the pub is a large taxi rank and so transport would be easy for them if they were called upon.

It takes about 15 mins to get there and we went to the Lord Louis pub, this is where we were told they were drinking. 1 of the lads went inside, surprise surprise, no one there. We called the Plymouth lad who was in contact with Cardiff to find out what was going on. The message came back that they were defiantly in Plympton but were not sure which pub they were in, so we went for a drive all around. Just as we were about to give up Mr "D" said there was one last pub to check. As we drove past it we seen loads of lads on the front patio leaning over the railings dressed in the usual CP, Stone Island etc. I thought to myself, that's Cardiff and there is not one copper to be seen. We got straight onto the phone to call the lads back in the city centre telling them to come up in taxis. We parked the car up about half a mile away and thought by the time we walk back the taxis should be arriving. Mr "G" was eager to get into them a bit quick and we found ourselves getting nearer and nearer to them. I called the others up to see how long they would be but they said as they started leaving the pub, the old bill had sealed it off and would not let anyone in or out the pub. It seemed they knew something was up as everyone went to leave. At this time we knew it was up to us 5 and we were now just 50 yards from the pub. One of the Cardiff lads clocked us and ran back into the pub to get the others. We agreed that we were likely to get done because they out numbered us and so just to steam into them as we had nothing to lose. So that was it, 4 of us in our 30's and a youth lad walked up to the pub and what seemed like loads of Cardiff spilled out. I think they thought we were going to back off but we kept walking towards them. We noticed that it was a younger mob, mainly early 20's. What must have been there main lad walked towards me, I asked him "How many you got?" He replied "14, how many more you got coming?" I said "This is it" and banged him right on the jaw with a left hook, knocked him right down and out. The other Cardiff seemed stunned at first and stood off for a moment. We took advantage of this and Mr "G" shouted "Come on you welsh cunts" and we steamed right in. With that the Cardiff lads started lobbing bottles, glasses, ash trays, whatever they could get there hands on. A bottle smashed against the side of Mr "D"'s head and cut him open from his check to his ear, he was furious and covered in blood went back in for more. Mr "G" ran into a small group of them knocking a few of them off balance but took a bottle in the back of the neck for it. Mr O grabbed one of the group and stuck him on his ass with a nut.

The main lad who I had hit first was still out for the count, at no stage did it cross any of our minds to kick him when he was down, not our style. Punches and kicks were traded for a bit

149

longer and the whole thing just seemed to keep going on and on. If I have to be honest it was probably only a minute but that's a long time in a situation like this. The fighting started to spread out from the pub onto the main road. Another stand off occurred as the 5 of us grouped up and Cardiff were all around us. 2 of the 5 were covered in blood where they had been glassed but the other 3 of us were unmarked. Even now we started to go back into them, surely the 14 Cardiff must have thought fair play to them for keep coming at us. Not one of our lads had even hit the deck and that's a fact, a fair few of theirs had gone down. If at this point they had re grouped and steamed into us they would have probably battered us but they didn't. Instead one of them, said alright lads that's enough, old bill will be here any second, lets just all fuck off. So both groups backed off.

As we were making our way back to the car we thought Result, we were buzzing. I'm not saying we did them but we gave as good as we got, but when its 5 against 14 that's a result. I had a phone call the other day from Danny telling me that in the soul crew book one of the Cardiff lads gave his account of the incident. This lad said things like, Plymouth bit off more than they could chew and they were sent home with bruise egos. Come on lads, I have always had respect for Cardiff and you normally tell it as it is. If it was the other way round and it was 14 TCE against 5 Soul Crew we would hold our hands up to you and say fair play. We will call that one a stalemate, we are happy with that, Keep it real . Mr S.

That pretty much takes us up to date. Its November 2008 now and we have a game with Cardiff at home next week, I wonder if we will be reading about that day in a future book. All real lads from Plymouth have nothing but respect for Cardiff, on there day they can match anyone. I don't agree with any club being number one or having the biggest mob, but Cardiff they are certainly in with a group that can't be touched on their day. Danny

Chapter 21

At The New Den Millwall v Cardiff
By Chesea Pat (Pat Dolan)

Wednesday night December 9th 1998 (Auto windscreen shield cup 1st first round)

I remember when this draw came out of the hat, the first phone call I made was to Annis to confirm that Cardiff were going and the second was to Ginger Bob to invite me over.

I didn't need a second invite being a nosy cunt and the night game in a Mickey Mouse cup game at Millwall had all the ingredients of a messy and ugly night out. Anyway over at Millwall there was a bit of a slow turnout at the meet probably 50 or 60 grizzlies in the bar. The mobile phones were soon going and the story was that Cardiff were at the Elephant and Castle.

Gregor (QPR) who was guesting, jumped in a car to go and have a look with some bushwakers. He rang back and said "you wont believe it, but they've started to walk down the Old Kent Road about 100-150 handed with no escort". The atmosphere completely changed and the talks was how are we going to get to the Old Kent Road to meet our Welsh Counterparts. Vans and cars were mentioned and as the wheels were put in motion another call had come through saying that Cardiff had cut off the Old Kent Road and were heading back to London Bridge. Apparently they had been arguing, that no one knew where they were going and they would probably miss the match if they got lost. Fair enough, I suppose and that is Cardiffs problem they should unite more and would then be probably the no1 firm in the country with their numbers.

Anyway about half an hour later someone runs in the pub and shouts "their coming off the station" with that the mob was now about 80, steams out and runs down towards the Cliftonville pub by the railway bridge leading up to the stadium. We all stood on the corner as the Cardiff escort turns the corner and heads towards us "BLUEBIRDS, BLUEBIRDS" chant the Welsh hooligans as they move towards us. "come on you Welsh cunts" as the Millwall charge across the road at the front of Cardiff's escort.Some Cardiff had got through the escort but the numbers were so small that got through, that they eased off when they saw the amount of Millwall that had filled the road.It was getting dark now and the street ahead looked a nasty sight of what I could see with two mobs baying for each other.

Fucking hell, Millwall were rabid to get at Cardiff and the old bill were really struggling to hold them back. One guy had got rugby tackled by two coppers and he was still crawling on his fucking hands and elbows towards the Taffs shouting threats, what a fucking head case!

As they marched under the railway bridge, Millwall charged the escort from behind with a deafening roar. Fair play Cardiff turned and fought back, some Cardiff picked up the police railings and threw them into Millwall. Cardiff went through the old bill and brought the fight to Millwall. Respect, the old bill were then smashing both firms knee caps with their steel batons and a police van drove between them. The old bill then did a charge and charged Cardiff down under the bridge, whilst a second lot of old bill lined the road to stop any Millwall following.

A bit later on I was stood with Terry, Ginger Bob's brother when what I can only describe as a two legged woolly mammoth came over for a chat, fuck me he looked like giant haystacks big brother. "well Terry, you got to give it to Cardiff, not many would come here for a nothing game in the night and come looking for it, lot more than Chelsea or West Ham would ever do" said the mammoth.

I glanced at Terry out of the corner of my eye to see a nasty smile playing on his face, "have you met Pat from Chelsea, he's one of their boys" (cheers Terry you cunt!) "oh sorry mate" said haystacks "I didn't know you were Chelsea", "thats alright bruv, don't worry about it" I said, Phew, to be honest that big cunt could have said Chelsea got battered by Orient and I wouldn't have said anything. Later Bob was laughing when Terry told him what happened. "what do you lot eat to get so big?" I asked Bob, "grilled West Ham fans with Chelsea sauce" shouted Terry across the pub. "That makes sense" I laughed.

Anyway during the game or during the second half a couple of Cardiff valleys had the bright idea to leave early obviously to get home. Bad fucking move. They were captured by a nasty mob of Millwall who came out of some houses as they walked past. Apparently the Taffy's were given a savage beating and one of the Millwall filmed it on his phone and texted it to a Cardiff lad in the ground to wind Cardiff up. Fucking sick or what?

I tell you what, and this is honest knowing Millwall the way I do, them Taffy's got off lightly. When it comes to things like that Millwall are fucking ruthless. They were really lucky they didn't get cut or fucking worse, end up brown bread.

I was in the area with Gypsy Ben, when Millwall rioted after the Brum game with the old bill. Trust me, when you've seen as many riots as I have, you know what your talking about. Seeing a police horse getting chased down the road with no one riding it showed me something. Millwall are absolutely radio rental.

By the way after the game was a non event, The old bill had the area well sewn up.

I would just like to make a friendly comment to some of the Cardiff lads, Your problem is that you have to much in fighting, if you were all as one you would no doubt be the NO1 Firm in Britain with your numbers. I came down to the launch of the 1st Diary of The Real Soul Crew, I was looked after second to none as usual. There was an amazing turnout over 700 lads, probably a Record attendance for a book launch, but I noticed the usual in fighting. This time it was over Swansea, putting a photo and a made up story about a lad called Christian as being mates with them in Milan ect. What a load of Bollocks in the years I've known Christian he is 100% Cardiff and a very game lad with it. How can you let your worst rivals put a split down the middle of your firm, thats exactly what they wanted to achieve. Now come on Cardiff be as one and you will be awesome.

Chapter 22

A NEWS PAPER REPORTERS VIEW ON CARDIFF, MILLWALL AND HOOLIGANISM By TONY REES (Ex News of The World Reporter)

I would like to Thank Tony for writing the following story and giving his views on Cardiff, Millwall, West Ham, Stoke etc and hooliganism in general .Tony has worked for the News of The World for 10 years and has since written for The Times, The Sun, The Mirror, The Daily Star and many other news papers.

The idea that the London-based newspapers cover the exploits of any club east or south west of the Severn Bridge through gritted teeth was fully confirmed by a short call on my mobile 22 minutes after a League One Millwall-Cardiff City clash kicked off on a dark December Saturday afternoon almost nine years ago.

I had been sent by the *News of the World* to scroll a report on the Bluebirds' match at the New Den - a mid-table encounter that, to the Red Top's sports desk, promised a lot more than two teams hoofing a piece of pig's skin between a couple of goal nets for 90 minutes. To Mike Allen, a bald aggressive deputy editor, South London would be a war zone between the both club's notoriously violent pockets of fans - an opportunity to sort out old differences that had spanned three decades of numerous collisions in various competitions.

There was, however, no question in my own mind that Allen's thoughts were concentrated on events that had unfolded at Ninian Park a mere four months earlier on the opening day of the 1999-2000 season. For after a low-key 1-1 draw in which the Millwall goalkeeper Tony Warner was alleged to have returned a coin hurled at him by a Bluebirds thug in the direction from which it had been propelled in the Grange End stand, all hell broke lose.

Hundreds of furious visiting Lions fanatics jumped the barriers, brushing a feeble line of stewards aside as they sought vengeance in the swiftest possible time. Led by ring leaders, much of MILLWALL'S following stormed onto the pitch as they began to try and invaded the lower grandstand. Many were intent on storming into the Victorian stadium's bowels via the player's tunnel, others gestured menacingly up into the press area where the late and wonderful Phil Suarez bellowed for assistance on the public address system. It was certainly one of the few occasions that I became a trifle concerned for safety, the anxiety easing only when a jet of water from a powerful hose was turned on the advancing throng by worried City staff.

The only time that I had seen such a violent invasion previously had been when Chelsea came to the Welsh capital for a dust up in the old Second Division in the mid-Eighties. The Stamford Bridge outfit had come to Ninian Park as section leaders but found themselves 3-0 down by the hour - three late goals, including the most dubious of penalties I have ever seen given, giving the Londoners an undeserved share of the points. Yet, in the eyes of most, the result probably headed off a riot - even though there were serious crowd problems before and after the clash. If my memory serves me correct, many Chelsea followers had got into the upper grandstand prior to kick off and had ousted many Cardiff season-ticket holders out of their normal seats - the utter pandemonium continued long after the final whistle too.

In those days, CARDIFF'S reputation was for having a legion of teak-hard, gnarled supporters amongst their ranks. The Bluebirds might have been floundering in the lower echelons of British soccer, but segments of City's following were at football's top table in terms of lawlessness. There was no question that this downturn in behavioural patterns commenced as the Mod-Rocker confrontation era ended.

During CARDIFF'S match at Leicester in August 1970, most the windows of a train carriage carrying City's supporters to Filbert Street were shattered after the Bluebirds' 1-0 victory. I recall a home League Cup tie against Bristol Rovers being disrupted as opposing fans charged each other on the Popular Bank - welcome to a decade when violent confrontation released some soccer supporters' socio-economic frustrations with the incessant power cuts encapsulating the relentless economic struggle.

Almost 12 months before Sam Hammam, the former Wimbledon owner and eccentric Lebanese millionaire, was seduced by the CARDIFF supporters' tarnished reputation, leading tabloids were becomingly curious to how the Welsh club's thugs would cope with fresh battle grounds such as Millwall, hence a journey sending me from Porthcawl to the London Docklands via three train switches.

Allen's abrupt tones boomed out on my mobile: "How's it all going?" he enquired - my response giving him the then goalless situation. "If I wanted to know the fucking score I'd have looked at the fucking Delete. What about the fighting? Have you seen anything go off yet?"

It was crystal clear to me that the only performance that interested Allen was how the Metropolitan Police coped with separating the two sets of braying fans. I reported that the Bermondsey area had been ringed by a gauntlet of steel beforehand - that had Allen positively salving Needless to say that particular 600-word match report contained little of a Neil Harris brace in Mill wall's comfortable 2-0 win, it was simply a summary of how many arrests and hospitalisations - punctuated by a few quotes from the club's respective managers pillorying violent fans.

In truth, the game itself was a non-event. An overcast day typified the action - colourless and witnessed by a crowd of less than 10,000. There again, without wishing to offend MILLWALLS diehards, this encounter represented the Lions' home really well. I always perceived the New Den to be a soulless place, so different from the giant imposing open terrace of Cold Blow Lane - a concrete slab occupied by a large contingent of one-eyed Dockers know to have followed their team for generations.

Barry Bridges, Bryan King, Barry Kitchener and the legendary centre half Harry Cripps these are the Millwall names that trip off the tongue. The Den, the Lions' original lair was demolished for new housing in 1993 - this the imposing old venue that had contained so many past on and off-the-pitch wars. Some of my first memories as a reporter where of turning up to a venue surrounded by towering hi-rise flats. Many a unsuspecting visiting fans had been chased or lured into the catacomb of cul-de-sacs that punctuated the wastelands. The Den was a foreboding place where racism was rife - particularly 25 years ago. All the more surprising then that on the opening day of the 1982-83 season and a 4-0 thumping by Cardiff, the Millwall fans commended the City winger Dave Bennett after an exhilarating show from the black ex-Manchester City winger - that type of things makes me feel that a large percentage of the Lions followers are some of soccer's true connoisseurs

Too often, though, the MILLWALL crowd show their ugly and unacceptable side - and this gloomy day 21 days before Christmas 1999 indicated what can happen if certain potentially explosive factors are in place. Robert Phillips, the BBC Wales Radio football reporter, wasn't oblivious to the dangers of visiting London SE16. The little flat-capped Welshman had parked his hired staff car miles away from the area on Shooter's Hill, catching a taxi into MILLWALL'S territory. He departed the game in the same manner - how I wished I'd taken precautionary methods myself around one hour after the final whistle.

Demands on copy meant I couldn't manage such a ultra swift exit. I was still locked into the New Den when hundreds of Lions fanatics charged the stadium's closed gates at about 6.30pm. Police were struggling to contain their unexplained fury - even Frank Burrows, the Cardiff manager appeared apprehensive about the worsening position. There was, at one point, a real threat of us all getting lynched by the Millwall mob who were loitering under two giant arches that the luxurious coach carrying City's team needed to negotiate. Then the unthinkable happened. As midfielder Willie Boland and defender Tony Vaughan climbed onto the bus four Lions idiots broke the police cordon - only, thankfully, to be met by the Bluebirds' assistant boss Billy Ayre. The Geordie, who sadly died of cancer when in his early fifties in 2002, laid the huge quartet on their backs with a flurry of well thrown punches bellowing: "Look, you fucking beat us, what more do you fucking want?"

My face was going a paler shade of white when Frank Burrows enquired as to what my problem was. I stuttered: "I have a bit of a dilemma," I replied, "I have no way of getting back to my tube station in one piece." Frank gestured for me to get on the bus with the City players, it was the start of a tense journey through the back streets which saw every passenger laying low in expectation of the windows being put through at any given moment. We had a small police escort for only part of the way into central London - breathing became a lot easier for everyone once we had passed the Elephant & Castle.

Frank's maroon Mercedes was parked nearer the M25 than the city centre. And after giving me a lift to my destination point, the great man disappeared into the night, his briefcase poised, yet another piece of business to conclude. Frank was so like Harry Redknapp it was untrue - the two men firm friends from their days at West Ham together. I liked Frank. His life involved around the next deal and his lovely wife Wendy. I found him to be kindness itself. The same went for his number two Billy - I cried the day he passed away. I remember going to his funeral in Ormskirk, a picture book village where he had lived. Billy was well loved - a man's man that called a spade just that. We had become firm pals ever since I broke the story that he was fighting deadly cancer in *The News of the World*. I'll never forget the emotional headline of that it read 'The Bravery Behind the Ninian Park Power Struggle.'

At the little church Billy's sister-in-law spoke about his life - a real who's who turned up to pay their last respects including Steve McMahon, Jan Molby, Colin Caulderwood, Wayne Allison and the Cardiff players Mark Bonner and Paul Brayson . There so many beautiful women too - whatever Billy possessed he could have bottled and then sold and made an absolute bloody fortune. God bless you Billy! God bless you Billy!

Covering CARDIFF for my numerous publications and over so many seasons, you would get to hear about the leading fighters of the day. Although I have brushed shoulders with so many of the present warriors, it would not be beneficial to one's health to name any, of course. I have, though, not encountered any problems - it's strange how people soon know that you are, indeed, a football fanatic like them. Legends of the past included Frankie, and Peggy - these were the leaders who had encountered the enemy throngs and headed up blood-curdling pitch battles at places like Derby, Leeds and Blackburn Rovers, Sheffield United, Portsmouth, West Ham and Tottenham.

As a reporter I always felt the heat at Upton Park. A visit to the old Boleyn stadium used to evoke a plethora of childhood memories from within. The Saturday nights of watching the Hammers play on *Match of the Day* and the commentary of Kenneth Wolstenholme, who I was fortunate to know well later in his life, and David Coleman's fluid off-the-cuff deliveries, are still strong in my mind. When I first visited West Ham as a reporter everything was as I envisaged it would be. Getting off the Tube I walked past the rows of pie and mash cafes. There, additionally, were the quick-talking geezers and their shops - Aladdin café establishments that peddled anything from Christmas trinkets to doggy household accessories all year around.

I adored WEST HAM UNITED Football Club and everything it stood for in the British game. Both the stadium and the famous training ground in Essex were studded by characters from the bygone years - real people that could talk about England '66 World Cup heroes Bobby Moore, Geoff Hurst and Martin Peters from a position of authority having known them personally. Somehow, a Cardiff defeat in the East End was always a little easier to take. In the years I visited West Ham for the *Daily Mirror* and *Daily Star*, the extremely erotic Hammerettes all-girl dance troop, a member who is currently with the Welsh international defender James Collins, complimented an intriguing backdrop from the main press area. There was something magical about watching a bevy of sexy women gyrating to the latest up-beat hits and a cluster of hi-rise flats in the background - a scene straight out of Johnny Speight's Sixties controversial sitcom *Till Death Us Do Part.*

Yet it was the traditional London pubs that ringed WESTHAM'S home which caused more than a little anxiety for me. Parking was a relentless problem when visiting this old stadium - as was spotting the thugs within the Hammers following. Getting through a curiously positioned door into the sanctum of the media zone was often precarious because you were forced to walk through tasty looking Armani and Burberry-clad local lads who totally scrutinised your appearance and accent. I am ashamed to say, but I did put on a fake cockney drawl just to survive the experience. Maybe it was the adrenalin rush, but I always relished a visit to West Ham.

I knew that a section of the Hammers fans carried a bit of a reputation - the movie *Green Street* tended to confirm what many of us within the game already knew. Yet, if I had lived in London or worked in the English capital more regularly I would have supported West Ham. I loved everything that the club stood for - particularly from the production of gifted players from the exalted Academy.

The Hammers had an academy system years before the Football Association big wigs dreamt up the concept from their ivory towers. Sir Trevor Brooking, now such an influential governmental figure in British sport, came off this conveyor belt - along with Alan Devonshire, Harry Redknapp, Frank Lampard senior and junior, Moore, Hurst, Peters, Rio Ferdinand, Jermain Defoe, Joe Cole, names that trip off the tongue. In past managers Ron Greenwood, John Lyall and Billy Bonds and Redknapp they had a mix of individuals who knew how soccer should be played - from a cultural and physical perspective. Without appearing to be xenophobic, why has the club replaced locally-raised Alan Curbishley with the inexperienced Italian manager Gianfranco Zola - to me, breaking from proud tradition is a complete mystery, a disaster waiting to happen.

Common opinion insisted crowd violence could be eradicated if stadia was comprehensively revamped and its design brought into the Twenty-First Century. The concept of an all-seater sterile citadel emerged from the aftermath of the Hillsborough - a tragedy that saw 96 Liverpool fans lose their life after being crushed at the Lepping Lane End during an FA Cup semi-final against Nottingham Forest in April 1989 that was abandoned after six minutes - this the deadliest stadium-related incident in British history. Terraces and fences were always going to be dismantled after this - and the action has certainly changed the experience of attending a match in British football's top two tiers.

Crowd tragedies had happened before that fated afternoon in Sheffield, of course. A flash fire in May 1985 consumed the whole of one side of Bradford City's Valley Parade ground - 56 people dieing near half time of a Third Division clash that was supposedly seeing the Bantams crowned league champions before an encounter with Lincoln. A report later deducing that a discarded cigarette in a polystyrene cup had ignited old rubbish and dust acuminated over 20 years in a gap under the ramshackle 2,000-capacity main wood stand

In January 1971, 66 fans, amongst them five Fife school pals, were crushed dead as they descended the Ibrox Stadium's stairway 13 after a match involving Rangers and Celtic, another 200 injured. Yet, arguably, because of the extensive media coverage, no UK sporting disaster has attracted such intense focus since Hillsborough. The way we watched our soccer was destined to alter after a comprehensive and expensively compiled Taylor Report which named failed police control as being an integral contributor in the disaster occurring.

Hence, multi-purpose stadium housed on expansive retail sites was always the direction that football's administrators wanted to go. If Scunthorpe United's Glanford Park was British soccer's first construction box, others have now followed - Bolton's wonderful Burnden Park, surrounded by its chippies, dismantled to make way for the Reebok Stadium in the Nineties. Cardiff will quit 99-year-old Ninian Park for a new 27,500 all-seater arena at nearby Leckwith next summer and Swansea departed their crumbling Vetch Field for the Liberty Stadium three years ago last July. Even if Everton and Liverpool eventually move from Goodison and Anfield respectively, rivals such as Arsenal have already taken the plunge - the Gunners' across-the-road switch from Highbury to the Emirates Stadium a resounding commercial and emotional success. Plenty of clubs have re-housed - amongst them Derby County, Shrewsbury, Manchester City, even Wembley Stadium's hallowed Twin Towers have been destroyed in the quest of progress.

Unlike many of my university lecturing peers, I am not convinced that positive and non-violent mental states are born in the deluded from dismantling the terraces. A visit to the Potteries and assignments at STOKE CITY can always provide a potent counter argument. I went to both the Victoria Ground and the Britannia Stadium - the sense of unease was a constant companion until your vehicle spun southbound back down the M6. Not content with utilising Tom Jones' *Delilah* song for their own chilling battle cry, the Stokies always, it seemed to me, to harbour an intense dislike of anything other than their own.

I recall covering a tense Stoke-Cardiff Division Two first-leg play-off encounter in May 2002 - Leo Fortune-West and Rob Earnshaw scoring in a match that the Bluebirds won 2-1. I managed to scroll a front-page *Daily Mirror* lead later when the City owner Sam Hammam's top-of-the-range A 8 Audi Quattro was allegedly attacked by rogue Stoke followers after the victory. I narrowly escaped a hiding myself later as a huge group of furious Potters followers marauded around the arena seeking unsuspecting souls to brand.

I was fortunate enough to spot them from 100 yards. At the time I was deep in conversation with my old journalistic pal Phil Blanche, now sports editor with Media Wales, but then a *Western Mail* reporter. It took me three seconds to finish the dialogue and leap in my brand new green S-type Jaguar - it was one of those occasions when possessing a fast car was crucial to well-being. I got away by the skin of my teeth - a near-hospital experience I repeated at Blackpool just before Christmas that same season.

Now a visit to the north-west Lancastrian playground was always something I relished. Blackpool is, to some, extremely tacky - these days a stag and hen night stamping ground. But to me, the Golden Mile, the pier shows, boisterous pubs and a lap dancing club called Aphrodite's are monuments of great wonder - any excuse to make a pilgrimage and stay in the resort's North Beach Hilton Hotel is taken by me.

Yet even if I had manufactured a London accent to stay alive at Millwall, Tottenham and West Ham in the past, I was grateful for the Welsh droll before Cardiff's game at Bloomfield Road in December 2001. Snaking between a row of terraced houses and a shop, I attempted a short cut to the stadium up a dark ally and encountered around 50 City fans coming straight towards me. It was once of the few occasions that I realised quite the edge some of the more hardened Bluebirds supporters carry. Without being overdramatic, I swear that if the shaven-headed group leaders hadn't detected my valley slang I wouldn't be here to write this chapter - it was a terrifying situation that I never want to encounter again. It was, though, the start of a weekend that saw the local police resources fully extended. Taking a stole near the Tower rooms after the 1-1 draw you could hear a mass brawl and CARDIFF chanting - I would imagine the scene might have been lifted straight from the Wild West.

Something similar accrued years later. I was in Milan to report on Wales' European Championship qualifier against Italy at the San Siro - it was September 2003. Walking through the fashionable City's centre I spied a group of CARDIFF followers moving in on some SWANSEA counterparts - with the Azzurri riot police in hot pursuit. Eventually the authorities managed to move between the two warring sets. Sirens pierced the autumn air and startled shoppers gazed on totally confused just why the Wales supporters should be fighting amongst themselves. A poignant question indeed. The scene saddened me greatly because I felt that all club differences should have been pushed aside in the drive to see Mark Hughes' Dragons reach the Euro finals in Portugal 2004 - that whole episode was a nonsense that I put down to cheap booze. The result didn't yield any comfort either - the Welsh lost 4-0 with AC Milan striker Fillippo Inzaghi getting a second-half hat-trick.

Unless politically encumbered, clubs will, invariably, attempt to defend the unsavourily element amongst their supporter group. This, a controversial viewpoint that many chairmen and directors would care to dispute. Yet, it must have been difficult for the Cardiff board to explain the events that followed the Bluebirds' 2-1 FA Cup third round victory over then Premiership leaders LEEDS UNITED in January 2002.

Records show that 2008 FA Cup finalists CARDIFF, were then more famed for having a formidable terraced firm than playing prowess. Trouble was rife in the Welsh capital that afternoon Leeds visited and as the Sky Sports cameras rolled live, 30 City followers were eventually arrested as police with dogs and on horseback attempted to stem trouble between the warring fan factions - pitch-invading Bluebirds thugs hurling missiles and abuse at counterparts in the Grange End. Disruption even sparked outside the Ninian Park boardroom later - the Leeds manager David O'Leary restrained by his then chairman Peter Ridsdale as he charged up to confront Sam Hammam.

Former Wimbledon controller Hammam, who typified his old club's Crazy Gang mentality, was not a stranger to controversy. Prior to a kick off that had seen the legendary Wales international star John Charles paraded in the centre circle, the diminutive Lebanese eccentric had strolled around the pitch stoking up the already hostile atmosphere that worsened as the clash unfolded - England defender Rio Ferdinand limping off early before Alan Smith was red carded for a high challenge on Cardiff's Andy Legg. A curling free kick from Bluebirds skipper Graham Kavanagh levelled Mark Viduka's fine opener, but Scott Young's late winner was only a minute part of the tale.

Chapter 23

FROM WORZEL TO TAFFY
BY Alan Swain Bristol City

I've known Alan now about 14 years, he use to be one of the doorman in a club I had in Somerset, for a couple of years I would go on about Cardiff and say why don't you pop over for a game and he would go on about his team Bristol City and the days when he would come over with their lads. When I finally left the area, we kept in touch and then finally he said wouldn't mind seeing a couple of games with me. The main thing I can say about Alan is that the area in (Bridgwater) Somerset that the club was, didn't half respect him and you knew when Alan was working, trouble was always well under control. Annis

My name is Alan Swain, I am 51 years old and have lived in a small Town in Somerset all my life. I have been asked to write a few lines by my friend Annis about some of my experiences at matches. I was brought up supporting Bristol City, but in the 60's, Cardiff were probably the biggest club for miles and there for most all the big games were at Ninian Park. One of my first ever games was as a neutral , I went to see Cardiff v Arsenal in the late 60's in the FA Cup, the crowd was over 50,000 and the atmosphere was absolutely brilliant and I was hooked on football.

It wasn't till I was about 15 years old until I went regular to watch my club Bristol City with a few of my mates, we always use to go by train and it wasn't long before we met up with other lads from my town Bridgwater and other lads from a near by town Taunton. Of course this was in the mid 70's and going to football for a ruck was the in thing. Many a time we have been in fights at or near Bristol Temple Meads train station with rival fans. Some of the good ones being against lads from MILLWALL, WBA and QPR. Other notable ones being at away games at WOLVES, where we were chased all the way back to the train station. Fights broke out every where that day and when we finally got to the train station, they were waiting for us, we had to fight our way out, they battled with us all the way on to the train its self. As the train pulled out, everyone thought that was the end of it, until one by one the windows were coming in, they were all on the tracks, some throwing bricks others trying to get on, it was unbelievable.

I remember 10 of us Bristol lads coming down to see Cardiff v MAN UTD, we got of the train from in Cardiff Central station and arrived at the same time as a train full of Man Utd, we thought we would stick with these lot as it might be a bit safer, no such luck, on the way to the ground, Cardiff came out of every side street, they were everywhere, they ended up running the Utd lads and us everywhere., the game itself was more about how many missiles you could throw, it was unreal. Walking back to the train station, there were just houses and shops smashed up, one after another. We were just glad to get on that train and get back to Bristol.

One of the games we most looked forward to was our rivals from the other side of the bridge, CARDIFF, yes Rovers are our main rivals, but you were always guaranteed a ruck, if we went to

Cardiff or they came to us. Nearly every time Cardiff came to Ashton Gate, they would manage to get a few hundred of their firm in the corner of the East End part of the ground and afterwards fighting would go on for over an hour sometimes longer, it was unreal, they never wanted to go home they seemed content to fight us all day and night. The fights we would have in Cardiff by the Grange end were endless, Cardiff in them days had hundreds of skinheads and they were fucking mad, but the Bristol lads would love coming over as they new they were guaranteed a fight.

As I got older I was going home and away with Bristol City regular, but I could see that the police were getting wiser and things were starting to get on top. Then it wasn't long before I got banned from Bristol City, I was nicked at Blackpool, Fulham and Wolves away for fighting on their ends, in the end I was banned. So I stopped watching football for a few years or shall we say they stopped me. I started going up to Spurs for a few games, but by the time I was 30, I started working in pubs and clubs on the doors. That's where I eventually met Annis.

Annis a keen Cardiff fan was always going on to me about going to watch Cardiff and kept saying it was still like the old days down there with the atmosphere and terracing etc. So eventually after 2 years of him going on, I did come and see them. The game was against SWANSEA CITY away, their most hated rivals. It was the first time in ages that visiting fans had been allowed to go. We had to meet at the Ninian Park car park, Cardiff were only allowed about 800 tickets and everyone had to be bubbled in by coach and police all the way to Swansea.

When we arrived in Swansea , nearly all the locals on the roads to the Vetch, made the effort to be outside their homes or caravans as Cardiff would say, they certainly let Cardiff know what they thought of them, it was everyone from granddads, grannies down to kids who could barely walk., with the usual swearing, hand signals and abuse etc. When we got to the ground we were put straight in there, barriers were all around us and a mass of old bill in riot gear.

Like I say I've been all over, but I've never been to a ground where to sets of fans hate each other so much and from the second I entered to the time I left both sets of fans were at each others throats, its was surely an eye opener to someone like me who isn't from Wales. It was just pure hatred between each other, I can never see the bubble trips being lifted, as the hatred seems to be not just about football, but they genuinely seem to hate each other in normal day life.

After that game I started going home and away to watch Cardiff with Annis, I soon got to know Mac, Simmo and many other lads down in Cardiff and I've had the mick taken out of me for following Bristol, but in a joking way. Cardiff has always had a reputation for being one of the most violent fans, and I could see why, but I've never seen them attack rival fans who didn't want trouble. It seemed where ever Cardiff went the other teams firms started making an effort and turning out .even when I went to CAMBRIDGE away, 8 of us ended up fighting 20 of them and it was right on top, we were in the old town and some Japanese tourists were running around clicking like mad their cameras. I honestly thought we were going to get done, until one of the lads got a fire extinguisher out and started spraying them with white foam, they didn't know what hit them and all backed off. The police arrived and the CAMBRIDGE lot all ran off laughing .But later at the game we found out they ran straight into Macs lot and soon had the smiles wiped of their faces.

I was watching them when they were in the fourth division, with home crowds of sometimes just over 2,000, but they always took a good following away including loads of lads. People talk about how great it is in the top tiers, but even in the lower leagues it can be very interesting, I remember MANSFIELD v Cardiff, they had a good mob out for Cardiff, but I'm pretty sure they had a lot of Forest with them.

Of all the places I have been to watch football, Cardiff was one of the most intimidating I have been to and I've been to them all over the last 35 years.

Chapter 24

NEVER LOOKING FOR TROUBLE, BUT FINDING PLENTY ALONG THE WAY! By GWYN DAVIES CCFC

The years that I have known Gwyn our support has only grown from strength to strength up the Valley's. Gwyn formed The Valley Rams, became president, spokesman, organiser, peacemaker, stood his ground when he had to (Don't forget he was World Judo Champion) and made it possible for fans who didn't have much money to follow their beloved Cardiff away. It was a big mistake when the authorities stopped working together with him and keeping to their end of the bargain. Annis

I started watching Cardiff City at the age of 10 and my first game was sometime in 1965. So I was there at the start, I was there at the peak and I'm still here during the decline of "Football Hooliganism" and for those amongst us that say "it hasn't declined and it is sill active" my reply would be that if you had been the in the mid to late 70's, you would realise how much it really has declined.

The 70's
People who have been involved or simply caught up in any incidents of "hooliganism" will often describe the buzz and the kick they got from such events, in most cases this is the adrenaline rush caused by the "fight or flight" situations that are part of our make up. Many people will keep searching for more such buzzes or even bigger and better buzzes and these are often the lads who develop into active hooligans rather than accidental hooligans, who I think if I'm honest most of us, are.

During the madness around the mid 70's, people were getting killed on a regular basis at games, serious slashing and stabbings weren't even making the headlines because it was such a regular occurrence. People nowadays talk of a hooligan code of honour or rules of engagement so to speak, but in the 70's it was survival of the fittest, there were no rules and very little respect for the law. These were the days where you would go somewhere on a football special train with 7 or 800 full on nutters and get off in some City or town centre and not see one copper waiting for you, sounds un-believable, but true none the less.

Usually when you travelled in such numbers you could look after yourselves in most cases. But going to somewhere like West Ham and arriving in Paddington at 11am, would soon see that mob of 700 break up into smaller groups all doing their own thing, there was very little organisation and basically at most times it was every man for themselves. Getting to the ground was a challenge on its own, when you got inside the ground, some places would have recognised away ends, but in most cases you just headed for sections which weren't seen as the home fans end. Often at the less infamous clubs, groups would mob up, infiltrate and have a go at taking the end, but you didn't go to West Ham, Millwall and the like intending to take ends, unless you had a death wish. In lots of grounds there was no segregation, hardly any police presence and if there weren't enough of you to stand your ground or look after each other, then you just split up and blended in trying to look inconspicuous.

Mind you when you went to some of the big Cityclubs in your Wranglers (jackets and jeans) and wondered why you stood out like a spare prick in a wedding until you looked around and seen all their fans wearing fashions you had never heard of, let alone seen, we may as well have turned up with flashing signs on our heads saying "here I am, please come and kick and stab me".

Whilst I may be making light of it now (having come out the other side in one piece) these were seriously scary and dodgy times and why I, or others would put themselves through that week in, week out is beyond me.

It makes me laugh now when people walk the walk, wear the gear and think that they are the new face of "hooliganism" My god, nowadays you spend half of your time being covered by CCTV cameras, escorted by 100's of coppers and 100's more stewards, helicopters, mobile phone tracing, pre-match combined police force and club meetings, picking through the intelligence and information they have gathered pre match. You have more chance getting into a scrape down your local Tesco's than at the football.

I would love to see the police and authorities having a couple of months off and seeing what happened. I doubt if lots of the brave teenage gesturing and threats would take place if they new that outside in the street they would have to back up such actions.
We have all seen a rival fan, safe behind his fence, his row of stewards and line of police giving it the big one with his cut throat gestures and the big you and me outside hand signals, knowing that he had more chance of meeting the Queen than coming face to face with you. It would be great to see such fans step out of the ground and left alone to back up their actions.

The organising of arranged offs with rival groups did not really get into full swing until the early 90,s and the advent of mobile phones and the "Tinternet", prior to these times old scores were still settled and fights still arranged and there were planned punch ups, but most of the trouble was sporadic if not inevitable at certain games.The mobile phone and internet era gave birth to a different type of "football violence" and far more offs and meetings were set up away from the stadiums.

The new technology proved to be a two edged sword though, and just as the hooligans were getting more up to speed with the new technology, so were the Police but at a faster and more advanced rate than the rival crews up and down the country.

There is no need for me to go into any detail about what technology is available to the police, but suffice to say whilst it isn't James Bond it's a bit more advanced than a Police whistle and a two way radio. When you are shown a photograph taken from a helicopter 100's and 100's of yards up above you in the sky, and in that photograph you can read the label on your shirt, then you soon realise you aren't going to get away with much. Does this mean there will be no more trouble at or around football? I very much doubt it, but it will never get back to the scale we witnessed in bygone years.

Now with regard to the title of my chapter "Never looking for trouble, but finding plenty along the way" I would never consider myself a football hooligan. Mind you my definition of hooligan will not be the same definition as everyone else.

I have witnessed mob rule and anarchy at football, I have seen people rob smash and destroy service stations, pubs and shops, vandalise things just because they knew they wouldn't get caught, I have seen bullying at its worse, away fans robbed of their money clothes and any other possessions the other group wanted, cars tipped over and windows in houses along the route smashed with bricks and bottles and at times Cardiff fans have been some of the worst.

Now that is my image of hooliganism and whilst witnessing many such incidents during my younger days and being on the fringe of things, I can honestly say I never vandalised or bullied others just because I could, in fact wherever possible I would step in to prevent bullying and also whilst getting caught up in many fights over the years, I will do anything needed to get the upper hand and stay on top, but I have always known when enough is enough, and also stopped my mates from causing serious harm when we have had the upper hand. I am not trying to paint an holier than thou image of myself, but most people that know me, know how I function, and in reality most of my close mates act and think along the same lines, or they wouldn't be my mates.

Some of my best memories in regard to trouble at football, involve situations where bullying by larger groups as been turned around and the larger group have come unstuck. I'm not going to write the typical 10 of us backed of 60 and me and my two mates chased off 20 other lads, that all gets a bit tired and for those of you who have won every fight, and come out of every scrape unmarked having never taken a backward step, then I take my hat off to you.

QPR
But I swear that at times past if I couldn't have run faster than the twenty boys chasing me on occasions, then possibly I would not be here writing this, but sitting in a wheelchair sucking soup through a straw. One such occasion comes back to me in QPR. It was a typical London game, back in the early 70's. There were possibly, 2,000 or so City fans that had made their way up there one way or another. No major trouble before the game, but there were 20 or so of our headers who got into the loft, had a 20 second kick off and then get onto the pitch, only to be booed by every Rangers fan in the stadium, and cheered by all the City fans in the away end as if they were heroes returning home from a successful conquest overseas.

The match passed without any serious trouble the final whistle goes and we all pour out of the ground, some going this way some going that way and within minutes everyone split up and spread all over. Well that day I'd gone up there with two mates from Aberdare, Jeff Francis, and Needsy, both of them a year or two older than me, and at 17 I was the baby of the group.

Now this was early Doctor Martin era, and many grounds would either not let you in or make you hand over the laces from your boots or even make you leave your boots at the turnstile in some cases. Now Needs! being the great thinker that he wasn't, thought he'd get around this problem by taking a spare pair of trainers (or daps as they were known then) with him in a carrier bag (mad but don't ask!).

Well we make our way back to the tube for our return to Paddington station., Now whilst not being well known for mass mob hooliganism in those days, QPR were well known for ambushing rival fans on the London underground and had it off to a fine art. I wished someone had told us though, we were like lambs to the slaughter, we went on to the platform and stood amongst 100's of other fans, some Cardiff, some QPR, most dressed similarly as skinheads or suede heads as they were called, similarly dressed to us (or at least we thought) any colours were blue and white, so no difference then. The atmosphere was tense but not seriously threatening, however when the tube arrived and we jumped on, things started getting a bit hairy.

The tube doors opened and every carriage seemed to be packed full with QPR skinheads, we had to get on and just brave it out, but that was the longest couple of stops in my life. Small gangs of QPR were working their way through carriages interviewing and handing out slaps to individuals or small groups of Cardiff they came across, there was no organisation and unlike today most of us didn't know which ones were our fellow Cardiff fans and without having a Frankie (undisputed top man at the time) type leader on board none amongst us planned to make themselves known and were just keeping their heads down.

We arrived unscathed at Paddington and thought we were home and dry, loads got off and we just hung back. When we walked up the stairs and went to cross the bridge over the platform, we could see possibly 50 or 60 QPR boys standing at the top of the other stairs. Well they clocked us straight away and we had a choice to either turn and run, or just take our chances. We kept walking towards them and suddenly the meanest looking one stepped forward "are you Cardiff he says" what could we say? "no Buttie, we are from Notting Hill, Honest!"

We stopped in our tracks, Needsy still with his daps and Carrier bag stuck under his arm pit, he goes to grab the bag either, to hold it whilst running down the stairs or to keep them safe whilst we are getting kicked to fuck, but for what ever reason big bad nasty skinhead lad jumps back shouting "look out he's got a gun" couldn't make it up could you, well that little jump back was just what we needed, we were down those stairs like Colin Jackson closely followed by this gang who must now have realised that 3 dopey boys from Aberdare are unlikely to be walking around London with a shooter in a carrier bag so they really wanted to hurt us big time now, well for those of you that know Paddington, you'll know how long the platforms are, and this one was the mother of platforms, we had done the Colin Jackson sprint, we were now looking at the Paula Radcliff marathon we were running and laughing with fear and you could feel their breath on the back of your neck.

We had no plan other than make sure you could run faster than your mate, but seriously you new you'd have to stop and take a kicking if they caught any of your mates, not that 3 against 50 would have done much better than 1 against 50, secretly I was just glad that Needs was carrying his trainers rather than wearing them, that could have kept him ahead of me in the race for survival and you don't want to be in last position during those races.

It's hard to workout how you can be running flat out and still have daft thoughts racing around your head, but one thing I vividly remember was that all three of us whilst running for our lives, were laughing out loud almost hysterically, but there ahead of us was our get out of jail card. Frankie and 50 of Cardiff's finest were drinking in a bar which was right at the end of the platform; they had seen our little chase and were pouring out of the bar, we were running so fast that we went through the Cardiff fans and had got 20 yards out the other side before we had slowed down to a stop.

The Rangers fans weren't as lucky and by the time we had turned around there were a dozen or so Rangers fans sprawled over the platform and some of the lads were chasing the others back up the platform, whilst others were still taking care of business.

They didn't look like they needed any help off us, and thank God, because we were breathing out of our arses. Now seeing those lads sprawled out across the platform, some with blood pouring from their noses, others with dazed looks and eyes that appeared to be spinning in different directions and all looking sheepish and trying to slope off from further damage, whilst I was so glad it was them having the kicking and not us, deep down I still hoped that it didn't get taken too far, justice had been done and they'd been sorted, but I did wonder would they have let us get up and walk away with a few slaps, or would we have been kicked to hell and back or even stabbed, these were seriously mad times and you never new how far things could go. At least my conscience was clear and I could sleep easy, and in my own bed rather that in St Mary's Hospital as would have been the case if not for Needsy's trainers.

This was my first taste of fun at Paddington station, and it would not be the last, we have had a few run ins around there over the years and even now at 30 years later I still keep looking over my shoulder around the station even if I'm up there on a shopping trip.

From The Year 2000
Well that's enough of the last century, so what about this century. Well this Century started with a bang, it was the Sam Hamman era, and the Valley Rams era. I wont bore you with how the Rams were formed or why we walked away from organising travel 1n 2007, but whilst those involved with running this group have stepped back officially, a lot of what the Rams created still exists and the people running coaches from all 4 corners of South Wales are more or less the same people who were key to the Rams organisation, suffice to say the Police, the club and authority's now spend far longer chasing up people to find who's going where and tracing their movements on route now that the Rams hierarchy has stepped down.

We had set ourselves to be used as scapegoats in the latter stages it was beginning to seem as if any fan that was seen as drunk or being a nuisance was automatically assumed as being part of the Rams group, and what were we going to do about it. It was almost as if they were no longer Cardiff fans, nothing to do with the club and only our responsibility, fuck me we were the only ones doing this for fuck all amongst all those involved, we had the Police, the club, the Stewards even the football licensing authorities all paid employees, yet it was down to our little band of volunteers to ensure that these 1,000's of lads behaved like choir boys, when 6 years earlier the authorities were amazed and grateful that we had finally helped to stop the major disorder that had plagued our club.

Whilst the pubs had stopped being trashed, the services no longer robbed, that was great but the biggest problems now were "Johnny is standing up to watch the game, and not even standing behind his allocated seat number" scuse me, I thought we were helping to stop mass disorder and we had, now they were trying to turn us into Big Brother and the thought police.

One such instance springs to mind during the last year or so of the Rams, we were in COVENTRY'S Ricoh stadium, placed in our segregated end with large sterile areas each side of us, keeping us safe from the Massed Coventry firm NOT!
However what this sterile area did do, was allow the same Chavvy teenage element I mentioned earlier (you know the ones, hard as fuck behind a fence) had the opportunity of being within shouting distance of our fans.

Most of our fans were standing as usual to watch the game, no problem, other Cardiff fans; those that want to sit-down will usually go in front of these lads or sit around the fringes, job done. We sort it out amongst ourselves and we all get to watch the game as we prefer, whilst standing or sitting next to the mates we choose to.

Well for this match showing my age I had sat on the right hand side of this group, about 4 rows lower than us was a group of four lads all around 15 years of age, they were no problem, looked like decent enough kids with their feet on the first rung of the watching football away with my mates, rather than my dad ladder.

Well the match was well under way, the normal chanting going on, Cov's chavs singing at us and pointing etc. our fans responding. Well along comes big hard bully boy steward and his two side kicks, he grabs the lad nearest to him and shouts "oi sit down in your seat or you're out" a bit heavy handed and looked like he was picking the easy option considering we got a 1,000 gorillas ten seats or so across doing the same. The young lads looked quite frightened, they didn't argue and just sat down.

A few minutes later the old chant goes up, "ten lads, you've only got ten lads" and our young lads are singing along to this and pointing over at the Cov fans. Well Billy the bully boy steward comes across and threatens the lads again; saying that even though they were now sitting down, if they pointed at the Cov fans again that would be seen as threatening gestures.

In all fairness to these now shook up young lads, they stopped gesturing and kept watching the game. Well fuck me 5 minutes later, bully boy is back again, but I can't work out what they have done wrong now, so I listen in and hear him saying he's seen one of the youngsters looking at the Cov fans, and if he looked at them again instead of looking at the game, he'd be out on his ear.

Well that was the straw on the camel's back for me, I had to intervene, and said to the steward if they have paid to come in, and want to spend all the match looking at Cov fans, then they would and he could do fuck all about it, and if he didn't fuck off he'd have a 1,000 nutters climbing over the seats to make sure he fucked off.
He chose the wise option now that a "grown up" had got involved and he went and hid somewhere else, mind you I spent the rest of the match waiting for a tug for daring to stand up to the thought police, there are people out there who really want us to watch football in a different method to the one that most football fans want.

It is a major concern and whilst we can't allow trouble, or racist abusive chanting as such, the day we have to sit down all match, not sing, not point and are even told where to look, is the day when I and many others will chose to spend their money elsewhere.

A couple of scrapes that I have got caught up in over recent years have been caused by Police ineptitude or stubbornness, rather than a group of lads out looking for trouble.
I will mention two of these that spring to mind, the first being SHEFFIELD UNITED away in around the season 2001-2002.

Now if you ask most football fans across the board who their least favourite football related police forces are, then I would almost guarantee that The Yorkshire and West Midland forces would be in most fans top three, and this is partly why I use these two examples to highlight such events.

Part of our initial success at the Rams in helping to limit problems breaking out at games, was discussion with away clubs and their police forces. Now you wont need me to tell you two of the forces who didn't want discussion with us, and basically who the fuck did we think we were offering to have some constructive discussion and team work to help things run with no problems. The reply we would have when trying to make contact, was thanks but no thanks, your fans like all others will be treated firmly but fairly, and we all know what that means, firm is "you will be met by officers in full riot gear, there will be no communication and you wont be told what's happening other than hearing the odd shouted threat or order, you will be herded, pushed, shoved and goaded, and if you complain you'll be assaulted or arrested, is that FAIR enough"
The Match for Sheffield seen us taking 16 coach loads of Valley Rams up for the game, now the only instruction we'd had was you will arrive in your coaches at 2 pm on the slip road/bridge at junction whatever it was on the M1.

What we had planned to do was make our way up and stop for a meal and a drink in a small town called Chapeltown. We had used this town on a few occasions and the three or four pubs and the British Legion club used to welcome us with open arms and ask us to call back whenever we could. We built up such a rapport with these business's that we would tell them we were coming, give them the time and numbers etc. and they would get on extra bar staff, and for some games they even laid on a free buffet for us, good business all round for all parties.

Well on the day in question everything went to plan, until the Police became involved. We had visited Chapeltown, had a great out day with no problems. Our coaches had loaded up and were on route to get to the rendezvous point at the allotted time.

Well my coach was the third or fourth coach there, we were met by a load of Police, told to stay on the coaches, and no other info was given, we waited ten minutes or so then started moving off, but little did I know that only eight coaches were allowed to travel and they held the last eight back in the lay-by. My phone started going with all the reps off the other coaches asking me what was going on, so I phoned our Welsh Police FIO's (football intelligence Officers) They came back to me saying that the master plan was to take our eight coaches in and the bring the other eight in closely behind us. Not ideal for those stuck there in the lay by, but just another example of the joys of being a City fan.

Anyway our coaches get to the ground at around 2.30pm and I'm off and waiting for the next 8 to arrive, but arrive they didn't and actually I found out they hadn't even moved, so basically they had been stuck there for 30 minutes or so. Twenty five to three, twenty to three, quarter to three, still no movement. I'm bouncing by now, balling out our FIO's who in all fairness I had a good working relationship with, and they new that I didn't just moan and stamp my feet for nothing and so they were doing the best they could to get our other coaches moving.

Three o'clock comes and still no sign, I go into the ground and then the phone starts going mental. They had finally started moving our coaches in, but the match had already started and they were still ten minutes away. Then (from what I found out later) they stopped the coaches a mile or so from the ground and just sat there again, well by now the lads on board had cracked, they could see the floodlights and were just stuck on these coaches like dummies, with no coppers telling them what the hell was going on.

The doors open front and back and 400 lads jump off the coaches and start walking to the ground. Not looking to smash anything or anyone up, just wanting to get to a game they'd travelled 200 miles to see. Well this throws Yorkshires finest into chaos, what are these fans doing, who do they think they are?, and suddenly every copper within a 10 miles radius is heading for this mob of warlike hooligans (or read frustrated football fans, depending which outlook you take).

Next thing they are surrounded bubbled up and marched to the ground (which is where they wanted to go anyway) now from what I was told by many sources, everyone in this escort was now seen as a criminal and fair game for the fair but firm approach (my arse).
Several fans get arrested for asking why they are being hit with staffs and called Welsh C's by loads of coppers frothing at the mouth.

Pandemonium! and by the time these lads get into the ground, the place is bouncing and you can cut the atmosphere with a knife (it's lucky they'd left the knives on the coaches.LOL).

The game was a real cliff hanger and added to the tension, and at the end of the game part of me was dreading what may happen next, I get wound up like a coiled spring by certain police and certain policing methods, especially where commonsense plays no part in events and you have some public school educated knob sitting in his ivory tower sending out orders and instructions to his Officers on the front line, having never ever been to a football match himself and having no personal knowledge of how things are, other than what he's read or been taught in a lecture.

How many times have you as football fans asked a copper why they were doing this and it was mad, and they would say "I know, but I'm just following orders" in all fairness, not all coppers are knobs just as all football fans aren't hooligans, but how they can work under such constraints sometimes is beyond me.

Now for those that have been to Bramall lane, you will know how things work. You come out of the away end and the coaches are there waiting in the road for you. No problem you would think and for this match possibly because of the tension that had been created, the Police blocked each end of the road off to stop any Sheffield fans walking through this road holding the coaches.

Sounds straight forward and it should have been, but coming down onto this road at 90 degrees were a couple of side streets. Now this one particular side street must have been a couple of hundred yards long but at the furthest end of the street you could see the Sheffield fans making their way down the adjacent road. Suddenly they must have had a rush of blood, they mobbed up and started running down the street to have a pop at the Cardiff fans, there were a couple of coppers mixed in with us trying to get us on the coaches, and a couple more at the end of the street, but not enough to stop a couple of hundred Sheffield fans looking for a scalp.

Well those Cardiff fans on the coaches were soon back off them and joining in with the others still milling around outside the coaches. Now for anyone that has been in this type of situation body language and expression can tell you a million things. The Sheffield fans had broken through the handful of coppers at the top of the street and thought they would pour down on the Cardiff fans and scatter them.

Well I could see ours grouping up and all excited for the scrap and running up towards the Sheffield fans to meet them half way (bless them, must have thought they'd save them running to far) and you could see the approaching Sheffield fans slowing down and their faces showing the realisation that the ones in the front row were going to be the first to have it, rather than being the ones who could brag later that they had Chased Cardiff everywhere. The next thing is the "dancing" so synonymous with these sorts of scraps, you know the things where people are bouncing on their feet side to side, arms wide spread saying come on then, blah, blah, blah.

Well just as Sheffield are mid dance, bang! Cardiff are straight into them, now I did say earlier that I didn't want this piece to be the typical, ten of us chased fifty of them and we never lose a fight etc. but this is how it is and what happened, and in all fairness with regard to numbers the 100 plus Sheffield fans who'd braved it were now being met by double or treble those numbers wanting to kick them back up the road. I don't want to glorify matters and unlike the Swansea comic that was written last year, why lie?, there were hundreds there who know what happened and they would soon know if I was lying or exaggerating events.

Within less than a minute or so, the police had regrouped their numbers swollen with dozens of the Robbo cops who had been stationed at each end of the main road, where nothing was happening. They'd put a couple of lines in between both sets of rival fans who by now were nearer the top end of the street where the fight had now taken them. These coppers are now pushing the Cardiff fans back down the street and towards the coaches, but whilst this is going on the Sheffield fans are regrouping at the top of the street and what seemed with extra numbers from those fans still pouring out of the ground, just as the Cardiff fans are within yards of the coaches, the Sheffield fans start making their way back down the street for round two.

Now instead of leaving a line of coppers up that end of the street to stop such a thing happening again (seems quite straight forward to a numbskull like me) all of the coppers are down with our lot, now these coppers don't seem to have any plans to stop these Sheffield fans from coming down at us again, so if they aren't going to stop them, there are 5 or 600 Cardiff loonies who are more than ready to.

Chaos prevails, you now have a couple of rows of Robbo cops laying into Cardiff with everything they've got, a mad few minutes there are lads in tee shirts and jumpers standing toe to toe with coppers in suits of armour hitting them with shields and staffs. One sight I'll never forget is seeing one copper, helmet less for some reason (a real ginga head as well) now he'd been standing down by the turnstiles in normal police outfit rather than body armour, I could see him running in behind the Cardiff fans who were standing facing the other way toe to toe and still bang at with the riot cops.

Well our ginger cop had lost the plot big time, and he was lashing out at everything with his staff, he was splitting heads for fun, and not just legitimate targets so to speak, he wasn't picking targets just lashing out at everything in reach. Well he'd gone to far into the crowd now for his own safety, and I could see two fists the size of cabbages smashing into his face, he fell backwards but before he hit the floor he must have been booted by a dozen or so different people, and not all stereotypical lads that you'd expect, lots of them had blood running down their heads so no doubt, these were some new friends he'd made earlier on his lone charge of the light brigade.

It was hard to feel sorry for him, you don't want to see anyone badly hurt, but this copper was a bad egg and out of control, it was frightening to see how much hatred was coming his way. Luckily for him, some of the Robbo cops had seen him go down and got to him before too much damage was done. Strangely rather than make things worse, this seem to bring some order to events and things started calming down. The Police had finally worked out that if they got the Sheffield fans back up the street, then things would improve and improve they did, mind you a Dai Taxi's coach had to stay up there for a few hours after the game parked outside Casualty waiting for several City fans to get stitched and bandaged up before returning home. We heard later that our ginger friend had a broken arm and quite a few lumps and bumps, so luckily nothing to serious, and a good result for the Police (not) with a score of 5 injuries to 1 in their favour.

One of the few positives to come out of this debacle was a bit of communication for next year's game. The following year they approached our club and Police asking them for some discussion about planning that year's game, they still wouldn't talk to us fans directly, but at least all parties could have some input. One of the things that forced this change in approach was the realisation that their firm but fair approach may wind up seeing someone killed, and after the Hillsborough disaster from years earlier, I'm sure they realised their force could not take another enquiry and the findings that would come up with

One comment that came back to me from one of those meetings, was one of their FIO's saying that he'd seen nothing like it and in his words he said that in his experience when dealing with football fans, if you threatened a fan saying you would be forced to draw your staff, then in most cases people would back off, those that didn't usually did when you actually did draw your staff, but when dealing with Cardiff fans he said none of these approaches worked and the more you hit them, the more people wanted to join in and fight you" I think this made them realise the Firm but fair policy needed a back up plan.

The following year after listening to our input and asking us what could they do to limit the chance of trouble, we made several suggestions such as finding us somewhere to have drink before the game on masse, not delaying us at rendezvous points unnecessarily, having some dialogue and communication, and not being met by coppers in riot gear brimming with aggression.

That years game saw them meet us at a Roundabout on the M1, as each bus got there a friendly copper got on, welcomed everyone to Sheffield and hoped they'd have a good day. Each bus was then taken within seconds by a Police bike into Rotherham, where they had basically given us the whole town for a drink and meal. When the coaches arrived in Rotherham, they were met by small groups of coppers in short sleeve shirts, smiling and showing you the way to the pubs, having a bit of banter, saying such and such a pub had the cheapest beer, but it tasted like shite, and this other pub had the best bar maids, fuck me human beings in uniforms, you could see our boys smiling and realising they may be treated properly if they behaved properly, at least they were giving us the chance.

Well I won't bore you and dwell on the positives, but what a day. I must have had 4 or 5 phone calls off landlords thanking me and asking to pass it onto the fans, several of them saying it was the most profitable Saturday they'd had since they'd owned the pub.
The day passed with no arrests, no incidents and can be summed up by a sight I though I'd never see at Sheffield, when I noticed one of our Stone islanded beauties sitting on a police motorbike with a police helmet on, and arm around a copper's shoulders and both of them smiling broadly whilst his mate took a photograph. A slight difference from scenes witnessed a year earlier, in fact things worked out so well that day, that by half time they had sent home half the coppers home because there was no threat and things were going so well.

It seemed so simple to us, and worked so well, other forces followed suit and thins did start improving for a few seasons, (West Midlands exempted) but more on that later.

WEST BROM away, now the game I'm referring to took place at the Hawthorns in the season 2003-2004 (I think) I have never been one for stats such as dates and scores etc from games played previously and unless something totally dramatic happened on the pitch that particular game, then I have serious problems remembering anything about it, can't put it down to my age because I've always been the same.

However, if something happened with regard to the fans then usually it is stored in the memory banks for long term. Now that don't just mean remembering the trouble that might have broken out, but also the craic that occurs amongst fans, such as where I was when I first heard a particular chant, or saw someone in a mad outfit, or things like Ronnie rock at Tranmere (a well known harmless lad who is drunk more often than sober) I had gone down to the concourse under the stand at half time, to see Ronnie Rock up against a wall with a copper facing him. The copper had both his hands on Ronnie's shoulders holding him against the wall, and I thought, oh fuck what's he done now!

I approached the copper in a nice conciliatory manner, trying not to make things worse than they were and said , "Everything ok officer, if Ronnie is playing up, I'll sort him out and get him away from here, even put him on the bus if he's causing problems", trying my best to stop him getting arrested and possibly banned. The copper smiled at me and replied "I ain't arresting him mate, I'm just holding him up" and as he started removing his hands off Ronnie's shoulders, you could see Ronnie sliding down the wall with both his eyes spinning and his legs collapsing like Bambi on ice, fucking priceless!

Anyway, back to West Brom, this game in the West Midland Police's wisdom had been changed to an 11am kick off. Again no consultation with supporters groups etc. just a case of this is what we are doing. Take it or leave it. Well lots of people left it, but I don't mean that they left it by giving the game a miss, what they left was the organised travel on the coaches, which had been proving so successful at so many other clubs we'd visited.

Now part of the reason they Police had arrived at this early kick off time was to stop our fans getting up there early hours and drinking in all the pubs in West Bromwich. Now if they'd have spoken to us in advance, we'd have explained that what we could arrange, as we had done at lots of other clubs, is stop well outside along the route in such places as Tewksbury, Worcester, Bromsgrove etc. in pubs that were glad to welcome us and would often ring me in advance to bring the till swelling revenue that we did with such gusto.
We would the happily turned up at their allotted rendezvous point for an escort on masse to the stadium, job done and quite straightforward.

Well what the forward thinking brains of Britain's finest police force hadn't worked out was, this early kick off would lead to loads of our fans saying, fuck them, we'll make our own way up (mostly by train) and either stay up there for a good drink afterwards, or wander into the centre of Birmingham and hang about New Street station, and have a scout about for any likely lads passing through, as so many do on most Saturdays of the football season.

So they created a nice little powder keg, which did lead to trouble breaking out in several areas in and around the station. What it also did was spread the match day police resources all over the place, instead now of having possibly 80% of the travelling fans coming on organised coaches, they were now looking at possibly 60% of our travelling fans coming from all directions and at various times. They had to have coppers spread out here there and everywhere, New Street station being just one of them, they had to have a presence on stations all around the West Midlands including the Metro type stations they have up there.
Also added to this lots of lads had taken up vans and cars, they were parking these all around the area planning to go back there after the game and have a few pints after the game.

So, all in all a policing nightmare. The City supporters club still had their normal allocation travelling on their coaches, and these are the fans you can count on week in week out to turn up everywhere, the numbers were pretty consistent and Vince who runs this club as got it off to a tee. Vince will be the first to tell you that whilst the Rams were taking so many coaches now to away games, there were more positives than negatives for him and the Official supporters club.

One of these were we at the Rams tended to attract and look after all the nutters (and I say that in the best possible way!) this left the family element who predominantly used Vince's coaches to travel unhindered and unmolested, my God I've been around the block a few times and there were times if I fell asleep on one of our coaches, then I would do it with one eye open. Also another benefit to Vince's group was the fact that until we had started using coaches, the supporters club tended to get the brunt of the silly over the top type policing with long delays at R/V points and top to bottom bus searches. Now in most cases when our group and their group turned up together, it gave the police chance to see which group tended to have the risk element on board so all their energy tended to fall on us.

Up until these times we used to believe with some credence, that the police and authorities tended to view all Cardiff fans as warlike Genghis Khan invaders out for rape and plunder, this now gave them the chance to see that this wasn't the case and often Vince's group would be allowed to have a separate escort, no searches and be taken quickly away from the R/V point, possibly to protect our own family groups(from the accompanying Rams coaches), who in all truth weren't out for trouble, just a good day out watching the football, having a day on the lash, letting your hair down and not necessarily breaking any laws, regulations yes, but that's a totally different argument and one that more or less lead to us finishing off the Rams travel group.

Where as at the onset they were happy to see that if they handled things well, then in most cases no laws would get broken, it soon got to the stage that regulations were now the main focus, yes we have to have rules and regulations, but we also need to have people that can apply these properly and use them to their advantage at times.

One of the daftest rules relates to alcohol, at rugby you can turn up pissed, drink in the stadium, even drink in your seat whilst watching the match and this is all good" rugger" fun, and the occasional mass brawl or damage in a pub is seen as a bit of high jinx. Yet at football you could turn up at a stadium and if an awkward copper was having a bad day, you could be arrested if he smelled drink on you, no matter if it was one pint or ten, and for those that say it don't happen like that, let me tell you I have lost count on occasions I have seen it happen and tried to stop someone getting arrested for such events.

Yes, if someone turns up pissed and staggering all over the shop, then fuck them off, and if they don't listen then yes you may have to arrest them, but there are so many variables to this equation and at the end of the day down to attitude and different approach from different forces and even different officers within that force, it's a bit like a risky lottery.
And then to compound this problem, they will enforce this law/regulation to the letter, yet when they do let you in, you are then allowed to drink to your hearts content as long as the game isn't being played and you're in view of the stadium, mad as fuck!

But the main law/regulation that caused most confusion and depending on where and who you were dealing with was the drinking on coaches law, applied to football mind, because rugby or horse racing didn't matter and you could fall off those coaches as drunk as a skunk and at will.

Now travelling on organised compliant coaches that turned up at R/V points at allotted time slots, was the one mode of transport where you weren't allowed to drink, Trains, cars, vans etc no problem, and even if you had a mini bus that this non drinking law applied to, in most cases you could get by un noticed and be parked up in some side street with no searches or delays.

So it was almost like an incentive to travel any which way you wanted to rather than in an organised method if you wanted to have a pre match drink, surely it would have made sense to do the exact opposite and say to fans "if you travel on recognised compliant coaches to the game, you can have a drink on board or we can arrange to find suitable premises near the ground where you can all drink together, whilst making things easier for us (the police) to look after things.

But there you are, who are we to have an opinion, even if it is one that when offered by forces, worked like clockwork in most cases.

Now back to WEST BROM and this was a classic example, the coaches were told they'd be searched on arrival and escorted well out of the force area preventing anyone having a drink before or after the game. So instead of possibly the 20 plus coaches the Rams would have had that day, we took around ten. This meant at least 500 of our regulars were now off the leash so to speak, and boy did those 500 (along with the few hundred regular independent regular travellers who would also be there) make them work for their money that day.

Our ten coaches had made their way up as normal, heading for the R/V point at the service station on the M5, just 3 miles or so down from the junction 1 turnoff to West Brom.The supporters club coaches at got there in advance of us, but were nowhere in sight, what had happened was they'd got there, hung around looking for the escort, which hadn't turned up, so after waiting a good while they decided to push on the last 3 or 4 miles on their own.
Our coaches were now doing similar things, and as they turned up in ones and twos, they had a quick look, see no coppers there and pushed on thinking "fuck you we came on time, you weren't there, so we are off"

What had happened, as we found out later, was the plans to meet and escort our coaches had been shelved last minute because Cardiff fans were arriving and showing up all over the place and the Police resources were reallocated to all these "hotspots" mind you someone had forgotten to tell all the coaches and they were just left to work it out and do their own thing.

This meant that you had the 8 or so supporters coaches ahead of us and in mixed in with the thousands of cars vans and lorries all heading off at junction 1, which is one of the busiest junctions in the country on a normal day, let alone on a match day at the Hawthorns.

By the time our coach had got within sight of the junction I could see the chaos ahead of me, it was gridlocked and the traffic was queuing down the slip road and hundreds of yards back down the slow lane of the motorway. After what seemed like ages lots of us had started getting well pissed off, we could see the floodlights but we weren't getting any closer to them, so people started getting off in dribs and drabs and walking up the slip road.

This all started off with good intention, but that soon changed when some of us noticed something happening up on the roundabout which was about 200 yards in front of us, we could make out that one of our coaches was surrounded by a good mob of 60 or so older lads who in fairness looked the part and not your spotty faced wannabe's we see so often.

We didn't know what had taken place, but it was quite apparent that something had happened. Now we found out minutes later what had happened, and it involved one of our Rams coaches that was being looked after by one of our Reps, Keith Harman ably assisted by his missus Joe. Now Keith new the score and had been in plenty of scrapes over the years, he wasn't a bully but he wasn't one to shy away from trouble so to speak, and what had happened was the bus he was in charge of had got stuck in traffic on the roundabout just as this group of West Brom had got there, now we'll never know if they had planned this, but if they had, then it worked out well for them in the short term, because Keith's bus had been isolated from the others who were stuck and spread out a few hundred yards back and then over the next half mile or so in the queue.

This mob, had managed to open the front door and were giving it the big one, now on a normal trip Keith's bus would have been rammed to the roof with some of our more dodgy characters, but these were the very ones who had now gone up on the train because of the WMP plans. So Keith's bus had mostly families and a lot of youngsters on board, so when Keith piled off the bus (with Joe backing him up) most groups of serious lads would have given them a pass, but not today you had one lad and his missus trying to calm things down and he took a real belting right hander off one of them. Joe managed to drag him back on the bus before he took a kicking as well, and luckily the queue started moving and they got away from the trouble. Keith was bouncing and when word spread (like wild fire as it does) everyone was livid and out for some revenge.

Well it didn't take us long to get a bit within minutes, because as we came up onto the roundabout we could see this mob had grouped up on the other side of the main road possibly waiting for their next victims, but this time we were on foot and not stuck on a bus.

I was in the front group which contained mostly lads off my bus containing Aberdare and Mountain Ash lads, not all blokes and we even had some kids along with their dads amongst us, but never the less we had 30 lads who I could count on if and when it kicked off, but the good news was just coming up the slip road behind us was another 30 or so lads and 100 yards behind them another 30 lads and this was being repeated back down through this nightmare traffic jam. Amongst all this chaos were two or three coppers with a worried look, you could see them thinking "oh fuck if this kicks off, we ain't going to be able to stop it" and kick off it did.

When West Brom saw our motley crew walking towards them, they came straight at us, we got the kids and their dads at the back and spread across the road as best we could, it started with a few small scuffles rather than an all in scrap, Puggsy from Mountain Ash was toe to toe with one and mad Andie was having it off with a big black monster of a lad, some were dancing around, but there must have been around ten or so small one on one scraps spread all over the road with these 3 coppers trying their best to calm things down. One of their lads was bending over one of our boys who was on the floor, I ran in and booted him off and five minutes later found his tooth stuck in my shin bone, great shot not!

Now in all fairness they weren't backing off and must have felt quite safe having a big wide road behind them leading up to the Hawthorns, with possibly 100,s more of their lads ready to back them up. But luckily for us, some of our other groups had seen what was going on and came running in from the side of these lads and had got amongst them from side on and behind them. This spooked them and their escape rout had been blocked off.

Now it's funny how things happen, and any one who's been in such situations will know what I mean, a group of 60 lads can within seconds turn into 20, somehow people just slope off, blend in or simply disappear, but I have seen it happen more than one occasion and if I'm honest I've done it myself in certain scrapes, or when two van loads of riot cops suddenly pull up all guns blaring so to speak

The 20 or so lads still having a go backed their way off through the now greater numbers, some of these sprinting up towards the Hawthorns shouting their heads off, the other 30 or 40 lads they'd had must have either blended in with us and were keeping their heads down or had just sloped off. I now new that we would soon be facing a load more West Brom lads when they'd heard what had gone on, and sure enough you could see hundreds of them making their way down towards us.

Our numbers though by now had swollen to more than enough to look out for ourselves and there was more joining all the time, not all blokes mind and as I've said there were quite a few kids and parents amongst us, but none the less enough of us for a full scale "off" if they wanted one. The police were now starting to get their act together and turning up here and there and you could the dogs giving it the big one. A couple of ours had been nipped or had their trousers ripped and now having a go at the coppers, there was the often seen pushing and shoving and lads shouting out "what's your number" and whilst all this is going on West Brom are still coming down the road towards us.

I have recently seen the Police footage of the next few minutes' action and it was strange to actually look at events from all that time ago. One thing I didn't notice at the time was how happy everyone was. It was mad, you had dogs biting people, some people arguing the toss with any copper who'd listen and a couple of hundred West Brom who were now no more than 50 yards away from us, but most of our lads present had big smiles across their faces.

The police had been caught with their trousers down, some older heads amongst us who had grown up with such events happening every other week, and it was like a throw back to their youth, re living what they thought were long lost days, as I may keep repeating, these blokes hadn't come intentionally looking for trouble, but if it happens, they wont be shy in coming forward.

Well it was on us now and the police were doing their best to keep a separating line across the road, I was up in the front with the Aberdare and Mount boys and could see them
Posturing and dancing around in front of us, with none of them really prepare to get into us when suddenly one lads lunges forwards, he gets knocked to the floor by a couple of stiff ones and next thing he's got this big fuck off Alsatian biting into him and almost lifting him off the ground an shaking him, he was yelping like a good un, it was funny as fuck.

A couple more tried to get into us and mad Andy still buzzing from earlier gave one of them a good clout just before a copper got hold of him and pushed him back on the pavement. It was all over bar the shouting now and you can see on the video all of their lads getting pushed up the road moaning like fuck, with all ours laughing and smiling as if they'd just been to the seaside.

We now had police coming in from everywhere, and whilst they'd missed out on the serious stuff and had been as much use as an encyclopaedia in Swansea, they were determined to regain some authority now and decided to bubble us up, walk us passed the way end and take us on a 20 minute hike before arriving on masse at the away turnstile 15 minutes after kick off.

But there we are we don't make these decisions we are just the people who have to live with results of them.

The West Brom matter didn't end there on that day mind, a good few weeks later we were playing Blackpool away and we had 5 coach loads of Rams stay up there for the weekend.

Well it came about that one bus load of the biggest, ugliest maddest lads you wouldn't want to meet in a church let alone a dark alley, decide to break up the return journey by stopping off for a pint on the way home. They decided that a pub in the Midlands area would be a good spot for a nice break.

So one of the large pubs used by West Brom fans was chosen and at 1pm 50 of our cultural attaché made their way through these pub doors. Big Sam reckoned later you have never seen so many people intently staring at the telly and afraid to look anywhere else, it's a bit like playing hide and seek when you're a kid, you know the scenario, if you close your eyes and can't see who's looking for you, then that means they can't see you either.

Wasn't the best plan and Ketty grabbed the biggest one in there "do you know who we are he asked" Y-yes came the reply, and "do you know that happened last month Ketty asked? I heard something about it the lad replied, but instantly added that neither he nor anyone else in that pub had been involved and the lads involved tended to drink in another pub in town, "no problem said Ketty phone them tell them we are here and we'll wait for them" You can imagine the landlord thinking "you dare mate and your banned for life"

Nothing came of it mind and the lad reckoned there was no one about. Our lads didn't create any problems there and didn't bully anyone, but the message had got out, sleep with one eye open if you hurt one of ours. I bet West Brom fans still check if we are playing Blackpool away every Sunday before popping down their pub for a pint.lol.

Chapter 25

THE ALBION WERE WELL UP FOR THIS ONE
by Big Jon Newey, West Bromwich Albion

Co Author of Sons of Albion due for release March 2009

I was contacted by John, after attending a casual clothes sale in Cardiff (www.casualsclobber.co.uk), held by a an Albion lad, John told me about his new book he had written and at the same time offered to write for me in mine, he also appreciated how much respect was given to the lad who ran the clothes sale in Cardiff . Annis

I am currently serving a seven year banning order after serving an 18 month prison sentence following trouble with our local rivals Aston Villa.40 years old born & bred in Birmingham, I was involved on the fringes of West Brom`s firms by personal choice from the mid eighties, I stayed on the fringes mainly due to internal wrangles within the firm, strange faces were not welcome so I stuck with my friends & we were involved in numerous if not many rows, from the mid nineties due to moving into the West Brom./Oldbury area. I became more involved with the firm, eventually becoming heavily involved in planning & organising our activities up until being dawn raided in December 2004 for the above mentioned trouble in 2005. I was sentenced to 18 months in prison as well as a 7 year banning order & that to be fair is the end of me, prison made me realise that I was being unfair on my family. I will be perfectly honest, I am not a top boy or main face, just a face who could be relied on in all situations, I feel honesty is the best way & that is my personal choice because that is the way I am. I have travelled the length & breadth of the country following West Brom & I have also followed England all over the world. I've taken in well over a thousand games with West Brom including visiting 86 grounds & I have visited many countries following England. Also I have followed Glasgow Rangers in Scotland & abroad for European games. To be perfectly honest in all the years I have followed West Brom, games against Cardiff have been very few & far between, infact apart from the games I will talk about in 2003-04, I find it very hard to recall any other fixtures between our two clubs, I do recall us playing Leyton Orient in an FA Cup game in the mid eighties in London & a firm of Cardiff led by a Mohican showed up after Cardiff's game at Brentford (I think) had been postponed, nothing happened between West Brom & Cardiff that day. We did ourselves play up, invading the pitch & fighting in the home sections of the seats & outside the ground afterwards.

The following is my recollections of our games Home & Away versus Cardiff in 2003 –2004.

Cardiff City V West Bromwich Albion. November 25th 2003

This fixture was much anticipated by our lads, as mentioned this fixture has not been a regular occurrence over the years & with Cardiff's reputation all of our lads were very much up for this trip, unfortunately the game was midweek but maybe that was a good thing, getting into Cardiff undetected would be maybe a little easier. Approximately 30-40 of us met in Oldbury early afternoon on the day of the game. We had hired two mini buses & the rest were due to follow us down in cars, numerous faces who were due to meet with us failed to show as per usual. So at around 2pm we left Oldbury & headed south down the M5.We arrived in Newport around 4 pm & entered a pub a short distance from the M4 Junction, as we entered the pub we noticed a fair few of our younger lads were already present along with a few of our well known older faces. When everyone had arrived we numbered in the region of 50,this was not bad & to be fair a good few lads present were well known faces, this was a tidy little firm. Obviously 50 lads would not be enough to take on Cardiff, we are not daft but we considered the element of surprise would stand us in good stead. To be honest the vast majority of this particular group were not interested in reputations or fear.

We sat & chatted for a time, with our phones constantly ringing with calls from lads also en-route to us & Cardiff At around 4.45pm we decided it was time to move, lads on there way to us were stuck in traffic etc so we decided as a group it was time to move. We arrived in Cardiff without incident at around 5.30 pm right on the main street in the middle of the city centre. All of our lads exited the vans & cars & entered a large boozer, to be honest after a short time in here we decided that we would be better off in a smaller bar because with only 50 of us present at this time we considered we would be better equipped to defend ourselves in a smaller bar, until our other lads arrived. Our best bet was to find a smaller place & plot up there & see what came to us.

We left the big boozer & crossed over the main street & entered Sams Bar, this was a smaller Bar & more or less ideal for us, we ordered our drinks & settled down in anticipation obviously Cardiff would now be aware of our presence, after only 5-10 minutes of being in Sams bar a small firm of Young Cardiff appeared outside, roughly 15-20 of them, we shot outside & to be honest a punch was not thrown. Glasses & bottles were thrown by our lot &the Cardiff group very quickly left the scene. This Cardiff group were all young lads, but we considered this little incident was probably the start of what would be an eventful night. We settled back into the Bar & no longer than 5 minutes later the police began to arrive outside, after a short time West Bromwich football intelligence police were also present so disappointingly it was now clearly evident for now the fun was over.

During our stay in Sams Bar the phones were very busy again with our other lads on the way down to Cardiff. We had arranged to travel down in a bigger group than we actually did, but to be fair with our lot talk & actual reality were two different things but over the years we have never worried about who had not turned up. We were confident in the 50 we had present & numbers never bothered us one jot. The Police completely had us surrounded, during the earlier trouble & the time it took the police to arrive, another group of our lot were on there way to us in the City Centre, this group numbered 30 but the police had got them before they managed to get to us, so for now their night was over as well they were escorted to the ground.

The Police held us in Sam's bar until around 7pm, they got us all outside & eventually escorted us to the ground it was a good walk & to be fair the Cardiff Police were ok with us, they mentioned that very few firms travelled to Cardiff on a Saturday, let alone midweek. We considered that at this point we had not done anything of any note but we had landed in their City Centre & above all else despite the fixture being mid week we had made the effort .If the police had not have collard our other 30 lads, we would have had a decent little firm, both numbers & faces wise.

We arrived at the ground shortly before kick off & entered into the away end. We had brought a good following as usual & the away end was full, it was quickly evident that many lads both young & old separate to our group had made the trip. The lads in the ground numbered easily 200+ & a lot of the well known good faces were present including a lot of the older 40+ year old lads who had travelled down on their own coach .This group contained some of the main faces, so all in all it seemed the night was still young & bearing in mind the lads present the game & afterwards could still be very eventful to say the least.

England had days earlier won the rugby world cup so many English songs were clearly in evidence, this added to the atmosphere & Cardiff were returning fire with anti English songs which wasn't a problem. After following England all over the world, I'd heard it all before & to be honest I think the English/Rugby songs were doing the trick & the atmosphere was superb with the old terrace in the away end adding to this, it was packed & our lads & fans were in the mood for a play up. The netting between the two sets of fans was ripped down by our lot & the away end was a scene of lads playing up & the Police/stewards just looking on doing very little. Albion took the lead through Jason Koumas, this just added to the atmosphere & the volume was raised even more, the game passed with Cardiff equalising & much of the same atmosphere continued from both sides.

The game ended in a 1-1 draw, the police held us in the away end for a time & when the gates were eventually opened the street outside descended into chaos very quickly. No Cardiff were present, here it was our lot & the police at war, I was quickly approached by our intelligence police & told to get my van & disappear or I would be nicked, this was quite a regular occurrence over the years obviously I had little choice unless I wanted to spend the night in Cardiff nick no offence I did not fancy that! I collected my van from a near by car park along with the other van driver, we drove along the main road by the ground on the look out for our lads. After passing the ground we shortly caught up with a large firm of our lot en route back towards the city centre, the police were present & after we pulled over, they made our lads get into their vans & basically then escorted us out of the area. They then made us join the supporters coaches in a police escort & it looked as though it was now definitely night over. The coach I mentioned earlier full of our older main faces had missiles thrown at it, they pulled over & chased the culprits without success. We were now indeed on our way out of Cardiff on our way home, the police followed us for what seemed miles until we were well out of the area, night over. We consider that action wise it was no big deal, we had turned up in Cardiff with a decent little firm face wise, a bit more luck & planning & it could have been a top night, no disgrace or result on either side, the atmosphere & play up in the ground was top drawer, a good night was had by all & I personally enjoyed my first trip to Ninian Park.

West Bromwich Albion V Cardiff City at the Hawthorns, West Bromwich February 14th 2004.

This game was much anticipated by our firm, due mainly to the fact that we had not played Cardiff for a good number of years at our place and also with Cardiff's reputation, we knew well beforehand that an eventful day would very much be on the agenda. The activities for this game started the evening before the game, rumour had it a decent sized number of Cardiff lads had booked into a large pub/hotel on the outskirts of West Bromwich called the Ridgeacre, this led to many of our lads including myself popping down there to have a look if indeed the rumours were true. We drew a blank and to be honest if the rumours were true no Cardiff were present in the pub when many of our lads paid a visit on separate occasions, that was Friday .

So we then went ahead with the pre planned meet early the next morning. We met very early doors in the Hargate Arms which is a pub a short distance away from the Ridgeace & roughly 2.5 miles away from the ground, by 12 midday we numbered in the region of 150-200,we kept a close watch on the Ridgeacre to see if indeed Cardiff were present in there, the rumours did have some substance because I drove down there myself to have a look & the place was surrounded by the police, obviously nothing was going to occur in that area now so for a short time we held tight in the Hargate to see what would develop. By 1pm nothing had happened so all of our lads present started to filter up towards the town centre & pubs up towards the ground, my Pals & I drove up to the Sportsman which is a bar close to Junction 1 of the M5, a brisk 10 minute walk to the ground, on entering, it was evident that numerous lads not present at the Hargate were in here, so it was apparent we had a good number of lads out today it was usually reserved for local derbies or very big games.

After being in here for an hour or so & many more of our lot landing here myself & around 10 of our older lot including Freethy, Micky R, Daz G, Peachy, Clem & others left the Sportsman en route to the ground, after a short walk we arrived at the motorway junction island, as we were crossing the exit slip road north bound we immediately noticed four coaches stuck in traffic on the slip road backing back onto the motorway. We slowed down & had a look, at this point 15-20 Cardiff lads exited their coach probably fed up with waiting, this led to a mutual confrontation between the two groups, we were outnumbered but we stood our ground, punches were thrown on both sides & to be perfectly honest, as this developed more Cardiff were getting off the 4 coaches to join in, this put us on the backward step a bit, because we were now starting to be heavily outnumbered, after a few phone calls were made our lads in the near by Sportsman & en route to the ground began arriving at the scene, our numbers very quickly grew to 150-200 lads. We were now on the front foot, I will not say that all the Cardiff present were lads because that was not the case, the coaches also contained shall we say normals/shirters whatever you may refer to them as. As a rule we are not bullies so in the main the Cardiff lads who were out on the road and involved in the row were our target. To be perfectly frank & honest we came out on top in this exchange, numerous Cardiff were dealt with on the slip road around the coaches, some were more or less chased onto the motorway. Following this part of the day it was said in numerous circles, we had attacked coaches full of supporters not lads, I can honestly say the initial row was between two sets of lads, some normals on the Cardiff side obviously did get involved but in the main I witnessed Cardiff lads & fans well up for the row & fair play to them.

Following the slip road exchanges our police were quickly on the scene filming & roughing people up, the small group of us present at the very beginning left the scene & to be honest left our younger lads to it. The chaos that followed on the main Birmingham Road was captured by the Police on video camera, this led to dawn raids on 20 + of our lads, the footage is available from hooligan DVD's. This footage shows our lads being pushed towards the ground followed by Cardiff off the coaches being escorted the same way, a stand off between the two firms followed which then led to our lads confronting Cardiff, where again punches were thrown, our lads made numerous attempts to get into Cardiff & Cardiff to be fair stood their ground & returned shall we say fire. The footage shows the police setting dogs on our lot & them making a sustained effort to get our lads away from the area, the footage is also a clear indication that the claims that the Cardiff coaches were supporter coaches to be untrue, it was evident a good percentage of the Cardiff present were indeed lads & handy ones at that! Following these pre game clashes the game passed without incident.

Cardiff were well supported at the game & they were very lively with it. It was rumoured that a decent sized firm of Cardiff without tickets had been allowed into the game to keep them out of mischief around the ground & surrounding areas. Due to the Pre-game incidents, after the game went without incident. The Police were all over us & they very quickly pushed us away from the ground, the two groups were unable to meet again, It was day over. To be fair to Cardiff they had made a good show & to be fair to us, so had we, any talk of us attacking supporters coaches was complete nonsense. Anyone involved in that incident was involved by choice, nobody was bullied & no coaches had windows smashed etc.

In the weeks that followed the game around 20 of our lads were dawn raided, in court the West Bromwich intelligence Police were pushing hard for violent disorder charges, in their desperation one particular unnamed Police officer completely fucked the case up.
The solicitors did their homework & found out evidence that the Cardiff coaches were supposed to leave the M5 at Frankley services to be then escorted into West Bromwich via Junction 2 of the M5 at Oldbury. The polices violent disorder charges & their cases against our lads amusingly fell apart, the violent disorder charges were dropped to lesser charges & our lads came away with fines & banning orders & nothing more, Result!!!

Epilogue.

Having witnessed Cardiff over these two games to be honest it's hard to judge & in my opinion unfair to do so. They showed at our place in big numbers & gave a good account of themselves despite us making a good show in Cardiff, a major off did not occur. A fair judgement from me is that Cardiff have obviously got massive numbers & a good amount of good quality heads, the opinion country wide is that Cardiff figure in most lads top 5-10,I do not argue with that, it's a fair assessment in my opinion. I have met numerous Albion lads from Wales over the years, these were good lads and they often brought some Cardiff lads to games with them, the Cardiff lads were also sound. I will always remember there amazement at a row between us & the police before an Albion/Wolves game regarding our numbers present & how mad we were, it was no big deal to us, it was a regular occurrence at this fixture obviously what the Cardiff lads had witnessed here led to us being added to their places to visit list when Cardiff were promoted to our division. One thing I would like to add because this book contains opinions Country wide, opinions will obviously differ, that is not a problem, football banter/violence is all about opinions one thing I will say about our lads is opinions/insults do not bother us one jot. Very few firms have ventured into our areas & although we do not travel often enough when we do we have both the numbers & quality to do a good job, we have & we do nothing more than that……….

Court refuses to b
brawling Albion fa

By Iain Robinson

Thirteen West Bromwich Albion fans who brawled with rival supporters are free to watch their team play in the Premiership after a court refused to ban them from matches.

The 11 men and two youths all admitted using threatening or abusive words and behaviour likely to put someone in fear of unlawful violence when they appeared before West Bromwich magistrates yesterday. The charges stemmed from a disturbance outside The Hawthorns shortly before a match against Cardiff City on February 14.

Andrew Cheung, aged 24, was among the West Bromwich A

Police chief calls on club to take action

Police chiefs today condemned a court's decision not to ban the 13 Albion supporters from matches after they fought with rival fans. And the club itself is considering possible action against the 11 men and two youths who were convicted yesterday.

By Iain Robinson

Senior police officers and prosecutors had hoped town magistrates would impose football banning orders on the defendants which would have barred them from all major home and international fixtures for three years.

Superintendent Bob Spencer, of West Bromwich police, said officers' only hope of barring the offenders from matches now lay with the football club itself, which has a reputation for taking tough action against unruly fans.

"This certainly was not the result that we expected and we are extremely disappointed," said Mr Spencer, who shares responsibility for policing Albion home games.

"We were following the government guidelines about attempting to reduce and remove this hooligan element from football, and a lot of time and effort went into that operation.

"It is clear from the video footage shown in court that there were young children who were part of that crowd who must have been terrified by what was happening," he said.

Mr Spencer went on to say "We will be asking the club to ban these men, but clearly that is a club decision."

A spokesman for West Bromwich Albion today said the club was aware of the court case and was considering possible action against the convicted fans.

"As and when we get an approach from the police we will deal with the matter and consider an appropriate response," he said.

The Crown Prosecution Service has also expressed disappointment at the sentences imposed on the convicted fans. But spokesman Vinny Bolina stopped short of criticising the magistrates. "We are disappointed by what has been said in this case, but we have to respect that and get on with the next prosecution."

Magistrates imposed two-year conditional discharges on all of the defendants and ordered all but one to contribute between £35 and £70 towards prosecution costs.

But the bench declined a request from prosecutors to impose football banning orders which have power to bar supporters from attending games for three years.

Chairman of the bench Mrs Brenda Moore said she had given defendants credit for entering early guilty pleas to the joint charge.

During the three-hour hearing, magistrates watched a police surveillance tape showing how the defendants had been part of a 40-strong group of Albion and Cardiff fans which clashed in Birmingham Road.

Prison

The defendants were Matthew Bolton, aged 19, of Dudley Close, Rowley Regis; Hayden Dando, 18, of Cophall Street, Great Bridge; Simon Hamblett, 30, of Charnwood Road, Hamstead, Birmingham; Thomas Oldaker, 19, of Castle Close, Cradley Heath; Philip Norton, 22, of Dorsett Road, Friar Park, Wednesbury.

Also Kevin Ritchie, 21, of Bassett Road, Friar Park; John Poole, 44, of Chester Road, West Bromwich; Stuart Pugh, 20, of Napier Drive, Tipton; Gary Ricketts, 34, of Greatfield Road, Kidderminster, Robert Simms, 42, of Sunbury Close, Coseley; Andrew Cheung, 24, of Wells Close, Tipton, and two Darlaston youths aged 16 and 17.

Ritchie is serving an eight-month prison term for violent disorder following a different football match.

Stuart Pugh, aged 20   Philip Norton, aged 22   Ro

SOCCER YOBS ARRESTED IN RAIDS

COPS swooped on suspected football hooligans during dawn raids in the Midlands yesterday.

Eleven men, aged from 17 to 35, were arrested and quizzed by West Midlands Police.

The operation was mounted following violent clashes before the West Bromwich Albion v Cardiff City match at The Hawthorns on February 14.

The men – from West Bromwich, Walsall, Sandwell and Kidderminster – were taken to various police stations.

Detective Inspector Carl Southwick, of West Bromwich Police, said: "We shall continue to clamp down on the minority of football fans who spoil the enjoyment of the game."

DAWN SWOOP ON SUSPECTS

Police seize Albion fans

BY STEVE JOHNSON

ELEVEN suspected football hooligans were behind bars today after being arrested in dawn swoops.

More than 50 police were involved in the pre-planned raids launched at addresses throughout the West Midlands at 7am.

The raids followed clashes before the match between West Bromwich Albion and Cardiff City at The Hawthorns on February 14.

The raids were carried out in conjunction with a nationwide football hooliganism operation codenamed Citadel.

The 11 men, from West Bromwich, other parts of Sandwell, Walsall and Kidderminster were taken to various police stations and were expected to be charged with violent disorder.

Genuine

Det Insp Carl Southwick, based at West Bromwich, said the men were aged between 17 and 35.

He said: "We shall continue to clamp down on the minority of football fans who spoil the enjoyment of the game for the majority of peaceful fans who visit stadia throughout the region.

"We will do everything we can to catch them and prosecute them.

"Nobody wants them in football, the clubs don't want them, the police don't want them and the genuine supporters don't want them."

Police intend to apply for banning orders against the men through the courts.

This will mean they will not be able to attend Albion games in the future and will also be prevented from attending away matches.

West Midlands Police have been working in conjunction with West Bromwich Albion FC to stamp out the hooligan element.

Soccer yob suspect
held in dawn swoo

By Katie Spooner

uspected soccer hooligans were targeted by police who
ried out dawn raids across the Black Country today in
nnection with violence at a West Bromwich Albion game.

en homes in the area were targeted by officers who made a total of
arrests as part of the Operation Citadel raids, which detectives
e hailed as a success. Those arrested after being raised from their
s were being questioned by police officers through today and police
I that they were expected to be charged by the end of the day.

The raids were made
after officers had studied
film footage of trouble
breaking out in Birming-
ham Road at Albion's
Valentine Day match
against Cardiff City.

The fans, arrested at
addresses in Kiddermin-
ster, Cradley Heath, Rowley
Regis, Darlaston, Tipton,
Great Bridge, Wednesbury
and West Bromwich, could
now be banned from
matches worldwide.

Detective Inspector Carl
Southwick said: "We intend
to continue to clamp down
on the minority of football
fans who spoil the enjoy-
ment of the game for the
majority of peaceful fans.

"We will do everything we
can to catch them and prosecute them.

"Nobody wants them
involved in football, that
goes for the police, the club
and the genuine fans."

Camera

The men, all aged
between 17 and 35, were
caught on camera during
disturbances at the match
last month.

They have been classed as
"Albion Risk Base" sup-
porters – a group of fans
who attend football
matches and seek out
opposing supporters.

Mr Southwick: "We are
sending a clear message
that we will not tolerate any
violence in or around the
football grounds.

" We want to bring foot-
ball back to the genuine
fans."

Today Albion, who gener-
ally have an excellent reputation throughout football
for their fans' behaviour,
play Crystal Palace at home
and police are hoping that
the fans will get the
message that if they misbe-
have they can end up in
trouble.

The police hope that the
supporters will back their
actions.

"We hope fans will see
this as positive action to
combat the trouble fans can
face at the match, said Mr
Southwick after the raids
today.

A suspected hooligan hides his face as he is taken to Wednesbury p

Sgt Lee Winters and Pc Mark Poxton
with heavy door- ramming equipment
at the start of Operation Citadel today

A police officer removes ev
the home of a suspec
hooligan on the Yew Tr

Chapter 26

"NEVER LEAVE YOUR MATES"
By Little Pete (Peter Lintern) CARDIFF CITY

I've got to know Little Pete, like you usually get to know most of the lads through going down the football, He's become well respected by all the lads over the last 14 years and for someone so small, he's one of the gamest lads about. Always found him easy to get on with and honest with it. He told me a story of how when Barnsley came to Cardiff in 2003, that one of their lads drank with Cardiff in the Game Keeper pub before all the trouble had happened and was respected and looked after. Pete then went back with the Barnsley lad to their pub and once inside within 2 mins, from behind was totally knocked out and was flat out on the floor in a pub with a 100 Barnsley lads in their. I asked about and it was totally true, Other Barnsley lads have agreed it happened and that it was well out of order. Pete to this day, is upset and believes they broke the football lads code of honour. I totally agree with him. Annis

My back ground......

I'm 33 years old and I was born and bread in a beautiful village on the out skirts of the wonderful city of Cardiff called Taff's Well. I went to school in Caerphilly with my old infamous mate Dai Thomas (I actually went to watch him have a trial for Cardiff when we were about 14 it was at Swindon and I even went on the youth teams bus to the game, sitting next to Scott young) . I have had an intense love affair with Cardiff city football club since I first went to watch them on my own. at the tender age of 12 in 1987.

As soon as I witnessed major violence at an away game at Bristol city in about 1989, I think I was totally hooked on football violence and that's all I ever started to think about, how could I become involved with that awesome fighting group of lads that I witnessed cause mayhem at Ashton gate. Anyway through hard work and getting involved in some crazy fights and situations over the years, I managed to work myself into the main firm of the Real Soul Crew, as I had now gained respect from some of the Top older lads, the main lads who made me really welcome and look out for me at the time were Simmo, Lakey and Ginger Jones (Ely's finest and maddest ha).

I have followed Cardiff all over England from the late 80s and then all through the 90's and the beginning of the year 2000. I've been banned since 2003, I was given a 6 year ban and a 6 month prison sentence for fighting with PLYMOUTHS central element out side Cardiff central station ! .

I first saw Annis at Walsall away in 87 /88 season, I think it was, and then over the years I got talking to him and became more friendly as time went on. When Annis rang me to ask if I would do a bit in his follow up of his first book, I was delighted to help him out as he his a well respected man in the football underworld and a true gent to go with it . I also know Annis is

Cardiff through and through and he was there through all the bad years.

Here are my 2 accounts in detail, about two serious clashes with MAN UTDS firm (the red army).

OLDHAM AWAY AND MAN UNITED........oh what a day !!!!!!!

It was our first game of the season and we had the long train journey up to Oldham, I had tried to arrange about 40 of us to meet on Cardiff central station but only about 25 turned up, as is the norm when you try to organise a little firm, always a few cant get out of bed because they have been out on piss the night before. On our journey up, my best mate Christian mentioned United were at home to Boa-vista in a pre season friendly!! So obviously mobile phones were used to get a United number which we got in about 5 minutes...United were spoken to by p so things were looking good for the day ahead .We were told United had about 25 to 30 but I will be honest, I thought they were lying just to trap us, but it turned out they were telling the truth so I really respect them for that to this day, as they could of easily had 100 plus for all we knew.

We were drinking in the Weather-Spoons pub near the station in Manchester and there were a good 100 Cardiff in there. So me and some of the lads spread the word that United wanted it before and after the Oldham game, me and my little crew of now exactly 18 solid, quality lads. Who I will now name, myself ,Pasty, the two mad brothers Christian and Shaun Thomas, the Rawlings, Clayton ,Chris Price, Scott from Carlisle) ,Goughy, Erricson, Bevon and kirkby, Jimmy, Big Ginger ,Mark Haynes and three North Wales boys who I don't know there names . We all stayed in the Weather-Spoons pub watching all the other Cardiff leaving the pub and heading for Oldham and, we were lets just say not fucking amused, they all make out they want it and here was their chance. I know who they are and they do, but I wont name and shame them !!!!

Whilst we were still in the pub, United were now ringing and calling it on, (I can't remember name of the other train station in Manchester) so we all agreed to meet at the other station in 5 min's time. As we where approaching the station, we saw about 25 of them approaching the station, so I told all the lads to just keep walking towards them. But as soon as we saw the United firm about 200 yards away, all the boys just ran straight at them, and United turned and ran, like fuck . At that time we didn't really know if they had the 25 lads as they had said they would have or there could have been 225(with the rest of their lads behind them),but we went straight into them without any hesitation at all. I couldn't believe we had just run United in there own city, it just seemed to easy. UTDS main lad then rang and said how disgusted he was with his firm running so easily and said that he would get more together to meet us after the Oldham game to make amends.

So after that little result we where bouncing, we couldn't believe what we had just done as that firm were part of UTDS main lads. So myself and the 18 gladiators got the next train to Oldham, which by now the game had already kicked off. We got in to OLDHAM about 3.30, so P then rang OLDHAMS firm to see if they wanted to meet as well, they didn't sound to confident. They said to us to ring back in about 10 Min's, so P did and they told him to go half a mile up the road. We were all on high now, so we all marched up to the pub where they said they were. When we were about 50 yards away, we saw the curtains shutting along with the front door !!!!!!So P kept ringing and ringing OLDHAMS firm, they would not answer there phones, surprise surprise. The only thing I can think of is why they didn't want it with us was because they had just heard, we had run UNITED 30 min's previously. Anyway nothing happened at OLDHAM and I have heard many stories from other Cardiff lads over the years that OLDHAM have always hid from them.

We then got escorted by 5 riot vans through an Asian area where we had some seriously strange dodgy looks from the locals. The police put us all on a train out of OLDHAM and back to Manchester we were headed.

When we where all on the train to Manchester P asked all the lads, 18 of them if they were ready and up for a meet with UNITED, for round two they all said 100 % YES. So P said are u all sure as UNITED could have loads more lads than earlier on in the day, as there was still only of 18 of us. They all said fuck it lets have a go, we only live once, one of the lads said. UNITED then said when u get into MANCHESTER City Centre ring us and we will come to u. So we made our way to a pub at the bottom of the steps by the big triangle monument, P rang them and told them we where we were and they said they would be there in 10 min's. I then told all the boys to be ready. I walked over to the pub and popped in to get a bottle of lager. Suddenly Big Pasty came running in and grabbed me and said they are fucking here now, so we ran out and with that we saw UNITED walking towards us at the top of the steps. Me and the rest of my real mental firm ran straight into UNITED without even thinking again. When we went into them they still only had about 25, but they were all big lumps, they had a big lad at least 6 and a half foot tall, he was like a   monster running into us and Chris price knocked him out with one of the best punches I have ever seen in my life, Scott from Carlisle had a bottle smashed into his face just above his eye and was bleeding heavily. Then fighting was just erupting everywhere for a solid 2mins proper, it was toe to toe fighting, not your hand bags. There was at least 4 or 5 UNITED lads lying on the floor as we had some serious big hitters amongst us like us, like Clayton ,Christian Thomas, Chris Price, Erickson ,Ginger and Pasty .We started to smash UNITED everywhere and they were now starting to back off and quite a few of them even ran away.

When I looked around I saw Big Ginger smashing two half cast boys in a shop doorway and they looked terrified. I then looked around again and I saw the 6 and a half foot monster getting his tongue pulled out of his throat by Scott from Carlisle. The Manc lad was in a serious condition. With that Scott then put him in a recovery position and shouted call an ambulance. We were gob smacked and surprised that UNITED had left one of their main lads knocked out and on his own. But we helped their lad out and sorted him out. One of the UNITED lads came back over to us, to see if he was ok and I told him that he and his mates were total wankers for leaving him on his own and his reply to me was to fuck off. With that I hit him as hard as I could, then I hit him again and again until Big Ginger jumped on me and said Peter he has had enough. I turned around and shouted at Ginger, I will decide when he has had enough.

So that was it the fight finished, major result for our little firm. The usual police noises were now being heard, so we then quickly made our way to a back street pub and all went straight into the toilets to clean ourselves up, as there was blood all over us. We then waited until the sirens of all the police had died down and then made our way back to Piccadilly station, where we then bumped into a couple of YORK CITY lads, they shit themselves when they saw the state of us and heard of what we had just done in Manchester. On the way home our phones didn't stop ringing until we got back to Cardiff. When we got back, we were met with a hero's welcome from some of our main players and doorman. At the end of the day it was a major result for a small firm against one of the best in the country.

MAN UNITED IN CARDIFF

WHAT THE DOCUMENTARY DIDN'T SHOW, THE REAL FIGHTING THAT DAY AND NIGHT

First home game of the season we had Wycombe Wanderers at home, the next day United were in their Cup final in the Millennium stadium .We all new Man United were going to bring a firm, so we were out in massive numbers that day....and by fuck could we have done with those massive numbers by the end of the night.

During the game we were all getting phone calls saying United firm were drinking in the Prince of Wales, so word soon spread around the terraces and stands for everyone make their way straight into town, straight after the game. I was with about 100 Soul Crew who marched into town and straight up the lane behind the Prince of Wales pub and walkabout. We intended to smash our way into the side door of the Prince of Wales to attack United ,but it was blocked by loads of old bill who forced us onto ST Mary street. Within the space of about 20 minutes, we must have had a huge mob of about 500 who were going mental because United were in one of our main pubs.100's of Cardiff were charging old bill on ST Mary street, when about 100 of us broke away down a lane by The Model Inn Pub, we then went down Wood street with no old bill with us. We finally got to the Prince of Wales, just as United had just charged out at same time and about 20 of them broke through the police lines and came straight into us, I managed to knock one of their front lads straight on his arse (best punch I have ever thrown). It was witnessed by many lads.. about 30 of us then managed to give as many United as possible a good few slaps until they had had enough and retreated back to safety of their firm. (Lakey mentioned this on the documentary) At the same time as this was happening the TV cameras were filming hundreds of Cardiff charging the old bill down St Mary Street. .they had missed the Real Soul Crew having it with the Mancs.

As the night wore on United were taken in a police escort down to what they thought, the safety of the Neville pub in Grange town.

We were drinking at that in the Borough Pub in ST Mary street and by now our numbers had gone right down to about 60 (a proper 60 "quality lads") ,it was about 10pm and a lot of our lads live a long way away in the Valleys . Myself Christian Thomas and Big Ginger told our lads to stay there, while we drove around in a car looking for United. Within about 20 minutes we found them drinking in Grange town, to our amazement no old bill !!!!!!!!! so we drove back to the Boro and told every one the score. All make your way to the Cornwall pub and when we are altogether go and attack united in the Nevill. So 10 of us got to the Cornwall, we were then waiting for the rest of our firm, but for some reason unknown to this day the, 50 Cardiff walking down, decided to attack United without meeting the rest of us !!!!!!!!!!!!!! .

The phone then rang saying they were hitting the Mancs from the front and you lot hit them from the rear .When me, Deacon, Simmo ,Big Ginger, Lakey ,Christian , Parker and a few others (cant remember names sorry lads) , ran from the Cornwall up to the Neville. This was going to be a proper firm on firm fight in middle of the road, we then went straight into United from behind them, dishing out as many slaps as we could , their faces were a picture they must of thought 100's of us were coming , but only us crazy 10 were there. After about a minute United realised our numbers and came straight back into us, Simmo knocked at least 1 clean out, but United were well on top by now and backed us off up the road towards the Cornwall, To be honest about it. If the old bill hadn't off arrived then we would have been mince meat, the old bill saved our mad arses. I'll never forget Deacon hobbling up on crutches on our initial attack and swinging them at United it was funny as fuck, and also Lakey hiding between 2 cars and jumping out slapping a United lad who was backing us off up towards the Cornwall quality Mr Rivers!

At the end of the day the result had to go to United fair and square and in my eyes are the best most up for it firm I've ever come across so far, so hats off to them. But what I cant understand is why these serious little fights have never been put in their books !!!!!!!!!!!!! ???????????

Chapter 27

We Didn't Go For Show
By BARNSLEY FIVE-O

The following was sent by a well known Barnsley lad who would like to remain anonymous. Annis

In the 2002/2003 season a fixture cropped up the, Barnsley lads had been waiting for, for a long time, CARDIFF away, it also dropped on a special day for most of the lads in Barnsley, particularly the older end, it was the anniversary of the death of a well known and respected lad "Robert "Gibsey", Gibbs who sadly passed away in February 2000.

The home game against Cardiff had been played in November 2002 and Cardiff had been in touch, a meet had been arranged in Wombwell, a village just outside Barnsley with the main Soul Crew who were travelling up on two 50 seater coaches, By 9 am we had 100 lads in a pub waiting for them to arrive, but unfortunately the old bill got wind of it and intercepted the Cardiff coaches and also shut down the pub our lads were in. Our mob headed back into Barnsley and the numbers swelled to 250 in "The room" on Eldon Street, rumours were doing the rounds that a large group of their boys had got into the town centre. So our lot tried to leave and confront them but riot police from all over Yorkshire blocked everyone in the pub, this didn't go down well with our lads and the lads attempted to smash their way out. The pub was completely wrecked as tables, bottles and stools were launched at the riot police, at one stage the pub was on fire, this forced the police to let everyone out, the mob headed through the streets, but the rumours of Cardiff in our town had been false and they were infact held in a working men's club just outside the town centre and were going no where.

The town centre was closed off to traffic for about an hour, as debris was cleared off the roads. After the match Barnsley numbers were massive, again it was mayhem, groups of Barnsley were all over the town trying to get towards the train station and bus station. Fighting broke out with the police all over the town, the riot police weren't local and had been drafted in from all over Yorkshire and were up for it, the fighting with the police went on for around 2 hours, with running battles up and down the town well into the night. Cardiff were probably halfway home by this time, but it was just one of those days

We were now looking forward to the away game at Cardiff. Leading up to the away fixture the phones were red hot, traditionally every year the lads would get together meet up with Gibseys family and celebrate his life as he would have wanted, a good piss up somewhere out of town or a decent day out at the football, these days usually ended up everyone getting back to Barnsley in the early hours, normally with half of South Yorkshire police in tow.

As the day got nearer the numbers going got bigger, as more realised it dropped on the day of

"Gibseys do" loads of the older end were up for it and some main faces were to be out for this one, the lads knew South Yorkshire Police would be wanting to spoil the fun so numbers were kept to a good 100-120.

The day of the game was an early start, 4.30 - 5 am for most, as many mini buses and taxis were booked and the idea was to travel separately to Sheffield and get into the station and on the 1st available train at the last minute, so everybody wasn't hanging about in Sheffield and hopefully get on the train without attracting any unwanted attention from the old bill.

This plan worked fairly well and by 7 am, 120 good lads we were on the train early doors, the lads had 3 carriages and as soon as the train left the station the booze was out, halfway into the journey the refreshments were in full flow and the lads were ready for whatever Cardiff had planned .The 4 hour journey went fairly quick and the plan was to get off the train at Newport and get taxis into cardiff and head for their 2 main pubs at the time , Sam's bar or the Philarmonic . Things were looking good, but soon as the train reached Newport the platform was packed full with riot coppers, everyone tried to get off but no chance, they wanted our lot straight into Cardiff and were obviously wanting everyone where they could keep everyone on cctv. Everyone was really pissed off by this time and thought it was game over for the day, the coppers had even said they might stick us straight in the ground which would have been a fucking disaster.

As the train pulled into Cardiff, a sea of old bill greeted us, they held everyone outside the station for about an hour, promising to get a pub open, as everyone was held there spotters from both sides were busy filming and taking notes of who was there and what they were wearing, a few lads were nicked for possession. As soon as it got to 10 am, the walkabout had finally agreed to open, everyone piled in there and everyone was at least now being served and having a beer and not been put straight in to the ground.

Obviously our lot were now in Cardiff and the Cardiff lads would have got wind of it and hopefully put in an appearance. After an hour or so, some Cardiff went past and soon more and more Cardiff lads drifted past, a few had chatted to a few of ours outside and they said they were turning out big.

10 - 15 minutes later the pub opposite started to empty, the Cardiff lads were trying to get at the walkabout front door, a roar went up and our lot charged at the front doors to get out, the old bill immediately pulled meat vans right up to the front doors, blocking the way out, they drew batons and cs gas... a few bottles and stools were thrown from both sides but the old bill kept control, although both mobs were trying their best to get at each other.

As the ob were still trying to force the Cardiff mob back, one of our lot stumbled on a fire escape that didn't have a padlock on, with a quick boot it was open and everyone piled out the back door, most of our lot turned right charging down the main street. Everyone knew most of the pubs would be full of their lads by know and anyone was fair game, about 20 of ours who left the walkabout last, went straight out into the car park at the back and bumped straight into about 20 of Cardiff's main lads. The timing was perfect and as the old bill tried to round the other lot of ours up on the main street, it kicked off in the car park big time, it was toe to toe for about 5 minutes, with each side giving as good as each other, one of our lads ended up with a broken collar bone, a Cardiff lad later said it had been their main faces the Docks boys.

The old bill were flapping like mad and it was kicking off down the main street, although many of the Cardiff lads in the pubs further down were caught unaware and couldn't believe where our lot had appeared from. Horses charged down the street towards us and eventually the old bill penned everyone in behind some scaffolding with batons drawn and cs gas out.

As more old bill arrived the streets were filling up with more Cardiff, word had spread fast and they were trying to get at the Barnsley lot, only the sheer number of coppers kept both groups apart. They shut off the main street and ordered some buses to get everyone to the ground, everyone was pissed off about this as a couple of Cardiff lads had said they were going to ambush the escort on the way to the ground. With Cardiff having such big numbers they could have probably done this by confusing the already stretched numbers of old bill.

As soon as they got our lot to the ground, everyone was herded straight in and we weren't happy, luckily they were serving ale and everyone carried on boozing right up until kick off.

During the game a couple of attempts were made by both mobs to get at each other over the corner of the pitch but the coppers soon put a stop to it. Half way through the second half our lads decided to leave, charging down the stand and towards the gate, the coppers weren't prepared and were flapping big time. The stewards tried jamming the gate but the lads carried on, the coppers drew batons and gas and it kicked off big time. There were old bill on the deck, bins were thrown at them, a gate was ripped off and hurled at them, it was mayhem, as the Barnsley lot battled against the coppers, the Cardiff lot were trying to get out as well. They weren't encountering as much resistance as ours, as most of the old bill were too busy trying to stop the lads smashing out of the ground. It looked like the Cardiff lot were trying to get out also, and Cardiff managed to and had got behind the old bill, the old bill would have totally lost control and it would have been game on.

More and more old bill arrived and finally shut the big iron gates, the coppers had kept both mobs apart by the skin of their teeth and had managed to drive the Cardiff lot back. The numbers of Cardiff outside the ground must have been 500 plus, with a few barmies in with them. Even as the coppers tried to get our lads on buses, we were still charging through at the Cardiff lot, with the old bill only just managing to keep them apart again. A Cardiff lad later said their old bill had been "fighting for their fucking lives" behind the stand.

That day the lads had done as much as possible to get at it, and the lads that travelled that day didn't give a fuck how many Cardiff were there. Cardiff have a good reputation and can pull massive numbers, a good mob of Barnsley had travelled and unlike some, had gone for it, not just a show, all the lads who went knew the score and had taken it to one of the biggest firms in the country! For our troubles many were dawn raided a while later from both sides.

Wales On Sunday 09/02/03
First report

CARDIFF .V. BARNSEY 2003.

Soccer violence: Four arrested FOUR football hooligans were arrested yesterday after trouble between Cardiff City and Barnsley supporters.
Around 50 riot police backed up by officers on horseback had to escort dozens of drunken visiting fans to Cardiff's Ninian Park for the match amid fears of violence in the city centre after a pub was damaged.

St Mary Street was closed for a short time before the 3pm kick-off.

A police spokeswoman said: "There was a greater police presence in Cardiff because of the football match.

"We were being extra cautious.

South Wales Police said about 360 visiting supporters were in the city.

Two Cardiff men, one aged 26, the other 35, were arrested for violent disorder and a public order offence.

Two men, one in his early 20s and another aged 33, were arrested for drug offences.

Echo 10/02/03
Trouble report
Soccer thugs clash before City game
VIOLENCE flared ahead of Cardiff City's game with Barnsley on Saturday.
Riot police and mounted officers had to deal with drunken brawling fans near Sam's Bar and Walkabout on St Mary Street.

Three men were arrested, a 26-year-old from Cardiff for violent disorder and a 35-year-old man also from the city for a public order offence.

A 33-year-old from Barnsley was arrested in connection with a drugs offence.

There was trouble between rival supporters at a number of bars in St Mary Street and police said one bar was left badlyconsiderably damaged.

At one point Barnsley fans tried to break out of the ground's visitors' section, but police using batons kept them at bay.

There were no further arrests for violence, but a Cardiff man was arrested for a drugs offence.

Police said there were no reports of violence after the game.

Supt Kevin Tumelty said: "The majority of games this season have passed without incident and it's disappointing that a small number of hooligans, from both Cardiff and Barnsley, were openly seeking confrontation with each other."

Echo 13/02/03
Police operation launched
More arrests in football violence probe
FOUR men have been arrested in connection with city centre clashes between rival soccer fans.

The arrests in West Yorkshire follow trouble in Cardiff before City's match against Barnsley at Ninian Park on February 8.

Officers involved in Operation Bolivia – a joint operation between South Wales Police and South Yorkshire Police – have been studying CCTV footage of the violence.

Today's swoop brings the total number of arrests to 20, with 12 having already appeared in court, two being cautioned and two released with no further charge. A South Yorkshire Police spokeswoman said: "Three arrests were made in Barnsley and one in West Yorkshire this morning after viewing CCTV footage."

"We expect a number of further arrests to be made in South Yorkshire as part of our policy of preventing public disorder at Barnsley games."

The trouble began when Barnsley followers began drinking at around 11am on the day of the match at the Walkabout bar in the city centre. City thugs massed in nearby Sam's Bar and damage was caused to both bars, with windows smashed and furniture damaged.

As officers tried to stem the violence, a large number of Barnsley fans ran up St Mary Street, with shoppers and traders caught up in the trouble.

Fans also clashed during the match, with stewards and police being attacked.

If you have any information about the trouble, call the Operation Bolivia incident room on 029 2022 2111 extension 30195 or Crimestoppers on 0800 555111.

Operation Bolivia Echo 11/03/2003

13 face court after hooligans run amok in city POLICE CHARGE FANS THIRTEEN men from South Yorkshire accused of taking part in soccer violence in Cardiff city centre have been charged by police.

Operation Bolivia – a joint operation between the South Wales and South Yorkshire forces – is trying to trace groups of Cardiff City and Barnsley football fans who clashed in the centre of Cardiff when their teams met at Ninian Park on February 8.

South Wales Police officers have been in Yorkshire this week to help track down Barnsley fans captured on CCTV footage.

The group of 13, who are all from Yorkshire, were charged with violent disorder and other public order offences.

It means 38 arrests have now been made as a result of Operation Bolivia, with 29 either facing court cases or having already appeared in court.

The trouble flared when Barnsley fans started drinking in the Walkabout bar in Cardiff city centre at 11am on the day of the match, and City fans congregated in Sam's Bar opposite.

Both bars were damaged, with windows smashed and furniture wrecked.

As officers attempted to intervene, the group of Barnsley fans broke up and ran up St Mary Street.

They made threats to officers and shoppers and traders caught up in the violence.

The rival sets of fans clashed again during the game, with stewards and police officers being assaulted.

Detective Chief Inspector Graham Lloyd, of South Wales Police, said: "As well as the 13 who have been charged, officers are continuing to question another five people from the Barnsley area who are now in custody, and further charges are anticipated.

"A team of four South Wales Police officers have travelled up to Yorkshire to assist in the arrests and will be there for the rest of this week, returning when further individuals have been identified.

"In addition, 20 arrests have been made in South Wales. We expect to make several more.

"We are sending out the message that anti-social behaviour and violence before, during and after sporting events will not be tolerated and, if it does occur, rigorous investigations will follow."

Barnsley 'fans' cause trouble in Cardiff

Monday, 10th February 2003

Game marred by hooligan element

There were clashes between rival fans before the Reds match with Cardiff on Saturday.

One Barnsley man was arrested in connection with a drug offence after what South Wales Police described as a "minor disturbance".

A spokesman for the force said a group of fans who had travelled from Barnsley plus Cardiff fans, were intent on fighting ahead of the match.

The incident occurred at St Mary Street in the city, which is a short distance from the Millennium Stadium.

"The majority of games this season have passed without incident and it is disappointing that a small number of hooligans from both Cardiff and Barnsley were openly seeking confrontation with one another.

"The game passed without any further incident and there were no further arrests."

The Oakwell fixture saw trouble earlier in the season when police in Barnsley had their biggest presence ever (over 300 officers) due to Cardiff's reputation.

Reds fans who made the trip to Ninian Park have reported a large number of unfamiliar faces among those inciting trouble in the ground while other unconfirmed reports suggested a number of Leeds hooligans had joined up with members of 'Five-O' - Barnsley's hooligan 'firm'.

Worryingly, reports of rascist chanting (against Sam Hamman) and 'No surrender to the IRA' songs also returned.

The police kept fans waiting inside the ground for an hour after the game while Cardiff hooligans were dispersed.

201

Chapter 28

THE TRUTH BEHIND THE WOLVES RIOTS
By Kevin Murphy (Big Sam) CARDIFF CITY

I've known Big Sam, right back to the dark old days, when our Support was at its lowest and lads like Big Sam were the only support we had. We've been to together through the good and bad days, stormed boardrooms, met every Chairman and rallied the fans when the club was sinking. You won't get a better fan than Sam, but he's also been one of our main lads from the Valley's. Annis

Kevin Murphy is my name, but most people know me as Big Sam. I am from the Merthyr area of South Wales and live in Aberfan, a mining village that has had more than its fair share of tragedy. Merthyr is a big Valleys town and along with many other valley towns and areas such as Aberdare, Rhondda Valleys, Pontypridd, Caerphilly, Mountain Ash, Tredegar, Ebbw Vale, Pontypool, Rhymney and loads of others there is a huge Cardiff City support. Even in my village there are around 30 season ticket holders plus others who go on a regular basis.

I have been following City for over 40 years and my first away game was Leicester City Aug 69, we won 1-0 and Tosh scored the winner. I was a 15 year old skinhead and along with thousands of others we love this club they call Cardiff City. Over the years of following City I have been involved in incidents up and down the country, it happens and I'm not apologising for it, in the bad old Div 4 days. Cardiff's lads were the only ones who used to travel, well not the only ones, but we were always there, I don't think there are many City fans who haven't been involved somewhere or sometime following our club anyway with rival fans fair enough, but the shit we had to put up with from various police "firms" especially West Midlands and West Yorkshire Beggars Belief, The Met ain't so bad really, they would rather give you a good kicking than do the paperwork bless them!!!

I have been asked by Annis to give a version of events of what happened when we played WOLVES Away in October 2004 and March 2006. I have known Annis for years; a few people slag him behind his back. You cut his arm and he bleeds blue 100% City Annis, good enough for me that. I remember the early days at MILLWALL where we had a go but shit ourselves the same time. Great respect for the "Wall" from the Valley lads. To LINCOLN CITY away in the early 80's where I'm sure the whole town had a go at us and other games like CHELSEA and WESTHAM etc. But some of them were so long ago I'd probably forgot more than I can remember, so here goes though, WOLVES it is.

WOLVES away, a special one to me was when I went there in the late 80's we won 4-1, Gilligan hat trick and as rough as fuck it was. A big game back then and a big game now. Wolves have always had a good crew and can pull big numbers as well.

WOLVES Away October 2004

As we were travelling up with the Valley Rams coaches Big Gwyn had to meet the West Midlands police "firm" Ha Ha. Police told him no alcohol on coaches, Gwyn said O.K then we will take 3 coaches and the lads will make their own way to the game. Police said O.K have a few beers so then we took 23 coaches and most of them were full of out Legions of the Neanderthals, Jesus Christ, we have some right beauties following our club. I honestly believe we have got more nutter's who follow our club than any other club in the country, must be something to do with the water down here, Or the "Bow".

During that meeting with the West Midlands Police Gwyn was told any Cardiff coaches turning up would be held, searched and put in the ground early. Charming, that!! So basically we were not welcome in that shit hole called Wolverhampton, so we decided 2 day's before to split up, as it turned out, our coach and 5 others went to Bromsgrove, others went elsewhere.

Bromsgrove, nice town, stopped there many times over the years for a few beers on the way home from away games oop north. Our 6 coaches were rammed with lads, so when we got there we split up. There are plenty of pubs in Bromsgrove so there was no problem getting a beer; we were all over the place and no trouble anywhere. We don't go smashing towns.... contrary to what people think. No plod, few beers.... Lovely. It was around 11 am police found us at 11.05 am ... amazing.

We had been in a pub about an hour when Tony Rivers (Lakey) came in with Gilly, Wolves main lad so we were told, I'd met Gilly before and he seemed a decent bloke. He told us Wolves had 200 lads in Bilston...where the fuck is Bilston????? I would have thought they would be in Wolverhampton where Wolves play, yeah but there you go and we knew we had a nice crew on the train. Now, many of our lads don't like fraternising with the opposition and told him to fuck off, so he went and took Lakey with him. ...Probably to another pub.

We leave Bromsgrove around 1.15pm – 1.30pm, can't remember exact time, Old Bill watching everything we do. Bromsgrove to Wolverhampton ain't too far. On the way one of the lads had a call to say there had been trouble in Wolverhampton already...interesting!!!

Police escort as usual all the way in, when we pull up, we get the usual warm welcome from the West Midland Police (Firm), you know the shoving, searching, bullying, verbal abuse and general intimidation. I wonder what these chaps are like when they get angry Ha Ha anyway, fuck them, we had come across these twats before, they are nothing but bullies in uniform and what a uniform wow!! They were a cross between Darth Vader and a Muslim woman. We could only see their fucking eyes and they were armed to the teeth, there is no talking to these twats, hate them and I'm not just saying this, but our lads don't give a fuck for them, we are used to being treated like shit, give Cardiff fans RESPECT and we are FINE, treat us like shit and you will have major problems. It was a half-mile walk to the ground across a car park and dual carriageway, down a hill, and into the ground, all nice and quiet before the game, the calm before the storm.

It was either half time or during the 2nd half one of their stewards said to Keith Cooper a referee (Cardiff fan and a retired ref) who was standing close to us, that a few weeks earlier Wolves were home to Wigan and after the game as the Wigan fans left the ground, the Wolves lot came down the hill and battered the Wigan fans and families as well. Believe what you want, he also said that they quite often attack visiting fans in that area after games and that the Old Bill know about it but do very little. Should be very interesting later we all thought.

Final whistle went and City win a belter 3-2, most stay behind to clap our team who thoroughly deserved the cheers and applause. Right, out we go, Happy as Larry, when we get out, all hell breaks loose. Wolves came steaming down the hill and were throwing everything they could, bricks, bottles, crash barriers the lot. Only this time they were playing Cardiff City, love us or hate us, Cardiff lads will always have a real go and if ever a club picked a wrong day to attack us, Wolves did, we had a huge crew out and as always, were up for it.

City's lads went steaming into them, no bouncing about or poncing about, this was football violence at its best/worst call it what you like, our lads were straight in and backed Wolves right up the hill, battering every one of them that got caught or tried to stand, I don't care what anyone says about that day, our lads were awesome. There was so much fighting going on between Cardiff and Wolves and Cardiff and West midlands police firm, you wouldn't believe it. I ain't naming names or anything, but all the known lads and young guns were having a real go and doing their selves proud, after all the Cardiff support were violently attacked by the Wolves firm who apparently do this quite often and get away with it, well not today, I won't describe in detail who was doing what or what was happening to this person or that person because these incidents only happened a few years ago and people tend to say aye aye he's bullshitting, but this we shall say was very tasty and Cardiff lads were quality.

Don't forget when the Wolves lot first attacked the Cardiff support there were families, women, and kids amongst them and when they were throwing everything, they didn't give a fuck who they hit, and a lot of people could have got hurt, and if it wasn't for our lads, a lot of people would have got hurt. A lot of our so called "proper" fans, and they are good people by the way, often put down the antics of our lads, but I can assure you, that over the years, at various grounds around the country, the so called antics of Cardiff lads have saved many of our "proper" supporters from having a real shoeing and this Wolves game was one of them.

After Cardiff backed Wolves up the hill, there was a bit of a lull, then Wolves came back again, this time they were vary wary and again Cardiff went at them and yet again we backed them off. This time though, the tosser's from the West Midlands Police Force had entered the fray, Robocop had less firepower Ha! Ha!. This police Force seems to hate most football fans and us in particular.

The shoving and pushing started, so the lads started shoving back. They then started to hit out willy-nilly with their truncheons so the lads fought back. Self defence – yeah? So now not only are we fighting the Wolves crew, the fucking police are having a go as well, fuck me, it was like being in the German Army during World War 2, we were fighting on two fronts. Cardiff support that day numbered around 2,300 of which at least 800 were lads and the West Midlands Police were cracking everyone, they didn't give a toss who they hit. It was chaotic, mad, there was so much happening all over the place and some of the situations going on were outrageous and hilarious. The police firm had formed a line ¾ of the way up the hill. The hill that City had sent Wolves packing up, these were the finest Robocop's, you know the ones, armed to the teeth, you can only see their eyes, they were trying to get Cardiff back down the hill, if you have ever been to Wolves, when you come out of the away end there is a hill to your right, that's the one the Wolves lot came down and went back up. By the way, there is another hill/incline right opposite the away end, the police were trying to get us down one hill and up the other to get us back to our coaches, cars, trains whatever. We had Wolves and police in front of us and Robocop behind us. A recipe for disaster me thinks…

At the bottom of the 2 hills/inclines, it started to go off with the police, about 20 yards up the second hill a patrol car pulled up. 2 Old Bill got out, they were surrounded by some Cardiff lads and I think they shit themselves because they forgot to put the handbrake on and the fucking car rolled down the hill and into a crash barrier. It was soon dismantled by some of the lads. All of a sudden a shout went up, a lad from Pontypridd, who now lives in Cardiff said I've dropped my phone and unbelievably the Old Bill and Cardiff lads involved in this particular fracas bent down and picked up, not his phone but the police radio out of their wrecked car, it had a curled Arial on it, we burst out laughing, the Old Bill went potty so we started fighting again, fucking amazing.

Not only had we seen off the Wolves lot, we were now having a go at the Old Bill, big time. Our lads were going mad, now a police van had its windscreen put in, the lad then took a packet of biscuits off the dashboard of the van and anyone who was walking up the other hill must have seen the little dance routine of this line of Robocop's who came jogging down the hill behind each other towards us. The last one tripped and a few of them went down like skittles. Wicked that.

The trouble finally died down and we made our way back to the coaches, trains, cars whatever means of transport we got here with. There were some comments made by police, which personally I did not hear, but very good friends of mine did and I totally trust and respect their word. These are a few of them: -

"It was like watching boy's fighting their fathers and Cardiff are the daddies."

"Fuck me, Cardiff got 800 no-necks."

And on the way back to the coaches, a great mate of mine was approached by a copper who said "Well done, those wanker's deserved a kicking they've been bullying other fans for years." My mate said yeah, a police officer saying that, the copper said, "I'm a BAGGIES fan!"

I've not mentioned anyone's names or who done this or who done that because this is recent history and you never know what the West Midlands Police fucking Force might come out with. All I know is Cardiff City's lads, firm, supporters call it what you like were violently attacked and responded with a venom that few, if any other club in these isles could manage, its just in us and always will be.

The West Midlands Police Force are hated by most football fans up and down the country, bullies, that's all they are and whoever was/is their match commander on that game October 2004 & March 2006 want's shooting. The man/woman is a complete tit.

WOLVES Away 11th March 2006

The game 2 years later nothing happened between either set of fans, but at half time, there was a major incident under the stand where Cardiff's fans were, I was at the game but because I don't like spending at away grounds, I stayed on the terrace, Ha Ha.

Here is the eyewitness account of a 16-year-old girl who was there with my youngest daughter who was also 16, hardly battle-hardened hooligans. The young girls name is Jamie Lee Francis and my daughters name is Kate Murphy.

Please read it and make your own mind up.

"The day of the Wolverhampton Wanderer's away game was a complete and utter palaver. To start off, we were told 2 different rendezvous points, then when we eventually arrived at the correct point, we were kept in a yard for at least an hour. We were then taken straight to the ground, along a retail park road on a Saturday afternoon, utter chaos as you can expect. No premeditated thought as per usual from the West Midlands Police Force. What's the point in bussing us in and bussing us out in a so called "bubble" game with no freedom, if they are going to allow us to walk side by side with the Wolves fans to the ground without blocking the road off and diverting the other fans?

When we eventually got to the ground, there were maybe 4 turnstiles and easily 1,000 fans trying to get in all at the same time. Instead of staggering the bus arrivals, they forced us all to arrive at once and we descend upon the ground together. I myself missed the Kick Off due to this lack or organisation.

Despite what other people and the police say, to me, there wasn't a bad atmosphere that day in the ground. At half time, ma and my friend went under the stand, and we went to the bar to get a hot drink. As usual the underneath was busy full of fans, singing and queuing to get served. I can honestly say that I witnessed, one of the bar staff serve not one but multiple fans with alcohol. Then for some reason they refused to serve one bloke for beer. As they said, "we cannot serve alcohol at half-time" to which he replied, "I've just seen you serve people for beer." And with this the fans started singing "we want beer!" There was no threatening or violence in this, just general banter. The bar staff with this, stopped serving all together, and started to pull the shutters down. The next thing I know, a swarm of riot police came wading into the packed bar area.

I moved out of the way and was shielded by a few men. Some of the police officers were like something possessed, swinging their collapsible batons with intent. They hit anything in their path without concern for age or if there were women or children caught up in the commotion. It got so bad at one point we were forced back up into the stands for our safety. The next thing we knew the police had come up into the stands and were battering fans who had not even been in the bar area. Many fans and myself were forced onto the pitch for pure fear of being hit by the police. The violence in the stands continued for well over 10 minutes and forced the second half of the game to be delayed. The West Midlands Police were totally out of order that day and have still not been reprised for their actions.

A few weeks later there was a meeting chaired by Sam Hamman, which I attended to state, that I witnessed beer being served that day. Not only was I called a liar by one of the more ("mature" shall we say) stewards at the club, but it was also suggested by Sam himself that I mistook a cup of coffee for a pint of beer, to which I replied "I may be only 16 years old but I know the difference between a cup of coffee and a pint of beer." It was also suggested that people had purchased beer before the game and a statement that stuck in my mind was, "By half-time that pint would have been as flat as a witch's tit, and there was no way it was bought before the game." That still makes me laugh to this day. It infuriates me that the club once again refused to support the fans and still to this day, to me, the events have been swept under the carpet."

That's a totally honest account of a 16-year-old girl. After this game, Jez Moxey, Wolves chief Executive and a right arse hole in my mind banned Cardiff fans from Molineux for fucking what????? For being hammered by those pigs... Mad ain't it?!?!

Most Cardiff fans believe the West Midlands Police wanted revenge for what happened 2 years earlier and I repeat we were attacked by Wolves fans. That's not a problem we defended ourselves and done the biz, the police didn't have a clue what to do and started having a go at us so we took it to them and they didn't like it. What do they expect us to do? Lie down and let them batter us????? Fuck that.

If people leave us alone we are fine, fuck with us and you've got major problems.

Daily Mail, Monday, March 13, 2006

HAMMAM HAILS FANS DESPITE MOLINEUX SHAME

WOLVES	2
CARDIFF CITY	0

CARDIFF chairman Sam Hammam left himself open to accusations of condoning hooliganism as he responded to insisting his club's Molineux by saying "some of the supporters were 'some of the best in the country'.

Seventeen Cardiff fans were arrested, seven during clashes with police inside the ground and 10 as troubles spilled into the streets afterwards, prompting the FA to launch an investigation.

All those arrested are expected in court today and West Midlands police revealed several officers had been injured, two seriously.

Yet Hammam insisted: 'Our supporters are well respected. They had a bad reputation as among they are now accepted as the best in the country.

'People will criticise because police are involved, but nobody should make sweeping statements about Cardiff fans. I cannot speak highly enough of them. They've been wonderful.'

Trouble flared at half-time when the bars were shut behind the lower tier of the Steve Bull stand,

where about 1,200 Cardiff fans were housed, and the restart was delayed by almost 15 minutes as stewards and police, some in riot gear and carrying shields, struggled to restore order.

Repeatedly the police were met with violence as they attempted to force back fans and officers lashed out with batons to try to stop the problem spreading.

The pity for Wolves was that this ugliness over-shadowed their return to the playing with what manager Glenn Hoddle described as 'probably our best football of the season'.

Denes Rosa tapped in from a yard after superb work by Jeremie Aliadiere in the 15th minute and Kenny Miller capped a brilliant individual display for the Wolves' second goal from the spot in the 53rd minute, after Darren Purse's clumsy challenge on striker Tomasz Frankowski.

Looking for trouble: riot police restore order among Cardiff fans at half-time

Chapter 29

THE ZULUS IN CARDIFF
By Sooty Jason (Older Zulu and J (Young Zulu) BIRMINGHAM CITY

I was contacted by some lads from Birmingham who wanted to give some accounts of their visits to Cardiff, I was away on my honeymoon in 2006, so I cant comment, What I've been told was that The Zulus didn't arrive till really late, but when they did they were really up for it. The numbers they had in the ground that day were massive and in today's age that doesn't happen very often. The Zulus in the 80's and 90's were always one of the biggest firms around and one of the gamest and judging by what they brought to Cardiff in 2006, they are still very active. I would like to thank Sooty Jason (Zulu) for helping to get these stories to me and being a sound lad.

Cardiff City V's Birmingham City 2006

On 26th August 2006 Birmingham City were due to play Cardiff City at Ninian Park for the first time in a number of years. Due to previous incidents involving the two teams supporters, in both fixtures of years gone bye and in recent years when the Blues have played final matches at Cardiff's Millennium stadium, and also simply because of the fact that both sets of hooligan groups belonging to the two clubs would like to think of themselves as, on their day, one of the top hooligan firms in the country the fixture promised to be a some-what explosive affair in terms of off the field activities.

Because of the interest that this fixture would also undoubtedly generate from our friends at West Midlands and South Wales Constabulary, the Blues lads planning on making the trip down to Wales that day knew that something a little different was in order if we had any chance at all of avoiding police detection and/or getting any sort of hooligan firm anywhere near their Cardiff companions. So at 6am on the day of the game a good firm of Zulus both young and old met up at one of the Zulu pubs in the time 'Billy's Bar', by 7am the pub was full and shortly after many of the lads set off for South Wales in cars with the intention of rendezvousing in Newport, Gwent . Before moving on to Cardiff, However a good firm of 50 Zulus, a large percentage young, who were travelling to South Wales on a coach had decided that taking a coach down the motorway towards Cardiff would bring unwanted police attention onto the rest of the Zulus who were meeting up in Newport, so therefore would go a different route to Cardiff taking them a good hour out of their way but avoiding any South Wales motorway, as well as the all important police check points.

After a long journey through South Wales, across to Merthyr Tydfil then down the A470 and some other winding Valleys A-Roads the coach of 50 Blues lads finally landed at a pub in the Welsh town of Barry only 9 miles away from Cardiff. But as it was the other side of the city we expected no police attention. The Blues lads had a quick drink in Barry whilst three 15 seat mini-buses and a 7 seat taxi were called to take them into the Canton area of Cardiff. The plan was that the taxi's would meet up, again to help avoid police detection, at a location inside one of the large parks that are right next to Canton where the firm of Zulus could then walk together unopposed, out into the Canton streets towards where they believed that the main Cardiff pubs at the time were located. However due to part of this park being closed off on that specific weekend added to the fact that two of the useless mini-bus drivers hadn't got a fucking clue where they were going, so the firm of 50 Zulus from the Barry coach were forced to reunite at a pub just outside the Sophia gardens park on the edge of Canton. Which was the only factor that I believe alerted the South Wales police to the arrival of the 50 Zulus right in Cardiff's back yard.

As soon as the last mini bus taxi arrived at the pub, so did one police van who could only follow, radioing frantically for back-up. They could not contain the firm of 50 Zulus as they started to walk through the Canton back streets towards where the Cardiff pubs were believed to be located. The firm of Blues after only a couple of minutes of walking through the streets were alerted by the shouts of some Cardiff fans at the end of one of the side roads, the police following then started shouting for the firm to keep walking straight ahead. So the Zulus of cause started to pick up the pace and turned down the side street. Once the firm of Blues turned into this street they saw that on the left hand side of the opposite end of the street was a pub, one of the Cardiff City hooligan firms pubs the 'Kings Castle'. The 50 Zulus started to jog up the road towards the pub as did the police. As the firm of Blues reached the pub, a firm of Cardiff hooligans burst out of a side entrance into the road chucking beer bottles and pint glasses at the Zulus. The Zulus not tooled up in anyway made a brief charge towards the pub and with only a handful of punches exchanged sent the Cardiff lads tripping over themselves backing off into the doorway, that they had just burst out from. From the look of shock on the Cardiff lad's faces who appeared in the road first, I believe that these lads at the Kings Castle did not anticipate the number of Zulus that had suddenly appeared to face them in the road right outside one of their main pubs or the Zulus willingness to engage. A second van of South Wales police had arrived from round the front of the pub who together with the van of police who had been shadowing the Zulus now formed a line in the road with their backs to the pub and batons drawn facing the firm of Zulus now started to force the firm away from the pub and down a main road in the direction of Ninian Park.

Although it was later brought to light that Cardiff's main firm on this date were in fact at a different location in the Grangetown area of Cardiff before kick off, as this incident took place, the firm of Zulus were not to know this at the time and I personally believe deserve full credit for making the effort that they did in getting a firm of 50 lads into the heart of Cardiff's territory with very little police presence. At no time did Cardiff ever know we were coming and thats how we work. A South Wales police officer was also quoted in saying to one of the Zulus "Fucking hell I've never seen the Cardiff back off like that before, they normally don't even back off from us" a quote which generated much amusement amongst the firm of Zulus throughout the day.

The Cardiff City Soul Crew are without doubt, on their day one of the best firms in the country and this very minor incident outside one of their pubs is not by anyway seen as a firm on firm result. It was just a brief incident that took a lot of effort and planning on the Zulus part to be executed in an age of football violence when it is hard for a firm to even move without the long arm of the law breathing down their necks, let alone come face to face with their rivals. It will be interesting to read/hear the Cardiff City Soul Crews take of the day's events but hopefully the respect that I know a lot of Zulus have for them will be reciprocated.

Throughout the rest of the day incidents took place of both firms attacking the police whilst trying to reach one another although this incident mentioned that took place outside the Kings Castle was by far the only real chance that the two firms had that day to properly exchange pleasantries. After the incident at the pub the police slowly started to descend on the firm of Zulus as they continued to walk through the streets of Canton and within about 5-10 minutes South Wales' finest had 50 of Birmingham's finest cornered in a Cardiff back street. Fair play to Cardiff as the police now escorted the Birmingham Zulus through the streets taking them the long way around the ground to the away turnstiles the streets, all around were filled with what looked like hundreds of Cardiff lads trying the best they could to break through the police lines and get to the road where the Zulus were being escorted. But sadly the time had already past and the police were now well on top of the situation, the 50 Zulus were then escorted to the ground without further incident.

Inside the ground mid-way through the first half trouble between the Birmingham City away following and the police occurred as a result of the Cardiff stewards trying to forcefully eject a Blues fan. The South Wales police entered the away end at the front of the stand which sparked off a crowd surge that forced the police back down the stairs over the advertising boards and onto pitch side. The police were then pelted with bits of ripped up seating from the front of the stand and lumps of concrete terracing from the back. This trouble inside the ground later resulted in prison sentences for some of our lads.(photos of this can be seen in The Diary of The Real Soul Crew 1.)

Although no major disorder really took place on this day it was, for those involved, one of the most eventful away days that you will get to experience in modern times following football. What I have a written about the days events is an eye whiteness account of what took place, although because of the recentness of the day in mention added to the fact that I am still an active member of the Birmingham City Zulu Warriors I hope you can appreciate why I have failed to specify any personal involvement in the day's events.

'J' A Young Zulu

2003 IN CARDIFF FOR THE CUP FINAL By Sooty J (ZULU) BIRMINGHAM CITY

Firstly I would like to thank Annis for the chance to give my views on the disorder between the Zulu's and the Soul Crew. Although I have not had the chance to meet Annis, I have spoke to him a number of times over the phone thanks to a good friend of mine Chelsea Pat, who I've known for a number of years.

2003 saw Birmingham City play Liverpool in the Worthington cup at the Millennium stadium. We set off for south Wales in the car around midday, calls were already made that there was already a good firm of Zulu's already in Cardiff. After arriving in Cardiff around 2.30pm, it wasn't long before we were spotted by some of the Soul Crew. "Birmingham are we?" said the one "Yeah I'm Birmingham" and he said" well your lot are in the RSVP bar up the road, we'll see you lot later". Knowing the Zulus were going to be in Cardiff in big numbers the Soul Crew were ready for us.

The afternoon passed off without any major trouble and by early evening we were 300 handed easy. Ten of us walked through the shopping centre and bumped into a few Cardiff lads. The chant went up "zuulluu". A handful of punches were exchanged and a couple of bins thrown, the police came in with their batons. Due to a heavy police presence it was hard for the Soul Crew to get into the centre of Cardiff where the Zulu's were drinking. So they had to wait till late evening.

During the evening a few pubs got smashed and a police woman got hurt as the Zulu's fought with the police at the Philharmonic pub. Shortly after, a number of Zulu's who were in a pub drinking with a few Liverpool fans were attacked by a group of Cardiff hooligans, the fighting spilled out into the street, till riot police came into force to split both groups apart which lead to many arrests. Through out the night incidents took place with the Zulu's attacking both police and locals. I remember walking through Cardiff with a small group of the younger Zulu's when we heard "ZULU" and the sound of smashing glass. We ran to a pub on the corner where it had kicked off with the Soul Crew. Bottles were thrown from both groups till the police arrived in numbers and separated both groups using dogs and batons, battles like this were constant during the night.

After I got split up from my group I walked up a road next to a group of lads who just happened to be Cardiff. I was on my own and expected a kicking. The one Cardiff lad who to this day has become a good friend of mine named Peter, he said I was "OK" and that they were "not bullies". I was then taken to a pub where there was a large group of Soul Crew, due to the incidents that had gone on through out the night with the Soul Crew, although very nervous at first I became relaxed in their company I now have a lot of respect for the Soul Crew. Due to the incidents that had been going on for most of the night between the Zulu's and the Soul Crew you could see Cardiff were well up for it. I would like to finish of by saying how well I was looked after that night. Although I wasn't involved in any of the disorder that night, many a time were the stories retold by other well known Zulu's from that fateful night. The Soul Crew are with out a doubt one of the best firms in the country and many Zulu's have a lot of respect for the Soul Crew due to three decades of similar incidents. The events mentioned are what I witnessed of the day in question.

212

Hooligans jailed August 2006

Six football fans have been sentenced for their part in violence at a match which left a steward permanently blinded in one eye.

Other stewards were hit in the violence at the match

Birmingham City fans threw seats, coins and a lump of concrete during a match at Cardiff's Ninian Park last August.

One of the missiles hit steward Roger Llewellyn-Mortimer in the face.

Five men were jailed for up to eight months and a sixth given a suspended sentence after they admitted affray. All received lengthy banning orders.

'No regard for anyone'

Cardiff Crown Court heard the men were identified from footage recorded at the match.

In a statement, Mr Llewellyn-Mortimer described how his left eye was hit with an "unbelievable" force.

"They paid no regard to the terrified men, women and children around them," he added.

Peter Davies, prosecuting, said one woman at the match with her children for a birthday treat was physically sick after leaving the ground.

Martin Bowman, 36, of Eastfield Road, Bordesley Green, Birmingham, was sentenced to eight months for breaking seats and throwing one.

Stamping on seats

Mark   , 31,   Birmingham, who stamped on a seat but did not throw anything, was jailed for three months.

Lee ———, 32, of '   .ks Green, Birmingham, who has 22 previous convictions and was given a football banning order in May, was sentenced to four months.

James ——   24,-   ., Lapworth, Warwickshire, was jailed for three months for stamping on a seat.

Chapter 30

OUR BITTER ENEMY
By Annis Abraham Jnr, CARDIFF CITY

The following story is not about our battles with the Jacks, as I've already written about them in my own book, out later on in the year, no this is more about how the hostility is still there and the hatred, but also showing how times have really changed in the hooligan world.

I've been to every Derby match that has been played against the Jacks in the last 30years, I've even gone down there when we have been banned on two occasions, the first time just as I was about to go through the turnstiles I was collared by the old bill and told "not on this occasion Annis", and as I walked away from the ground there were lads from the valleys standing outside shouting to each other "everyone do the ayatollah". On the other occasion so many of us managed to get in that eventually 400 of us were put into the empty away end behind the goal.

I have also been there on many occasions when we have swamped the town centre and taken over virtually every pub, well I suppose those days are well and truly gone but they were great days and any true honest Jack should admit it, Cardiff in the 80's would well and truly take over Swansea.

When the fixture list came out for the 2008/09 season every fan in Wales was looking for the fixture dates of the Cardiff v Jacks games, as it had been ten years since we had played them in the league and even more interesting was that we would be going to their new stadium.

So we knew we had them away in November on a Sunday morning and at home in April 09, but it was soon announced that they would both be bubble trips but that didn't matter to the lads and fans from Cardiff as they were going no matter what. So in the mean time we had Birmingham, The Worzels and Sheffield United to play.

Before the season had even started there was trouble at Swindon away and Ajax at home in pre season friendly's. At Doncaster away and Southampton home Cardiff fans were involved in scuffles and about 30 Southampton lads took a right pasting in the suburbs of Cardiff (Grangetown).

On Saturday August 30th I went up to Sheffield Utd with all the Bridgend lads, a great bunch of lads to be with, yes they like a good piss up and have a good laugh at the same time. They don't go looking for trouble but if trouble came their way, man for man they would match any mob that is around today. A mate of mine Dibs (Wayne Anderson) runs a coach to every away game from the Bridgend area and goes out of his way to pick me up at every game. I started travelling with Dib's lot in the last two seasons, one because they are a good bunch of lads who don't backstab and second like I say Dibs is a good friend of mine and I have always been good friends with the Bridgend lads over the years through another lad called Jaffa (Alun Griffiths).

Anyway back to Sheffield United away, we stopped off in Rotherham Town Centre on the way and just after we had got off the coach we were greeted by hundreds of other Cardiff lads celebrating like we had just won the cup, but in fact it had just been announced we had drawn the Jacks away in the 3rd round of the Carling cup. At first the old bill thought they were going to be attacked when everyone came running out of the pubs and the old bill retreated onto the main road, until they realised and were told by Simon Insole (our police spotter) that we were just celebrating drawing the Jacks in the cup. For the rest of the day and night that was all that was on everyone's minds and was the main conversation of the day. There was trouble at Sheffield that day and was mostly caused by their over zealous police force who seem to love whacking Cardiff fans with their batons even though United's lads had put windows through one of our buses, but that's a story for another day.

So for the next few weeks all that was on everyone's lips was how many tickets were we going to get to go to Jack land, we all knew that the away end held 3,000. Different rumours were coming out of the club, yes we could have the full allocation because it was the cup, the next minute it was being said that the police were against it, then the police said they were staying out of it and that the 500 police that would be on duty for the game could handle whatever we brought down to Jack land. Then Sky TV wanted to televise it live, which then gave the Jacks the chance to reduce our away support as they said the car park at the away end could hold no more than 28 coaches due to Sky and their lorry's setting up on it. The Jacks at one point offered us 1,100 tickets but eventually City agreed on 1,457; to me we were sold short. The fans offered to take double decker buses and the club then announced that the police were against it, but the police to this day insist it was the clubs, yet again will we ever know the truth.

So 1,457 Cardiff fans was the final allocation, the tickets were like gold dust and this upset and hurt a lot of the lads and fans. A number of lads did buy tickets in the Jack end but they knew the days of showing themselves had gone, not because of the fear of any of the Jacks, but of the courts and banning orders for just being in the wrong end.

The night before the game, my phone rang and it was Sam Hammam who was ringing to wish us luck and said he wished he could be there himself. He was still in Lebanon and said he kept up to date with everything that was happening at the club. He reminded me that the cup wasn't important and beating the Jacks wasn't everything, but promotion to the Promised Land was more important. He finished off with his usual words of love to every Cardiff fan and to my family; some times I wish he was still our chairman.

Well the day finally arrived and I drove down to Bryncethin nr Bridgend to a pub called the Royal Oak, with my brother in law Jamie and a good mate of mine Simon. We got there nearly 5 hours before kick off and on arrival nearly all the Bridgend lads were already down there, downing the ale as usual. Dibs had got a 70 odd seater bus so it meant we had a good group of lads. We then had to go all the way back on ourselves to meet the other coaches at Ninian Park, where there we were met by over 60 old bill including some of our spotters and the usual video cameras were out in full swing, I thought to myself, what's the point of all this as we were 40 odd miles from Jack land and yet the police were already in our faces. These police were going to travel down with us to make sure no one accidentally took the wrong turning. We were the last coach to arrive as usual, so we were the last to leave Ninian Park.

Soon we were back on the motorway, 28 coaches all in a line holding the M4 virtually to a stand still and the chants soon went up as we past Bridgend the place we originally left from. The buzz on the coach was unbelievable and the slow 40mph journey was broken up by laughter's and cheers when a valley lad got himself on top of one of the coaches and sat himself down as it moved along the motorway. As we past through the outskirts of Port Talbot and Neath there were some amazing sights, only a few miles from Jack land and many houses had Cardiff flags out their windows and the bridges above us on the motorway, banners were hanging over with Cardiff City and Bluebirds on them, it was a sight to be seen. Cars drove past, hooting their horns and people cheering us on as they past and I will repeat again ,this was on the door step from Jack land and 30 odd miles from the heart of Cardiff, "BLUEBIRDS".

The journey went quick, until we were taken past the outskirts of Jack land into a quiet trading estate and yet again as we were one of the last coaches to pull in it meant that we would be at least an hour waiting by the side of the road as the police took about 8 coaches at a time to the Liberty Stadium.

The problem for us was there wasn't even a toilet on the coach and tempers soon started to flare up as the lads asked for a piss to only be refused time and time again by the old bill. Every coach had at least five old bill standing outside the door in the middle of an empty trading estate, what was that all about? I ask you that's how trouble can soon start. We were all sweating as the air conditioning never worked, (thanks Dibs) and the driver was told the doors had to be kept shut, asylum seekers would have been treated better, but just as tempers were about to boil over, a sergeant saw this and allowed us one at a time to have a piss by the side of the coach, hooray common sense prevails.

Eventually we were off to finish our last few miles of the trip and the chants went up again and as we passed any man and his dog, up went the chant "you Jack bastards". We were all getting phone calls saying that the first few coaches had been attacked by flares and rockets. As we drove nearer the ground on the right hand side by some trees there looked like 600 Jacks all being kept back by riot police, dogs and horses. The Jacks looked a mixture of allsorts from lads to hundreds of kids and even women shouting abuse, well you can imagine the noise on our coaches .We were eventually put into a specially erected steel caged area (built in the last 2 weeks prior to the match especially for us). As we got off the coaches I looked around me and beside our coach of lads you had Big Sam, Ketty and Mogs's coach full of monsters and then you had Mac's lot even the Ely Trendies had brought their own coach led by my old mate Mikey Dye. Everyone tried to stand outside, but the police with cameras in our faces had opened double doors to the stadium, no turnstiles were used we were just pushed in, tickets weren't even checked.

Once inside, the bar was absolutely packed, I was shocked to see them selling alcohol as most places we go too, alcohol is banned to Cardiff fans, yet Swansea of all places were allowing us to drink, they must be desperate for money.

Jamie and I went upstairs to have a look, we had been here once before a few seasons ago to see Wales play their first ever match at the Liberty stadium. About 100 of us had travelled down there in cars and that evening, we never saw a Jack lad all the way to the ground and in the ground that night. The crowd had been a paltry 10,000 for the first ever Welsh game in the Jack stadium, there wasn't an atmosphere full stop. Anyway back to today's events as we entered the seats I was stunned, there was just an arena of hate all around us and virtually the whole ground was just pointing and singing hatred songs against us from pensioners, women, to school kids they were all doing the stupid "swim away", one idiot had the full costume on with a rubber ring around him. The hatred in their faces was unbelievable, now yes we hate them but their not the be all and end all, but you could see by their actions how much they hated us, jealously maybe, we are the capital, all the money comes to Cardiff, everyone has heard of Cardiff throughout the world and even Cardiff's lads "The Soul Crew" are known throughout Europe, I suppose you could say, what is Swansea known for? Not once did the crowd stop for breath, like I'd said earlier I'd been to their old ground the Vetch field and yes the North bank had been loud and always had a mouth at us but this was different all three sides of the ground were filled with sheer hatred.

The police had positioned themselves so that we could not move left or right or enter the seats down below, there were three lines of police and stewards betweens us and rows of empty seats and on top of that black sheets had been placed across rows of empty seats. How times have changed, none of this would of happened 10 years ago. As the match started the atmosphere got worse and their fans seemed to go into overdrive with their hate filled songs and they had actually managed to drown our singing which to be fair I've virtually never witnessed that before, I suppose there was 15,500 of them and only 1,400 of us. The atmosphere reminded me of when we played Leeds in the great giant killing FA Cup win at Ninian Park, this time the roles were reversed.

What I did notice was that the Jacks never had hundreds of lads, as most were just kids that were either side of us. On the left hand side I noticed Ledley getting continually abused, it was Toozey and his 40 cronies sat in the front rows by the half way line, well done to Ledley anyway the more stick they gave him the more he kissed his badge.

To the right of us the Jacks had no more than 100 lads, probably only 50 good ones at that, they had hundreds of wannabe kid fighters. I knew if there had been a proper outbreak of trouble at least 400 amongst the Cardiff contingent were proper old school game lads.

Most of the first half was just abuse going back and for and the odd coins and rubbish thrown at our players as they took the throw ins. We had played well for the first 20 mins but when they scored, from that moment the game went down hill and the longer the game went on the more it looked like they would score again. At half time and one nil down I went under the stand, bars were packed once again, everyone was wound up but felt we were like in a prison camp.

During the second half a lot of our lads just stayed down in the bar. Our end got quieter and quieter as we were continually drowned every time we tried to even sing, so most gave up just like our team, you could say. In the last ten minutes a lot of our younger Cardiff lads tried to push through the police lines only to be quickly sent flying back. For the whole game the police had cameras in our faces.

Whilst the game had been going on about 100 lads who follow Cardiff had sat themselves down in Port Talbot waiting to see if any Jacks came back after the game, they had originally wanted to meet in Neath nearer Jack land, but every pub had been banned from showing the match and any of the lads pubs had been closed down for the night. Five van loads of old bill sat there all evening monitoring the Neath and Port Talbot lads.

When the final whistle was blown, I really felt that the Jacks had deserved to win as their players had more desire to win than ours and it felt like our team never really bothered to turn up on the night, maybe Dave Jones hadn't wound them up enough of what the game meant to us. We were told we had to remain in our seats for 30 mins. Well for the next 30 mins, thousands of Jacks stayed in as well taunting us, at one stage a group of 30 older Cardiff nearly got over to them, The Jacks on the right of us, for about ten minutes fought with the police to get to us, but the ones on the left just sang their stupid song, The police just let them stay in the stadium, it would never happen at Ninian park in the year 2008.Toozies little firm had already left the stadium by now.

The Old Bill had moved in closer to us virtually not letting us breath, we were sitting ducks with missiles continually flying our way and the Old Bill more concerned with watching us. So Cardiff decided to try and leave and everyone steamed out the back, a few lads from the Rhondda managed to get up a fire exit left open by the old bill when they had dragged a fan out, a small charge occurred up the stairs with the Jacks retreating but the old bill soon got to the area.

As I stood in the coach car park, a hail of stones and bottles rained down on us, we were sitting ducks just like in the ground, Cardiff fans had had enough of it and it wasn't just the lads, everyone virtually near the fences tried to tear the fencing down, which did come down by the Sky TV lorry's but this only led to the main steel cages which got the Old Bill steaming towards the Cardiff fans. For a good 40 mins Cardiff refused to go onto the coaches and at one stage a lot of Cardiff fans decided to sit down on the floor as we were totally surrounded by old bill and steel cages. They eventually forced the Cardiff fans onto the coaches. While this had been going on (I've seen the videos of the following on ITV Wales, on the Net) about 800 Jacks and I mean mainly kids had running battles with the police, which later led to 20 having their mugs put in the local papers.

Finally the coaches were on their way, I thought we might be one of the first coaches out as we were one of the last in but we were about 8th and as we came out hundreds of Jacks tried to attack the first two coaches, everyone tried to get out the fire doors but as the coaches drove out, the police in their dozens were having to run by the side of each coach, whilst the rest of the police were chasing the Jacks back into their slums. Rockets and flares were fired once again by them.

The journey home was fast and the old bill let us go straight back to Bridgend (hooray), the Jacks never did go back to Port Talbot or Neath.

All in all I have to say even though not a punch was thrown between either side, the Jacks had got the message over to us, they hate us with vengeance and are jealous as fuck of us.

What this did show was that the hatred has never gone away and that if it wasn't for the CCTV, also hand held cameras by the old bill, black plastic sheets across rows of empty seats between us, a steel compound put up just for us, no freedom of movement outside the ground, every single supporter vented before they got a ticket ,bubbled in, surrounded by mass ranks of police and weeks of police gathering intelligence, there would have been fighting all over the ground and probably every street corner.

So the 80's feelings are still there amongst the fans and has never really gone away and if it wasn't for this mass operation by the police a guaranteed riot would of happened.

I've written just a short story on our league game down there, we were once again in our usual bubble. But this time the lads had to get up at 6am and report to Ninian Park for 7.30am, for a journey by car that would haven taken only 40 minutes.

The league game at the Liberty stadium at 11.15 am on Sunday November 30th 2008 had a larger police presence again and the atmosphere wasn't as bad, but the day still had its incidents. Cardiff were allowed a couple more hundred fans this time, the Jacks did they're swim away again including one of their players Pratley, when he scored in the 19th minute, he ran past the Cardiff fans doing the swim away with his hands, you could say that was inciting violence in its self, oh my mistake its alright he's a player and can get away with it and a Prat too ,maybe that's why his name is Pratley. Trundle and Tate got away with wearing t-shirts in the Millennium stadium with derogatory comments on them and holding a Welsh flag up with Fuck off Cardiff on it. Are they all obsessed with us or what? At the end of the game The Jacks did their pretend charge at the police, while a loan Cardiff fan stood next to them doing the Ayatollah and was smacked a bit and fell down the seats and in to the arms of one of our Spotters, probably the highlight of the day. The good news was he was put back in the Cardiff end. After the game the Jack kids did their usual stone throwing and then it was off home after a great match ending 2-2.

September 24 2006

Angry scenes at last night's tense derby

WELSH DERBY MAYHEM!

SWANSEA vs CARDIFF (23 SEPTEMBER)

What happened: The first big game between these sides in nine years ended with hundreds of riot police keeping Swans fans at bay as they reacted to away fans hurling bottles and other missiles at them. There were eight arrests and South Wales Police are trying to identify dozens more troublemakers in the aftermath of the Swans' 1-0 Carling Cup victory.

Tony's view: "This one is a complete madhouse – it retains the 1970s mentality that has left other rivalries. These guys don't care if they get nicked, it's more important for them to lay one on their rivals. Every kid is out for a fight and it's a rampage. It's not sophisticated, but they're off their nut so it's tough."

In April 2006, then Swansea striker Lee Trundle was arrested for displaying an anti-Cardiff T-shirt at the Millennium Stadium

SOCCER POLICE HIT BY CS GAS

AUGUST 29, 1987

Violence flares before City-Swansea derby

Cardiff City 1, Swansea City 0

FIGHTING RIVAL soccer fans let off a canister of CS gas at a police patrol before the start of the Cardiff City clash with Swansea this afternoon.

And there was more trouble inside Ninian Park when around 200 Cardiff supporters surged towards the Swansea fans.

Missiles rained down on dozens of police who desperately tried to keep the two factions apart.

Community Constable Jeff Richards was kicked to the ground and had to be rescued by a colleague.

Police dog handlers then moved in to clear the fighting fans and Pc Richards was treated by a police doctor.

Two policemen were taken to hospital and one man was arrested following the gas incident at the junction of Leckwith Road and Wellington Street.

Fans were searched as they entered the ground and close by officers discovered a gruesome weapon of a klaxon doctored to spray what was thought to be ammonia.

The policemen were taken to Cardiff Royal Infirmary for treatment to streaming eyes. They were later released.

At half-time the situation inside the ground was so tense that the officer in charge of police operations called in reinforcement units to prevent further possible confrontation.

CARDIFF City earned their first victory of the season when Jimmy Gilligan was again on target to give them a 1-0 win over Swansea in the fourth division derby marred by the first half sending-off of visitors' striker, Joe Allon, at Ninian Park this afternoon.

The opening minute of this encounter were marred by sporadic outbreaks of violence on the terraces forcing police with dogs to move into to deal with trouble from both sets of fans.

November 6 2006

Police arrest 27 over soccer riot

A TOTAL of 27 people have been arrested as part of a major police operation to round up football fans who ran riot after the Swansea versus Cardiff football derby at Swansea's Liberty Stadium in September.

Trouble broke out after the match, with glass bottles, bricks and other objects being hurled at police and Cardiff City supporters.

South Wales Police launched Operation Cybil to track down the culprits, many of whom were captured on fixed and mobile CCTV cameras.

Police issued more than 20 CCTV images of people they wanted to interview.

Chief Superintendent Mark Mathias said yesterday: "We are looking at every opportunity to identify, arrest, prosecute and ban those people who tarnished what was otherwise an excellent and well-behaved sporting event."

As a result of Operation Cybil, seven people have so far appeared in court, 17 have been bailed pending further inquiries, and a further three people have been quizzed but released with no further action being taken against them.

Police say they "have names" for another two people they want to speak to, and are trying to trace them.

October 3 2008

Three-year ban for flare hooligan

A FOOTBALL hooligan who threw a lit flare at a coach of Cardiff City fans in Swansea was yesterday banned from every ground for three years.

Darren Riley, 20, attacked the convoy of buses carrying City fans to the Carling Cup match last month.

Riley was one of hundreds of fans in a car park near the Coopers Arms pub in Neath Road before the game.

Prosecutor Andrew Fouracre said: "A police officer saw a large flame within the crowd. He could see Riley in the crowd holding the flare, which was burning with a bright red flame, above his head.

"He launched the flare into the road in the general direction of the Cardiff fans' bus. It rolled into the road and was kicked into the gutter by a policeman."

Riley was arrested when he was spotted by CCTV operators.

His solicitor Paul Jackson said: "He is very sorry for what he did. It was foolhardy. He insists there was no particular malice."

Factory worker Riley, of Clydach Road, Morriston, admitted disorderly behaviour. He was fined £375 and given a three-year banning order, ordering him to stay away from any football ground during games.

In a separate offence David Lewis, 18, from Townhill Road, Townhill, was fined £100 for swearing at a police officer after the same match.

Fans vandalised Liberty
Thursday, September 25, 2008, 09:00

CARDIFF fans went on a wrecking spree at the Liberty Stadium after the team were beaten by the Swans.

Sections of the 1,450 away supporters tore up seats in the stadium and vandalised toilets in a fit of rage.

Swansea City director David Morgan refused to comment on the details, but insisted away fans won't be banned at the next Tawe-Taff derby in November.

He said: "The atmosphere during the game was electric, possibly the best we've ever seen at the Liberty Stadium.

"Unfortunately there were problems after the match, but there are no plans to ban Cardiff fans when we next play them, on Sunday, November 30.

"If we do that, then it means the hooligans have won and genuine football supporters will have lost out."

During the match, police and stewards worked hard to ensure rival fans were kept apart.

The usual taunting and chanting took place, which dramatically increased when Jordi Gomez's free-kick hit the back of the net after 56 minutes.

Eye-witnesses say Cardiff fans tried to charge towards to Swans supporters on a number of occasions after this.

Lyndon Davies, of Glyntawe, was at the game with his wife.

He said: "I saw police using truncheons on the Cardiff fans to stop them getting over to our side."

After the final whistle was blown, the away fans pelted police with rocks from their fenced off enclosure. Hooligans on the Swansea side also clashed with cops, hurling slabs of concrete and bottles in their direction.

Police, who were armed with digital cameras, are presently scouring through hundreds of photos to identify the culprits.

The Post has been inundated with emails from genuine fans expressing their disgust at the scene.

The game was the first between the two clubs in nine years. Previous derbies have erupted into violence.

Swans director Mr Morgan added: "No-one wants to see that happen again."

While he refused to comment about the aftermath of Tuesday night's troubles, he added both clubs were doing all they could to help the police. However, Liberty Stadium workers have lifted the lid on clean-up operation.

One insider said: "It could have been a lot of worse, but there was quite a bit of damage done. "Cardiff fans ripped up seats and damaged the toilets as well as some electrical fittings."

He added: "The next game will be a different kettle-of-fish as it's on a Sunday afternoon — it also won't be the first game in nine-years."

Conclusion

So lets get something straight from the start I am not saying fighting at or away from a football match is right, what I am saying is that most lads have a fight when they're growing up, some continue it as they get older, other's move on, its just these lads and myself included got involved at some stage in their lives. Some in the 70s and 80s when it was the in thing at football at the time, others have got involved later in the 90s and even lately, But what I do guarantee is that in every town in this country there are street gangs causing ten times as much trouble than a football lad.

These lads have been named, shamed and lost their jobs in the past, for a fight at a football match against a like minded football lad. They then have to sign at a police station, hand their passports in and then say and proof when they are going on a holiday for the next 3 to 10 years and some of them for just sticking their fingers up or drunk at a football ground. I am not totally blaming the police for this as they are acting out orders from our Government. Hundreds of millions of pounds have been spent on cracking down on a football so called hooligan. There are times that it could get well out of control like the Cardiff v Swansea or Sunderland v Newcastle games and hundreds of police are needed , like I've shown in my story Our Bitter Enemy. But week in week out thousands are still spent on the every day match and lads/fans are treated worse than animals, with no rights at all.

Just the other month before STOKE C played at MAN UTD a few miles away from Old Trafford , 80 Stoke fans were just sitting in a pub, not chanting, singing or causing any nuisance in fact the report is they were quite boring. The police arrived in mass and under section 27 of the violent crime prevention act 2006, told them they had to leave. They were put on their coaches and held there for over 2 hours and then escorted back to Stoke City centre, even when some didn't even live there. No match was seen and No proper reason was given and guess what before all the do-gooders say they must have been known hooligans, they were in fact all members of the official Stoke City away supporters club, who have to be vetted by the police to become one. Apparently this Act can be used against football fans without justification, I wonder if it can be used on Rugby fans as well. I wonder how much that police operation cost and these fans were humans ,but where were their Civil rights. I have to say though what happened to those Stoke fans has been happening to Cardiff fans for the last ten years.

I could go down the route of the money spent on looking after and keeping asylum seekers here, but I'm not going to, as worse things are happening in this country at the moment. You've got the courts to scared to take a convicted Paedophiles passport of him ie Garry Glitter just one of thousands , because they thought it would be taking away his freedom. The papers wont put paedophiles faces in the papers and shame them as the Government wont let them. Every day all you hear about is murders, stabbings, children killed through neglect and Social Services haven't got enough staff, so they continue to make mistakes, Burglars now get a slapped wrist and continue to burglar another 60 odd houses before the courts decide to do something about it, probably probation. MP s have been involved in drugs in their past, even fraud but everyone says they deserve another chance, where as a football fan has supposedly brought shame to their work place and they are sacked.

I have been involved in pubs and clubs for 24 years, I've seen fights which make a football fight look like a playground scrap in an infants school. When they're locked up, they are given respect ,bailed and back in court for a £50 fine or most of the time cautioned and told don't do it again. Brownhills keeps getting mentioned by a lot of the lads, yes a lot of football lads use to drink in the pub in the late 80s, so did a lot of other people. It was known as a football pub and in the 3 years that I worked there, we had one glass inside smashed by a football lad, who apologised ,we had no doormen on football days and up to 400 lads would frequent the premises. On rugby days we had 6 doormen and by the end of the day, from the drain pipes being pulled off the walls outside, pictures and lights being pulled off the walls inside to the toilets totally being flooded. When a fight occurs, we are reminded its all done in good jest. The papers forget to tell you that on rugby days now, every train back up to the Valleys now has to have numerous police on them for the safety of the normal public and that in the last few years, when rugby teams have been abroad on tour there have been bars wrecked by the teams and a number of rapes have been alleged.

At the end of the day all we football fans are saying, yes there is trouble at football, but treat us the same as every body else is treated in Britain. Most police forces treat Cardiff fans like scum, yes we've been naughty boys and have fought battles with like minded lads, but we haven't murdered anyone. What goes a long way in this world is "REPSECT" and if you treat lads/fans with more respect in the year 2009, the police would find that they would get it returned. We have two main Spotters Simon Insole and Wayne Palmer and they have managed in the last 5 years or so to gain Respect from some of our worst Nutter's and main lads, because they haven't stabbed them in the back and a lot of the lads know they can only go so far, they have also tried to stop other police forces from going over the top on our fans. Yes at the end of the day they're police and have a job to do. but I will say this and a lot of lads will agree on this, they have been fair and treated us like human beings .I just wish the Government and the rest of the police up and down the country realised were not the main criminals, actually players themselves behave worse than us, but I forgot their not fans their Celebrities.

Times have really changed for Cardiff, probably more than any other teams fans in Britain as "ALL" our big games are bubbles and the Club and the police vet every person who travels on the coaches, also we don't receive our match ticket till our arrival at that ground . Swansea, Bristol City, Bristol Rovers, Birmingham C, Millwall, Leeds, Wolves and West Ham away are All Bubble games for our fans. Yet Millwall v Leeds, Swansea v Birmingham, Wolves v Swansea etc this season, no restrictions. So the days out and the big occasions are over for Cardiff fans.

Most of the lads that I know have totally moved on, grown up, got families like myself and look back on it as part of growing up. This book is not saying yes its right what we did, what its saying is it happened ,its not a lie and did really anyone else get hurt other than a football lad. The book is also saying that a great % of these lads did and still do love and follow their clubs week in week out and most have no interest at all in fighting nowadays.

Anyway what is good now is that a lot of lads from the 70s, 80s & 90s all now have a lot of respect for each other and even turn up at each others events, ie Boro lads went to an event held in Hull to raise money for 9 Hull City lads families whilst they were in prison, this actually happens all over the country.

Only last December Chelsea Pat got rushed into hospital and was critical for a couple of weeks. Pat spoke to me every day and he said on many occasions how overwhelmed he was by the lads all over the country and especially the Cardiff lads as he had received over a 100

Get Well Cards and three quarters were from Cardiff with many giving money. Big Sam and the Valley lads had also contributed big time.

Pats Chelsea mates when they visited him couldn't believe how well thought of Pat was in South Wales and how we as lads were so supportive to Pat. So see were not all animals like the media and the government portray us as.

I know I keep saying it, but I will finish off by saying that thousands of lads have settled down, I certainly have. I believe as soon as you meet the right person and your child is born, it totally changes you and your family come first, as they're your future.

The memories of the 70s, 80s and 90s will always live with me.

January 2009 Annis Abraham Jnr.

November 26, 2008

FOOTIE HOOLIGAN ARRESTS UP 700

SOCCER violence is on the increase. Home Office figures revealed yesterday.

Cops arrested 3,842 yobs at domestic and international games last season up 700 on 2005. Official figures show violent disorder, possession of weapons and booze related crime are on the up.

Last year 1,048 new football banning orders were imposed, taking the total in force to a record 3,172.

Leeds United topped the league of shame with 152 outcast fans.

Three Premiership teams Aston Villa, Manchester United and Chelsea were in the top ten for banning orders.

Statistics show an average of 1.21 arrests at every top flight game last season – most concentrated in a few flash-

By DAVID WOODING, Whitehall Editor

points, with no arrests at seven out of ten games. There were 1,225 alcohol-related offences – up 18 per cent. Champions Man United had 248 fans arrested, up 17 per cent on 2007-8, and Arsenal 105, up 35 per cent.

Arrests for violent disorder were up ten per cent to 373, weapon possession up 12 per cent to 46 and alcohol offences up 18 per cent to 1,225.

Shadow police reform minister David Ruffley demanded more police on matchdays.

● CLUBS with the most banning orders by October 2008 were: 1 Leeds 152, 2 Cardiff 136, 3 Millwall 117, 4 Portsmouth 91, 5 Wolves 85, 6 Aston Villa 82, 7 Coventry 79, 8 Man Utd 78, 9 Chelsea 76, 10 Birmingham 76.

Don't treat fans like criminals

26th November 2008

Figures released by the Home Office this week prove what the Football Supporters' Federation have been arguing for years – there is absolutely no need to treat football fans as criminals.

The latest Home Office statistics show that 37 million supporters attended football matches in England and Wales last year and there were only 3,842 arrests made – one in every 10,000 fans.

Only one in 10 of these arrests were actually made for acts of violence - the majority related to consumption of alcohol, pitch incursions and public disorder offences.

Of these offences the majority were committed away from football stadiums, meaning less than half a fan per game, per stadium was arrested inside a football ground.

And the FSF are extremely concerned with the manner in which police increasingly choose to use legislation in order to criminalise normal football supporters.

FSF National Council member Amanda Jacks said: "The vast majority of football supporters are normal, law abiding citizens and we're very concerned at this portrayal of fans as violent, mindless thugs.

"The Government's own statistics show this is simply not the case, and we're pleased that Home Office minister Vernon Coaker has acknowledged this.

"There were fewer than 1,600 arrests inside football stadiums last year, a tiny amount when you consider a total of 37 million people attended games. And a large number of these were for trivial offences such as persistent standing or drinking alcohol within sight of the pitch.

"It's very difficult for many supporters to challenge fairly minor, non-violent charges. We've heard from people who have been put off from contesting dubious charges purely because of the expense involved or have had their cases thrown out due to lack of evidence – although these still appear in the arrest figures.

"Supporters are frequently treated like criminals, and we hear of far too many worrying cases."

Recent examples of this include 80 Stoke fans rounded up in a Greater Manchester pub before their club's visit to Old Trafford and forcibly taken back to Stoke, while in another shocking case last month, Chelsea fan Cliff Auger was victimised for protecting his teenage son.

Annis' first book,
'From Shattered Dreams to Wembley Way', released 28th June, 2008.
On sale from www. annisabraham. co. uk

My two previous books are available from:
www.annisabraham.co.uk

"From Shattered Dreams to Wembley Way"
£16.99 inc p&p

"The Diary of the Real Soul Crew"
£9.99 inc p&p